Praise for *Hands-On Smart Contract Development with Hyperledger Fabric V2*

Check out this book if you want to get a deeper understanding of Hyperledger Fabric and gain expertise with creating permissioned blockchain networks.

—*Brian Behlendorf, Executive Director for Hyperledger*

One of the best books covering Hyperledger Fabric to the degree of breadth and clarity that this piece captures. From component overview to practical examples within a relatable context, it uniquely explicates Hyperledger's inner workings in a way that is hard to match.

—*Jim Murphy and Jason Jaan*
Financial Transformation Partner, KPMG; Transformation Delivery Manager, KPMG

A well-balanced comprehensive literature. This book provides that balance with an approach essential in blockchain architect skill-building. While many of its concepts may focus on Hyperledger Fabric, they are portable to other blockchain frameworks and platforms. A must-read for all aspiring blockchain architects and developers.

—*Nitin Gaur Director,*
Financial Sciences and Digital Assets, IBM

A great practical hands-on guide to developing smart contracts using Hyperledger Fabric on popular platforms. This book provides detailed step-by-step instructions for developing, testing, deploying, and maintaining smart contracts on popular Blockchain as a Service platforms.

—*Todd Little, Oracle Blockchain Platform Architect*

Clean, clear, and clinical, this thoughtful, deep dive into Smart Contracts is a boon to blockchain development and a must-read for Hyperledger.

—*Joseph Raczynski, Technologist & Futurist, Thomson Reuters*

This book makes understanding Hyperledger concepts extremely simple and easy by serving technical and nontechnical audiences to understand Hyperledger from the basics and then build on top of it. The authors allow anyone to understand the intricacies of building an enterprise blockchain application using Hyperledger.

—*Andile Ngcaba,*
Founding Partner & Chairman of Convergence Partners

This book is the gold standard in smart contract development. This comprehensive examination understands the challenges facing enterprises interested in implementing blockchain solutions and offers concise direction. Zand, Wu, and Morris supply readers with valuable insights for smart contract development through the hands-on techniques discussed in the text.

—*Bobbi Muscara, Hyperledger TSC Member;*
Chair of the Hyperledger Learning Materials Working Group;
Director of Education, Ledger Academy

I have been building enterprise blockchain solutions for five years, and *Hands-On Smart Contract Development with Hyperledger Fabric* is my go-to resource for creating new blockchain use cases and improving existing solutions. This book should be in every HLF developer's toolkit.

—*David Havera, Chief Blockchain Engineer, GE*

Anyone interested in smart contract development on Hyperledger Fabric should get this book both for a cover-to-cover read as well as an ongoing reference. Well written, well organized, and eminently understandable. Zand leverages his years of development training experience to deliver highly consumable foundational, strategic, and tactical knowledge for builders in the Hyperledger ecosystem.

—*Eric Hess, Host of The Encrypted Economy podcast and*
Managing Partner of Hess Legal Counsel

Comprehensive, easy to read, and state of the art: the first book that intuitively supports both software developers and product managers in developing real-world enterprise blockchain applications.

—*Robin Pilling, CEO & Founder, Dis3bute*

Hands-On Smart Contract Development with Hyperledger Fabric V2

Building Enterprise Blockchain Applications

Matt Zand, Xun Wu, and Mark Anthony Morris

Beijing · Boston · Farnham · Sebastopol · Tokyo

Hands-On Smart Contract Development with Hyperledger Fabric V2

by Matt Zand, Xun Wu, and Mark Anthony Morris

Published by O'Reilly Media, Inc., 1005 Gravenstein Highway North, Sebastopol, CA 95472.

O'Reilly books may be purchased for educational, business, or sales promotional use. Online editions are also available for most titles (*http://oreilly.com*). For more information, contact our corporate/institutional sales department: 800-998-9938 or *corporate@oreilly.com*.

Acquisitions Editor: Michelle Smith	**Indexer:** nSight, Inc.
Development Editor: Gary O'Brien	**Interior Designer:** David Futato
Production Editor: Christopher Faucher	**Cover Designer:** Karen Montgomery
Copyeditor: Sharon Wilkey	**Illustrator:** Kate Dullea
Proofreader: Charles Roumeliotis	

September 2021:   First Edition

Revision History for the First Edition

2021-09-08:   First Release

See *http://oreilly.com/catalog/errata.csp?isbn=9781492086123* for release details.

978-1-492-08612-3

[LSI]

Table of Contents

Part II.   Introduction to Hyperledger Projects

Part III.   Developing Smart Contracts with Hyperledger Fabric

Part IV.   Blockchain Supply Chain with Hyperledger

Part V.   Hyperledger Fabric—Other Topics

Preface

Blockchain is currently the forerunner technology in shaping the next generation of fintech by offering transparent and fast transaction processing, higher financial data availability, better security, and tremendous cost savings in the financial industry. By introducing decentralized authority that makes third-party and middle actors obsolete, blockchain has initiated a paradigm shift in the way traditional financial institutions and other industries run their business operations.

A recent Gartner survey showed that more than 40% of companies have at least one blockchain pilot project in progress. Gartner also predicts that 30% of global blockchain projects will make their way to the production stage. Likewise, the global blockchain market is growing, manifested by a large number of Forbes Global 2000 companies currently experimenting with digital trust implementations.

Gartner (*https://oreil.ly/XPsUK*) has predicted that 90% of enterprise blockchain platform deployments will require replacement within 18 months from 2021 in order to stay competitive and secure, and to deter obsolescence. Gartner also predicts that by 2025, the business value generated by blockchain will move up gradually to $176 billion and then surge to surpass the $3.1 trillion mark by 2030.

Because of blockchain popularity, the developer community has passionately contributed several private and public distributed ledger technologies (DLTs) for building blockchain applications. Among the existing DLTs, Hyperledger is a leading platform for building enterprise permissioned blockchain applications. By design, Hyperledger has embedded features, functionalities, tools, and libraries for building, scaling, and managing enterprise blockchain applications.

The aim of this book is to show you how to build a private enterprise blockchain system using Hyperledger Fabric and how to combine various components of Fabric to create and maintain a robust, secure, and scalable blockchain application.

We have been offering blockchain consulting, development, and training services since 2018 through our companies, Hashflow and Coding Bootcamps. At Hashflow (*http://www.hashflow.us*), we advise companies of all sizes on leveraging blockchain technology and fintech to either overcome business challenges or help bring about foreseeable values through brand-new visions. We also are partnering with pioneering companies in industries like fintech, healthcare, music, and energy to build software-as-a-service (SaaS) products using blockchain technology. Our team is composed of industry-leading practitioners who have applied the blockchain framework to achieve desired benefits within both classical business models and novel ventures.

In addition to Hashflow, we started a training company to build capacity and capabilities for prospective employees looking to build and deploy blockchain solutions internally. With regard to our (individual or enterprise) training experiences, we noticed that the majority of beginner students lack prerequisite skills (like Linux bash scripting, Docker, or Go programming) that are essential for mastering Hyperledger Fabric. As such, at Coding Bootcamps, we have tailored our training programs to meet multiple business requirements. You can start by visiting the following pages on our company website:

- Coding Bootcamps (*https://www.coding-bootcamps.com*)
- Self-Paced Training (*https://oreil.ly/LyEyN*)
- Live Group and Hybrid Training (*https://oreil.ly/YOk59*)
- Intense Blockchain Bootcamp (*https://oreil.ly/N8Wks*)

Our blockchain courses are offered in both English and Spanish. Also, for Hyperledger we offer two courses: Fabric System Administration and Fabric Development. While the system administration course prepares students for the Certified Hyperledger Fabric Administrator (CHFA) exam, the development course covers topics in the Certified Hyperledger Fabric Developer (CHFD) exam.

From all the offerings that we have created over the last few years, we are most proud of our Blockchain Engineering bootcamp. It provides over 180 hours of live and recorded instruction, with many hands-on labs and a certificate of completion upon finishing the quizzes and final project. We offer our blockchain bootcamp multiple times per year, and we update and improve it with every cohort. The online program is the first of its kind, in that the top students in each group are also referred for employment to our employer network.

How to Build Enterprise Blockchain Applications with Hyperledger

One industry after another is currently experimenting with blockchain. The prominent industries currently leading blockchain use cases are real estate, healthcare, government, higher education, logistics, aviation, finance, and energy. Among these industries, finance has been more receptive to adopting a variety of blockchain use cases. For example, based on a report by the Bank for International Settlements (BIS), 80% of global central banks are researching the advantages and disadvantages of digital currency.[1]

Based on our personal experiences with clients in fintech, including private banks, many financial institutions and independent entrepreneurs are exploring the idea of digital-only banks. In doing so, they want to utilize blockchain technology to offer banking products such as digital currency, digital wallets, peer-to-peer payments, loan and credit, utility tokens, and security tokens. Likewise, we have experienced growing demands from banks for implementing Know Your Customer and Anti-Money Laundering guidelines for their digital banks, where we typically use Hyperledger DLTs like Fabric, Aries, or Indy to manage their customers' identities.

Regardless of use case or industry, invariably, all enterprise blockchain implementations go through four stages: proof of concept (PoC), minimum viable product, production that induces integration, and maintenance (which includes performance monitoring and scaling). Based on our personal experiences with enterprise blockchain development, most large enterprises run into two issues:

- Miscommunication between passionate technical teams and top management, which has only basic knowledge of blockchain technology
- Lack of proper planning for integration with current systems

To remedy the first issue, companies need to offer high-level training for their executives. For the second issue, developers need to have access to solutions like serverless architectures, which minimize interference with current system operation.

When building a private enterprise blockchain application with Hyperledger, you can take advantage of several DLTs, tools, and libraries. For example, Hyperledger Grid DLT is well suited for building and managing enterprise supply chain applications, as we cover in our final chapter. Although some Hyperledger tools and libraries are still in the incubation stage (as we will discuss in Chapter 2), once all Hyperledger family members become active, they will collectively provide developers and system

---

1 Codruta Boar, Henry Holden, and Amber Wadsworth. 2020. "Impending Arrival—A Sequel to the Survey on Central Bank Digital Currency." *BIS Papers*, no. 107, June 2020. *https://www.bis.org/publ/bppdf/bispap107.pdf*.

administration with a complete set of tools to build and manage enterprise consortium blockchain applications. Because of high industry adoption, Hyperledger Fabric is the leading DLT within the Hyperledger ecosystem. As such, we cover Hyperledger Fabric components that are essential for all enterprise blockchain applications.

Speaking from our personal experiences, we have seen time and again that successful production of an enterprise blockchain application depends on several factors, including scalable architecture, choice of cloud provider, performance monitoring, integration with existing systems, security audits, smart contract life-cycle management, off-chain data management, and documentation. Knowledge of chaincode or Fabric components by itself is not sufficient to successfully deploy and scale a blockchain application. For example, as we discuss in Chapter 8, choosing the right cloud provider requires several considerations, as each provider offers numerous features and services for building an enterprise blockchain in its platform as well as various ways to integrate and upgrade your application with other services offered by the same provider.

Who Is This Book For?

Topics covered in this book are geared toward beginners who want to build enterprise private blockchain applications with Hyperledger or take the Certified Hyperledger Fabric Developer (CHFD) exam. Nonetheless, at a high level, Hyperledger Fabric professionals have two major career routes: Fabric system administration and Fabric development. Each career route requires different skill sets and competencies, which can be validated by taking the Certified Hyperledger Fabric Administrator (CHFA) or CHFD exams offered by the Linux Foundation.

To become a professional Fabric developer, you should know how to design, develop, test, deploy, and invoke Fabric smart contracts. In short, you need to know the following seven topics (as covered in this book) very well:

- Defining transaction functions
- Executing simple queries
- Creating complex queries
- Defining assets using key-value pairs
- Identifying potentially private data
- Incorporating private data collection
- Submitting, evaluating, and querying transactions by invoking smart contracts

In a nutshell, as a Fabric developer, you should demonstrate your ability to package and deploy Fabric applications and smart contracts, perform end-to-end Fabric application life-cycle and smart contract management, and program in Java, JavaScript, or Go.

Overview of the Chapters

Chapters in this book follow a top-down hierarchy, from introducing blockchain technology through deploying smart contracts. This section provides a synopsis of each chapter.

Chapter 1, *Fundamental Concepts of Blockchain*, walks you through essential components of blockchain that are common in all blockchain platforms. In particular, concepts such as cryptography, consensus, and smart contracts are concisely explained.

Chapter 2, *Overview of Hyperledger Projects and Tools*, gives you a high-level overview of the Hyperledger ecosystem, including common components among all Hyperledger family members. It moves on to briefly discussing all Hyperledger DLTs, tools, and libraries.

Chapter 3, *Hyperledger Fabric Architecture and Components*, discusses the Hyperledger Fabric architecture as well as its main components such as the membership service provider, policies, peers, orderers, smart contracts, the Fabric network, and more.

Chapter 4, *Smart Contract Development*, shows you how to write your first Fabric smart contract using the JavaScript programming language. It covers hands-on topics such as defining smart contract classes, installing and instantiating a smart contract, validating and sanitizing inputs and arguments, running simple or complex queries, working with private data, and more.

Chapter 5, *Smart Contract Invocation*, shows you how to invoke smart contracts via the command-line interface, submit transactions, query a transaction, and more. You will also learn how to create and issue an application contract.

Chapter 6, *Testing and Maintenance*, discusses hands-on topics such as how to handle errors and process responses. It also shows you how to run unit tests on smart contracts. Further, you'll learn how to perform Fabric maintenance tasks by building a Fabcar UI web application that acts as a smart contract client. By adding functions to the Fabcar UI, we'll walk you through hands-on steps for testing and debugging a Fabric smart contract.

Chapter 7, *Building Supply Chain DApps with Hyperledger Fabric*, covers an end-to-end pharma supply chain built with Fabric. It is a complete project for putting knowledge obtained from previous chapters into practice. Along the way, you'll learn how to design an architecture for a blockchain supply chain, write a smart contract for tracking inventories, compile and deploy the smart contract, and more. In addition, you'll learn how to develop an application with Hyperledger Fabric through the SDK.

Chapter 8, *Deploying Hyperledger Fabric on the Cloud*, shows you how to set up and deploy Fabric on three popular cloud providers: Amazon Web Services, IBM, and Oracle. Through hands-on example projects, we'll walk you through setting up the Fabric network and deploying smart contracts on each cloud platform along with explaining main considerations for using each platform.

Chapter 9, *Hyperledger Fabric V2 Integration*, covers new features offered in Fabric v2 such as new chaincode application patterns, an external chaincode launcher, Alpine-based Docker images, and more. We also discuss how to update the capability level of a channel and upgrade Fabric components as well as the major considerations for upgrading to Fabric v2.

Chapter 10, *Overview of Other Hyperledger Projects*, covers four more Hyperledger family members: Hyperledger Aries, Hyperledger Avalon, Hyperledger Besu, and Hyperledger Grid. Specifically, we show how to harness the power of Aries in managing identities and use Avalon to move securely and process blockchain data off the chain. We also show how to use Besu to run both public and private blockchain applications using different consensus algorithms. Finally, we demonstrate how to use Grid to build and manage an end-to-end blockchain supply chain.

Conventions Used in This Book

The following typographical conventions are used in this book:

Italic
> Indicates new terms, URLs, email addresses, filenames, and file extensions.

`Constant width`
> Used for program listings, as well as within paragraphs to refer to program elements such as variable or function names, databases, data types, environment variables, statements, and keywords.

`Constant width bold`
> Shows commands or other text that should be typed literally by the user.

`Constant width italic`
> Shows text that should be replaced with user-supplied values or by values determined by context.

This element signifies a tip or suggestion.

This element signifies a general note.

This element indicates a warning or caution.

Using Code Examples

Supplemental material (code examples, exercises, etc.) is available for download at *https://myhsts.org/hyperledger-fabric-book*.

If you have a technical question or a problem using the code examples, please send email to *bookquestions@oreilly.com*.

This book is here to help you get your job done. In general, if example code is offered with this book, you may use it in your programs and documentation. You do not need to contact us for permission unless you're reproducing a significant portion of the code. For example, writing a program that uses several chunks of code from this book does not require permission. Selling or distributing examples from O'Reilly books does require permission. Answering a question by citing this book and quoting example code does not require permission. Incorporating a significant amount of example code from this book into your product's documentation does require permission.

We appreciate, but do not require, attribution. An attribution usually includes the title, author, publisher, and ISBN. For example: "Hands-On Smart Contract Development with Hyperledger Fabric V2 by Matt Zand, Xun Wu, and Mark Anthony Morris (O'Reilly). Copyright 2021 WEG2G LLC, 978-1-492-08612-3."

If you feel your use of code examples falls outside fair use or the permission given above, feel free to contact us at *permissions@oreilly.com*.

O'Reilly Online Learning

 For more than 40 years, *O'Reilly Media* has provided technology and business training, knowledge, and insight to help companies succeed.

Our unique network of experts and innovators share their knowledge and expertise through books, articles, and our online learning platform. O'Reilly's online learning platform gives you on-demand access to live training courses, in-depth learning paths, interactive coding environments, and a vast collection of text and video from O'Reilly and 200+ other publishers. For more information, visit *http://oreilly.com*.

How to Contact Us

Please address comments and questions concerning this book to the publisher:

O'Reilly Media, Inc.
1005 Gravenstein Highway North
Sebastopol, CA 95472
800-998-9938 (in the United States or Canada)
707-829-0515 (international or local)
707-829-0104 (fax)

We have a web page for this book, where we list errata, examples, and any additional information. You can access this page at *https://oreil.ly/smart-contract-development*.

Email *bookquestions@oreilly.com* to comment or ask technical questions about this book.

For news and information about our books and courses, visit *http://oreilly.com*.

Find us on Facebook: *http://facebook.com/oreilly*

Follow us on Twitter: *http://twitter.com/oreillymedia*

Watch us on YouTube: *http://youtube.com/oreillymedia*

Acknowledgments

We've had so much support from many wonderful people throughout the process of writing this book. Thank you so much to everyone who helped make it a reality! We would like to give an especially big thank you to the following people.

Everyone at O'Reilly has been fantastic to work with throughout the whole life cycle of this book. To our editors, Gary O'Brien, Michelle Smith, and Chris Faucher, thank you for your amazing support, constant encouragement, and thoughtful feedback. Thank you also to Katie Tozer and Jonathan Hassell for their support along the way.

Thank you to Ashwani Kumar, Sergio Torres, and Sushma Varadaiah, who reviewed the entire book and provided many helpful suggestions and insightful comments. Your reviews have made the final draft a better book. Thank you for your hours reviewing the book in such detail.

Thank you to Angelo De Caro and Sergio Torres for contributing to Chapters 2 and 3.

Thanks go out to Vivek Acharya from the Oracle team for contributing to Chapter 8's details about Hyperledger Fabric development on Oracle Cloud Platform. Likewise, we owe deep gratitude to Shikha Maheshwari from the IBM team for contributing to that chapter's information about Hyperledger Fabric development on the IBM cloud platform.

Thank you to Jason Jaan for continuing our good fortune of collaborating with forward-thinking entrepreneurs and progressive companies to work on a string of truly exciting and value-driven blockchain projects the world over.

Thank you to the other contributors who helped in various stages: Abhik Banerjee, Robin Pilling, Mohammed Nihal Ansari, and Jim Sullivan.

This publication would not have been possible without my coauthors, Brian (Xun) Wu and Mark Anthony Morris. Thank you for your friendship, your encouragement, and your endless patience. I am very happy we accomplished this publication together.

Brian (Xun) Wu

I would like to thank my family and friends for their patience and support throughout this endeavor.

Thank you to the talented team at O'Reilly who provided prompt guidance and valuable feedback throughout this project.

Mark Anthony Morris

Dedicated to my dear mother, Grace Morris—my inspiration, purpose, and strength to strive and never give up. Thank you, Mom. I love you!

Introduction to Blockchain

This first part of the book contains a single chapter, which introduces and explores the fundamental concepts of blockchain. This chapter will provide you with the knowledge required to begin designing and developing enterprise blockchain applications. The first prerequisite is understanding the fundamental concepts of blockchain. These fundamentals include blockchain's origin; its core components, consisting of a decentralized network, introductory cryptography, ledger implementation, consensus mechanisms, and smart contracts; and finally, its architecture and supporting technology and concepts.

## CHAPTER 1

Fundamental Concepts of Blockchain

It's important to understand that blockchain is not a simple concept for most to grasp without a solid understanding of its origin, core components and architecture, as well as the debates surrounding blockchain. Blockchain has many slightly varying definitions that elicit some very dogmatic opinions, and this confuses many when first beginning their blockchain journey. This confusion happens because blockchain is not a tangible thing that can be touched or seen; instead, it is a concept born out of algorithms, technology, and fresh ideas for the exchange of economic value.

In this chapter, we'll explore the fundamental concepts of blockchain by first starting with a brief history of its origin. This background information will help you understand why blockchain has no single standardized and universally accepted definition.

Following our discussion on blockchain's origin, we will look briefly at several core components. Then we'll delve into its architecture, followed by supporting technology and concepts.

In our look at the core components, we begin with the decentralized network. Then we cover cryptography. You can think of cryptography as the secret sauce of blockchain because it is what makes blockchain work. Without cryptography, there would be no use for blockchain. Next, we discuss ledger implementation. The ledger represents the storage or database in blockchain. It maintains the state created as a result of the last committed transaction as well as the history from the beginning of the ledger's creation.

Next, we discuss the consensus, a protocol to find "agreement" among the nodes, which is the heart of blockchain. Consensus provides a secure means to complete transactions without relying on the traditional intermediaries in common transactional systems. Finally, we discuss smart contracts. The power in blockchain to perform complex transactions is a direct result of the employment of smart contracts. You can think of smart contracts as software programs.

This chapter will help you understand the following:

- The architecture and core design components of blockchain
- How ledger databases and world state databases work in blockchain
- The role of cryptography (such as public/private keys or hash functions) in blockchain
- The most popular consensus algorithms used in blockchain
- How smart contracts work in a blockchain system

What Is Blockchain?

In the generally accepted definition, *blockchain* is a subset of distributed ledger technology (DLT). Breaking down DLT, we get *distributed* by creating a peer-to-peer network of nodes, which are computers; together they form a distributed network (Figure 1-1). Each node processes transactions submitted by clients. These transactions become committed records—called the ledger—of a replicated database on all nodes. This ledger is immutable, and the records are grouped into blocks.

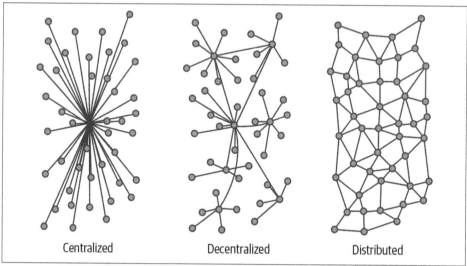

Figure 1-1. Types of networks

Each node maintains a copy of this immutable ledger, typically implemented as an append-only file or database. Blockchain relies on the employment of digital signatures and consensus to commit records. Most DLTs do not use consensus; instead,

DLTs require only digital signatures to be present to commit records. There is no consensus, just digitally signed transactions.

The records are committed to the immutable ledger. In this append-only database, each record is ordered in time, and each block of records is cryptographically linked to the prior committed block. Each block contains additional metadata along with the hash code of the prior block and a set of committed records. The records are typically represented by a hash tree known as a *Merkle tree* (Figure 1-2).

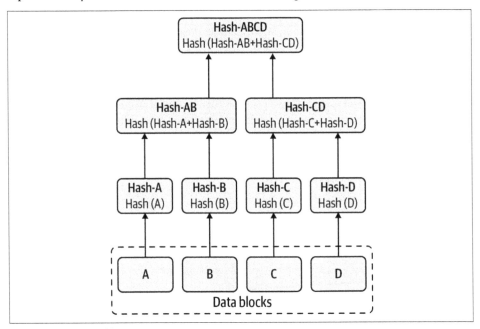

Figure 1-2. A Merkle tree

This gives you a general idea of what blockchain is. But we can begin to gain greater clarity when we look at its origin, its architecture, and its components. The origin explains why definitions diverged. Blockchain's architecture is the easiest aspect to grasp because it is the most concrete of the topics and provides a holistic view. The components are a set of legacy technologies and logical concepts, each of which can be separately understood. By examining the components, we can build a solid foundation for mastering the skills required to develop blockchain smart contracts and blockchain applications. Understand that blockchain technology is built on legacy technology such as digital signatures, peer-to-peer networking, and decades of prior work.

Synergistic in nature, blockchain comes into existence when several legacy technologies join together as a single, complex, integrated system performing the fundamental task of executing transactions. Many, when discussing blockchain, see it as a database.

Others see it as a transaction processor. Still others see it as a decentralized utopia free from any central control and a way to restructure society. Blockchain is all of these and more. Unfortunately, this paradigm is why it can be difficult to grasp the fundamental concept of blockchain.

Typically, new technologies or inventions are defined by a single purpose or well-understood solution to a problem. For instance, the concept of NoSQL databases is easy to understand. Even software-defined networking is not a stretch to envision and define.

Many try to understand blockchain by equating it with Bitcoin, the cryptocurrency that employs blockchain technology. This happens because blockchain technology is the underlying mechanism that facilitates the operation of Bitcoin, and thus they are seen as one. You should understand that Bitcoin is an application using blockchain technology. The Bitcoin use case is a peer-to-peer financial exchange. To understand blockchain, we will break it down into discrete components. Then you can combine them and envision solutions to problems you want to solve.

Origin of Blockchain

Most people date the birth of blockchain with the beginning of Bitcoin—more specifically, the Bitcoin paper authored by Satoshi Nakamoto and published in 2008. Who is Satoshi Nakamoto? Nobody knows, because they have never made themselves publicly known. They could be a person, group, company, or government agency, like the US National Security Agency (NSA). Regardless, Nakamoto remains a mystery.

There are those who claim to be Nakamoto, but no concrete proof has ever been presented. So, Nakamoto remains an unknown figure.

In Nakamoto's paper, "Bitcoin: A Peer-to-Peer Electronic Cash System" (*https://oreil.ly/HuDYt*), you will not find the term *blockchain* or *block chain*. The closest you'll find is *chain of blocks*. You must go to code line 596 in *main.h* to find the first instance of the term *block chain* (*https://oreil.ly/pwWUh*).

Satoshi cited eight papers, including "How to Time-Stamp a Digital Document" (*https://oreil.ly/Uz3ef*) by Stuart Haber and W. Scott Stornetta, which contains the phrase *chain of time-stamps*. This, no doubt, was inspiration for how to link blocks of transactions together in the design of Bitcoin. Other cited papers must have influenced the design. First was "Protocols for Public Key Cryptosystems" (*https://www.merkle.com/papers/Protocols.pdf*) by Ralph C. Merkle, who was famous for the Merkle tree (see Figure 1-2), a cryptographic hash tree data structure widely used in blockchain. The other paper of great influence was "b-money" (*https://oreil.ly/Fh6YV*) by Wei Dai, which was certainly thought about while designing Bitcoin to be a digital cryptocurrency for use as a peer-to-peer exchange of value.

The Blockchain Revolution

Bitcoin was the spark that ignited the revolution of blockchain, but not the fuel for it. It also generated a subculture around Bitcoin with strong beliefs and a sense of ownership. This sparse and federated community, bound together by the common belief that "blockchain is only permissionless," immediately took ownership of Bitcoin and replicated it into hundreds of incarnations. Some were identical and some divergent, but all united in a common thesis that represented an anarchist's view of a new world possible with Bitcoin.

Blockchain 2.0

Prior to Bitcoin, Adam Back, known for Hashcash (*https://oreil.ly/qwanr*), wrote about a proof-of-work system used to prevent email spam in 2002. Nick Szabo developed the terms *smart contracts* (*https://oreil.ly/JQTe8*) in 1997 and *bit gold* (*https://oreil.ly/u3Ole*) in 2005, which many consider the precursors to Bitcoin. As far back as 1982, David Chaum, called the inventor of digital cash and inventor of blind signatures, was working on electronic cash (*https://oreil.ly/xglEZ*). The concept of blockchain has a rich history and was fully developed in 2013 in "Ethereum Whitepaper" (*https://oreil.ly/Notob*) by Vitalik Buterin into what we think of today as Blockchain 2.0.

Prior to the Ethereum whitepaper, we had Blockchain 1.0, which powers Bitcoin and represents blockchain technology without the concept of the smart contract. In Blockchain 2.0, we have smart contract technology, which Buterin expressed in his whitepaper. It facilitates rich transactions far beyond the capability of Bitcoin, a platform for the simple exchange of value. With smart contract capability, intelligent stateful execution of complex transactions are possible. It is Blockchain 2.0 that started the blockchain revolution, the evolution of blockchain, and the attraction of enterprise organizations like IBM, Intel, Oracle, Amazon, Microsoft and many others, with the list expanding exponentially every day.

By 2015, after Ethereum became the first platform under Blockchain 2.0 to implement a single ledger, enterprise companies saw the potential of Blockchain 2.0. In December 2015, the Linux Foundation announced the creation of the Hyperledger project.

We cover the Hyperledger project in Part II, which contains two chapters. One covers the projects and tools, and the other covers the Hyperledger Fabric architecture and components. These two chapters provide the knowledge you will need for Part III, which covers smart contract development, invocation, maintenance, and testing. In the next section, we discuss, at a high level, the many components of blockchain.

Core Components of Blockchain

Blockchain is not a single compilation of source code. It may have a common executable, but both logical and physical components work together to form a functioning blockchain. This separation of logical and physical components may help create the confusion you see when discussing blockchain technology, along with the fact that blockchain is more of a concept than an implementation. Implementations of the concept are rapidly evolving and will continue to change and shift as more and more technologists and entrepreneurs enter the world of blockchain.

Common components form the central concept of blockchain. First is the decentralized network. Second is cryptography. Third is an immutable ledger. Fourth is consensus. And fifth is smart contracts. These five elements form the core components you need to create the concept of blockchain. The way they are implemented will evolve as new methods and algorithms are developed over time.

Which components you decide to use will shape your blockchain landscape and create a rich ecosystem of innovative solutions to new and existing problems. There are no rules.

Decentralized Network

A blockchain employs a decentralized network (depicted previously in Figure 1-1). *Public blockchains* allow anyone to participate, while *private blockchains* enforce membership, and only parties with a valid membership can participate in the blockchain.

Today there are two universally accepted types of blockchains: permissioned and permissionless. A *permissioned blockchain* requires a managing blockchain authority to enroll and grant membership to participate. The enrolled party may have rights to read only, or write only, or read and write. Hyperledger Fabric is a permissioned private blockchain.

A *permissionless blockchain* has no central authority, and anyone can participate. They can read and write the blockchain.

The network can be internal or external, or a combination. The network can be self-contained or span the world. Today we think of decentralized networks as made up of nodes when we consider blockchain. Any discussion, lecture, or presentation on blockchain will tell you that a blockchain must have a decentralized network of nodes. Depending on the speaker and target audience, the message will be biased to open, closed, or hybrid networks, but they're always decentralized.

Cryptography

Cryptography is the blood of blockchain. It is the art of creating and keeping secrets. Since ancient times, people have needed to create secrets and send secret messages. Today complex mathematical algorithms are used to create secrets. To send the secret messages, *protocols* are used, which are rules for connecting and communicating the messages between parties. Without cryptography, there is no blockchain or DLT. The primary use of cryptography is for encryption, keys, hashing, signatures, integrity, proof, and tamper resistance.

Digital signatures

Digital signatures employ asymmetric cryptography, which employs a private and public key. Keys are pseudorandom generated bit strings. The private key is never revealed and kept secret. The public key, however, is revealed and distributed to the public or a designated party. Digital signing algorithms use the private key to encrypt text. The encrypted text can be decrypted by only the public key. Because the private and public keys are a pair, they work together and facilitate the creation of the concept of digital signatures.

Digital signatures have three primary uses. The first is for *authentication*. When someone signs a blockchain transaction with a private key, the receiver can authenticate the party that signed the transaction by using the party's public key.

The second primary use is *integrity*. When a message is signed, any change in the message will invalidate the signature, and the receiving party will know the message has been tampered with.

The third important use is *nonrepudiation*. When a party signs a transaction and submits it, they cannot later try to claim they did not submit the transaction because their signature can be verified on the transaction submitted. They can claim only that their signature was stolen, but this too can be proven not true by employing additional signatures that belong to the device used to submit the transaction, including a timestamp and possible metadata that designates the location.

Hash functions

A *hash function* is a cryptographic one-way function. The function receives data as an argument, performs a cryptographic task, and then produces a string unique to the input data. If one bit of the input data is changed, the output string will change. If no bits are changed, the hash function will always produce the same output string.

Using a hash function in blockchain means you cannot change data, or the result will not match what is recorded. By linking the hash outputs into a Merkle tree, large numbers of records can be linked and stored in a block. The blocks are hashed, and the prior block's hash is part of the next block, creating the immutable chain of blocks.

The Merkle tree is a hash tree structure in which nodes are hashed together successively until a single node is created. This single node provides the integrity for the entire tree. The bottom nodes can be rehashed and verified for data integrity.

Several secure hash algorithms exist, but SHA-256 and SHA-3 are the primary ones used in blockchain.

Wallet

Private and public keys are used a lot in blockchains. Private keys are used to sign transactions and represent the secrets you want to secure and protect. You place your keys in a *digital wallet*, just like you place your credit cards in your physical wallet. You may have a wallet for each blockchain, or you may have separate wallets for different applications. Wallets are containers for your keys. They secure them, manage them, and can facilitate the function of signing.

The functionality of wallets is growing, and they are becoming more sophisticated. There are *physical wallets* that plug into your USB and keep your keys safe in a hardware enclave, and *software wallets* that can exist on your computers or in the cloud. As time goes on, the function and features of wallets will continue to grow and expand.

Shared Ledger

The *shared ledger* represents the database in blockchain. There is no standard format as with relational databases. The blockchain shared ledger has two hard-and-fast rules. First, it is immutable, meaning it is tamper-proof. Second, it is ordered. The order is by time.

These two rules create the feature in blockchain that makes it so powerful: a time-ordered record of immutable transactions. Combined with consensus and cryptography, the shared ledger yields a mechanism for delivering trust, transparency, and provenance. In Hyperledger, the ledger is divided into two components: the ledger database and the world state database.

Ledger database

The *ledger database* is a binary file. Blocks are appended to the file. Each peer locally hosts the file. The file cannot easily be read because it is in a binary format for performance purposes. Tools and an application programming interface (API) are available for exploring the blocks in the file. By exploring the blocks that make up the ledger database, every transaction can be read, and this allows the file to be replicated to new nodes if needed.

World state database

The *world state database* is unique to Hyperledger Fabric. It is a traditional database. You can plug in your database of choice. Hyperledger Fabric defaults to LevelDB, and supports through configuration CouchDB. By switching to CouchDB, applications can perform rich queries against the world state database. It is called the world state database because it represents the current state of the blockchain at any point in time.

Consensus

The concept of trust is the heart of blockchain. *Consensus* is the mechanism that facilitates the utopian aspect of blockchain by providing a means for disparate parties to transact without the necessary trust provided by intermediaries prevalent in today's transactional systems.

Another way to think about consensus is this: every time you use your credit card, several intermediaries are involved, each performing a specific function and collecting a fee, which you are paying for in addition to the amount of your purchase. You may not see the fees, but they are built into the transaction either implicitly or explicitly, and you are paying for them. In blockchain, the mechanism of consensus performs this function of trust, void of intermediaries.

Consensus has many implementations. Each is designed to provide trust based on probability. This probability is a function of agreement. Complete agreement is difficult to attain and requires a lot of time and resources, while partial agreement is faster and requires fewer resources, but is risky. How much risk is tolerable depends on blockchain governance and determines the attributes of the consensus mechanism used to reach agreement. Seldom, if ever, can the probability of agreement be 1, or 100%, and often less than 100% is acceptable.

Many consensus algorithms exist, and new algorithms are continuously being designed. You should understand four: proof of work, proof of stake, practical Byzantine fault tolerance, and proof of elapsed time.

PoW

Proof of work (*PoW*) is a consensus algorithm used in Bitcoin and Ethereum (note that Ethereum is moving to proof of stake). This consensus algorithm relies on energy by solving a cryptographic puzzle. The energy is represented by the hashrate, which is the number of hashes generated per second. To generate a hash requires a finite amount of energy. This energy is the electricity used to produce a hash. The more hashes produced, the more energy required. The cost of energy is critical to the number of hashes that can be produced. The puzzle is to find an input that produces a hash number with a certain number of leading zeros. The complexity or average time to solve is controlled by designating the number of leading zeros.

For Bitcoin, the number of leading zeros is adjusted to keep the solving time around 10 minutes. Depending on how many miners are hashing, this number will vary up or down. This consensus model is energy dependent because miners who spend the most energy have a higher chance of finding the winning input and thus are rewarded with Bitcoin and get to commit the current block.

PoS

Proof of stake (*PoS*) is a consensus algorithm that depends on both randomization of and vested interest in the blockchain. Several PoS algorithms exist, but most employ routines for generating a random number from certain criteria such as the amount of coins held or the age of coins held. The lowest or highest random number generated wins and gets to commit the current block and receive a reward. Once a stakeholder wins, their stake criteria reverts to zero; this effectively eliminates them for the next round.

PBFT

Practical Byzantine fault tolerance (*PBFT*) is a consensus algorithm that dates back to 1999. PBFT is a leader-based nonforking algorithm. It requires all nodes to be connected to all other nodes. All the nodes are known, and the algorithm does not permit random nodes to join the peering group. The algorithm supports up to one-third of the nodes faulting. As long as no more than one-third of the nodes fault, consensus can be reached.

PoET

Proof of elapsed time (*PoET*) is a consensus algorithm that uses a trusted execution environment (TEE). In this algorithm, random peers are selected to execute requests at a predetermined rate. The selected peers sample an exponentially distributed random variable. They wait for time to pass, determined by the sample, and the peer with the smallest sample wins the election and gets to commit the block.

Smart Contracts

Blockchain applications are segmented into a client, smart contract, and blockchain. The *client* is the frontend that a user, either human or machine, interacts with to sign and submit transactions. The submission goes to a designated node, or peer, which accepts the transactions and forwards it to the smart contract. The *smart contract* executes the transaction in concert with the blockchain. This interaction between the smart contract and blockchain incorporates an API that the smart contract uses to perform specific functions exposed by the blockchain (for example, read or insert).

A smart contract can't actually execute many functions against the blockchain because the blockchain is an immutable ledger. A smart contract can add or read data, but updating data is really an add data function that changes the current state. It cannot delete data even though it may execute an API for deleting data. The deletion is a change in state. This deletion would cause a read to return no data, but the data is there.

The data can be audited by using a special application called a *blockchain explorer*. This special program reads the immutable ledger at the lowest level, effectively crawling the data structure of the blocks and reading recorded data. A smart contract can do this too, but that would not be a typical use case.

A smart contract is best used to read the current state, perform logic on the state, and update (add) the state. Remember, the blockchain ledger is an immutable linked list of recorded data. That data represents the state. So the blockchain is really a running ledger of state transitions, a journal of immutable recordings. This is extremely powerful. Clients of the smart contract typically do the application-level logic and present the UX. Clients not only act as the interface to the smart contract, but in many ways, they represent the application to the user.

The thing to remember about the smart contract is it really isn't that smart. It sits between the client and the blockchain. This is actually a good thing, because you don't want the smart contract working that hard.

You don't want to be making a lot of round trips between the client and ledger—for example, a thousand reads to populate a list. You want to tell the smart contract to read a thousand states and send them to your client. This executes a single call to the smart contract, an expensive resource, and the smart contract can potentially bulk-read on the ledger.

The typical interface is asynchronous, so keep this in mind and use your callbacks effectively. Try to give the user the perception of a lot of work being performed, when in reality, the blockchain is a turtle, not a rabbit like the databases we grew up with. Used wisely, smart contracts are powerful instruments; they can work for you or against you, so think about how you are using them. As a smart contract developer, you always want to keep your client in mind and support them with the most efficient API, based on what we have discussed.

Blockchain Architecture

The architecture of a blockchain consists of a decentralized and distributed network of nodes. Each node hosts a copy of the immutable ledger. The immutable ledger is a cryptographically linked set of append-only blocks. The nodes execute transactions and consensus to add blocks to the ledger. Clients sign transactions and submit them to the nodes. Nodes forward the validated transactions to the smart contracts for execution. Executed transactions are ordered and placed into blocks. The blocks are appended to the blockchain. The core design of a blockchain consists of blocks, chains, and a network.

Nodes

Computers are called *nodes* because of the role they play in creating the distributed network. They can be virtual machines in the cloud that are hosted by physical servers. They can be laptops participating in distributed networks. They can be Internet of Things devices operating in decentralized industrial networks. They can even be smart light bulbs. *Node* is a general term representing an endpoint in a network. The network can be wired or wireless. Another name for a node is *peer*, as in peer-to-peer networks, which are designed for decentralized applications.

For the Hyperledger Fabric blockchain, you will encounter both terms. In Hyperledger Fabric, the term *peer* represents a computing node that executes the endorsement and commitment of transactions and hosts an immutable ledger. In Bitcoin, nodes are *miners*, and like Hyperledger Fabric peers, commit transactions to the ledger.

Blocks

Blocks contain the records of submitted and committed transactions. Each block also contains a header, a timestamp, and the hash of the prior block. The first block, called the *genesis block*, contains additional information that describes the blockchain, like policies. If it's in a permissioned blockchain, like Hyperledger Fabric, the genesis block will contain a list of member organizations and their certificates as well as policy information describing the number of organizations that must endorse transactions. It will also contain the identity of the orderer node responsible for ordering the transaction and creating the blocks that peers append to the blockchain.

The block contains additional data used to link the blocks together and provide integrity constraints, preventing any ability to tamper with the data contained in the block. The blocks are linked together, and this linking of blocks is responsible for the term *blockchain*.

Cryptography is used to create and maintain the blockchain data structure and linking. The block is tamper-proof because of the use of the cryptography.

The blocks together represent the immutable ledger, and many refer to them as the blockchain *database*. Blocks are appended to the last block created. Over time, this appending process creates a large data structure that must be managed. Other data structures are in use, like graphs, that are not linear and create network-like data structures. Data in a transaction is not always stored in the block and may be hosted in a traditional data store such as files or existing database technology.

Chains

Chains are a linked list of blocks. They are immutable and append-only. A blockchain architecture may have one or more chains. Chains can grow to an infinite length, or number of blocks. This can be prevented or managed by pruning, but pruning has side effects that reduce the trust in the blockchain network and remove the ability to explore and audit the entire chain. This can reduce the integrity of the chain.

Channels

Each blockchain in Hyperledger Fabric is called a *channel*, which is a consortium of organizations collaborating to execute transactions that are related to a specific purpose. Organizations in Hyperledger Fabric may belong to multiple channels. Bitcoin and Ethereum use a single main blockchain and multiple blockchains for test purposes.

Supporting Technology and Concepts

Beyond the components (decentralized network, cryptography, immutable ledger, consensus, and smart contracts), you need to understand, or at least be aware of, many concepts and supporting technologies in order to develop a solid foundation for understanding blockchain. Let's introduce each of these concepts and supporting technologies so you can later further your investigation and advance your knowledge over the course of your blockchain journey.

DLT

Distributed ledger technology is the parent of blockchain. With DLT, you use only digital signatures and do not use consensus, because you want scale and high throughput. It is consensus that creates the high latency and limits on scale in blockchain. This is why you see DLTs like Corda so popular in the financial and insurance sectors. When you have semi-trust among participants, as in insurance and banking, you can enforce remediation by relying on digital signatures; you can use DLT. But when you need a trust mechanism to enforce integrity among participants, as in supply chains, you want blockchain because the consensus mechanism provides this level of assurance and trust.

Decentralization

Blockchain is a *decentralized* technology. The ledger is hosted by a network of peer-to-peer nodes that form the decentralized network. The removal of a central control point is what creates the concept of decentralization. It is the ability to delegate control to all nodes that collaborate, to execute the goal of the network, that delivers power to blockchain. This delegated control and collaboration provides the means for performing consensus without a central authority influencing the outcome.

Peer-to-Peer

Blockchain networks are *peer-to-peer networks*. The network is designed to be decentralized. No central control exists in a decentralized network, and each peer (or node) is connected to one or more peers (or nodes) in the network. The peers cooperate to send and forward messages in the network. Using peer-friendly protocols like Gossip enables the fast replication of messages among numerous peers in a network. This allows millions of peers to receive messages within seconds. A peer-to-peer decentralized network facilitates the ability to maintain copies of a blockchain ledger.

Immutability

The concept of *immutability*, which means not changeable, or tamper-proof, is critical to blockchain, because it is the primary attribute of the ledger. Trust is created from the concept and implementation of immutability. Knowing that time-ordered transactions are immutable allows parties to create trust and finality.

Identity

Blockchain and smart contracts need identities to function. *Identities* represent the entities (humans and machines) that participate in executing smart contract transactions and blockchain administration. For enterprise blockchains, organizations that are members enroll identities to represent them and perform transactions on behalf of the organization. Identities are assigned private and public keys for digital signing and encryption of data. The digital signatures authenticate the identities and authorize them to perform transactions.

Accounts

The concept of accounts in blockchain enables us to perform a variety of roles and to execute a multitude of functions for a single identity. An *account* is a record of attributes that define specific rights for access and authorization to perform transactions on assets that belong to or are managed by the account. Roles are created and assigned to an account. The role defines a set of permissions mapped to an account. Identities are granted a role, which allows the identity to perform actions against the account permitted by a role. This means we do not need to create and manage an identity for every account permissioned to execute transactions on a blockchain. Accounts allow us to partition the roles and permissions available to one or more identities. Accounts can hold various forms of state and transact as a trusted entity on the blockchain.

SDK

A *software development kit* (*SDK*) is used to integrate or develop software for a blockchain. Most developers are familiar with this component because many applications provide an SDK to develop software for their application. Blockchain is no different; most blockchain platforms provide one or more SDKs, each targeting a programming language and specific component of the platform. Several SDKs are available for Hyperledger Fabric, including JavaScript, Java, and Go, for developing Fabric blockchain applications.

API

An *application programming interface* (*API*) is a software contract between the application and client, expressed as a collection of methods or functions. The API may be implemented with an SDK or as a RESTful interface. It defines the available functions you can execute. Some APIs have hundreds of methods or functions you can call to execute a variety of transactions. Others may have fewer than a dozen and target a very narrow and specific set of application features.

The API is the intermediary interface between the client and the application. It must be managed well and support the continued evolution of the application's life cycle. Versioning is often used to control and provide ease of migration to new or deprecated functionality.

Blockchain is an application and has an API. It is the API that smart contracts embed and expose to clients. The embedded API and exposed API are not the same intermediary. The *exposed API* is meant for the clients of the blockchain's smart contract facility, while the *embedded API* is an internal contract between the smart contract facility and the core blockchain software responsible for operating the node, or peer. The smart contract facility may or may not be hosted by the node, or peer.

Transactions

Clients submit *transactions*. These transactions are processed by the nodes, or peers, and, if accepted, committed to a block that is appended to the chain of blocks (or blockchain). Transactions can be anything, from a data update about an asset to the payment for a service or the purchase of a product. They may be simply the recording of information representing a known state or the execution of an action. Transactions can originate from human clients or machine clients. Transactions in blockchain are always timestamped and ordered. They are immutable and cannot be tampered with. Transactions are signed with a private key when submitted for processing and may be authenticated depending on the blockchain permission for transaction submission.

Incentives

Incentives are rarely discussed in blockchain, and this hampers the success of many blockchain projects. A strong *incentive* is needed to create the behavior required to succeed in blockchain. The miners of Bitcoin know what incentive is because it is what drives them to mine. As a result, they execute transactions for clients and maintain the immutable and trusted blockchain that facilitates the exchange of value that clients seek to perform for a small fee. Their incentive is a reward if they can solve a cryptographic puzzle. The reward is a sizable monetary grant represented in Bitcoin.

For blockchains in the enterprise, there has been little or no incentive along the lines of Bitcoin or Ethereum. The absence of incentive has been a major reason for so many projects failing to succeed. Without a strong incentive, external partners have little reason to become enthusiastic about changing their mature business processes. They see only added cost and risk. The financial modeling, if done, is not enough to convince them this is a better and more efficient way to execute the business processes performed.

Privacy

Keeping data and the identity of the participants of a transaction private is a major concern in blockchain. The ability to disclose selectively and operate on data that cannot be exposed is critical to blockchain's advancement. When several parties need to transact and exchange information, they should adhere to *data privacy*. Likewise, when specific parties want required data to execute their portion of a complex transaction, that data must be kept private.

One weakness in blockchain until recently has been the inability to mix varying levels of privacy within complex transactions. Hyperledger Fabric v2 supports the ability to perform transactions with private data. Within Hyperledger, work is being performed on zero-knowledge proofs (ZKPs). This cryptography facilitates the ability to prove facts without disclosing the source material used to determine a fact. Think of verifying an age without presenting the documentation that proves the age. This is powerful because it will allow transactions that protect the privacy of parties to the transaction. Because blockchain is a linked ledger and keys may represent parties or addresses, it is possible to build profiles that reveal enough information that could reduce the privacy a party thinks they possess. This is true with Bitcoin and Ethereum.

State

Blockchain has history, but it is the *state* we most often want. Being an immutable ledger of state transitions over time is what blockchain is built for. But when we put blockchain to use, we find it is the current state that manifests its power. We believe in the state because we know it was hard-earned, going through a gauntlet of validation and cryptographic proving. We enjoy the knowledge that it is tamper-proof, which adds even more value to the state.

But the state is not history. Blockchain has the history, but we find that accessing that history is expensive and not something the blockchain is really all that good at—that is, at scale. Because at scale, it is all about capturing state, reaching consensus, and committing it. We have learned to keep the state fresh and cached and to put the history in a traditional database. If we need to prove the history, we can walk the ledger and prove the history. But history is history. State is what matters. You make your decision based on state. State can be a rolling record—for example, sales to date. You don't need to run those reports to get state.

This is a sea change and a huge boost in productivity. Blockchain will change the world because the world will know the current state, now, not tomorrow, or at the end of the week or quarter. The ability to maintain accurate and trustful state is a powerful tool to be leveraged and exploited by smart contract developers to empower decision makers, be they human or machine.

Turing Complete

The addition of the concept of *Turing complete* to blockchain was a turning point for blockchain's separation from Bitcoin. It made blockchain a smart transactional engine for the 21st century. Smart contracts need to be Turing complete and deterministic to reach finality. Being deterministic allows them to be decentralized and scaled. Turing complete and deterministic capabilities enable consensus mechanisms to perform the function of intermediaries, delivering a means to reach agreement on state and finality.

Gas

Ethereum employs the concept of *gas*. This means you pay to compute, and the fees to compute are calculated by the instructions you execute. This concept is not new; mainframes charged users to compute, and calculated fees based on CPU time. In the world of the web, it is an explicit cost. We all pay fees to compute, but we cannot quantify them because of the layers of access and resources used. The closest we can get to the gas model is the Amazon Web Services (AWS) cloud computing service, which charges by the resource and time of use. AWS is much coarser than Ethereum's granular cost model.

The volatility of Ether and all cryptocurrencies is problematic for trying to budget and launch applications on the Ethereum platform. With AWS, the currency is dollars, so you have a reasonable expectation of your long-term costs to launch and budget the resources required to operate your application. Your costs effectively do not vary from day to day, let alone minute to minute, as on Ethereum.

In addition to the gas cost, you are using a shared resource and are thus competing directly with others who want to execute their application and will pay more for the opportunity. This can lead to a situation where you may never get your transactions executed or not get them executed within the time period required to achieve your goal.

Tokens

Most will equate tokens with cryptocurrency, but they are evolving and will continue to evolve as they move further and further from the Bitcoin and Altcoin communities. A *token* is a digital voucher that can be exchanged. Tokens can be classified into types.

The first is *cryptocurrency*, the first blockchain token. Note that cryptographic tokens have been around a long time and have been used for various purposes like identity and metadata. The newest token, a derivative of cryptocurrency, is called a *stable coin*. It is called a stable coin because its token value is designed to equal the token value of another token, currency, or asset that does not exhibit large value fluctuations. The term *pegged* represents this value relationship between the stable coin and the other token, currency, or asset, which the stable token is designed to mirror in value. For example, stable coins pegged to the US dollar are valued at one dollar plus or minus a very small change in value on the order of hundredths or thousandths of a dollar at any point in time. Stable coins were promoted by Goldman Sachs and Circle to create stability in cryptocurrency and offer a means for established companies to explore cryptocurrency.

Crypto tokens, in the world of blockchain, are classified as cryptocurrency, security tokens, and utility tokens. You will find a variety of other names, but you need to focus on security and utility tokens.

Security tokens are sold to investors through various means, including initial coin offerings (ICOs) and security token offerings (STOs). Security tokens are considered securities, which are regulated by the US Securities and Exchange Commission (SEC). Therefore, you cannot sell (issue) them without registering with the SEC. They are treated no different from stock.

Utility tokens are like Ethereum's gas. These are tokens you can sell, but have no air of investment surrounding them. The blockchain uses utility tokens as an internal means of operation. Creating and trying to sell utility tokens is risky. You should talk to legal professionals and seek a no-action letter from the SEC. You do this by submitting a detailed plan that explains how you will use the utility tokens. Some companies have received a no-action letter from the SEC and serve as a model for what the SEC considers utility tokens. Utility tokens do not appreciate and may fall in value, but no reward is associated with their purchase. They typically equal one dollar and can be redeemed for one dollar. An escrow account holds the funds exchanged for the utility token.

Tokens are an exciting opportunity for innovation in smart contract development and blockchain use. They can be smart, hold value, and represent assets and rights.

On-Chain

When we execute work on the blockchain, this is referred to as *on-chain*. Or, when we store data on the blockchain, it may be referred to as *on-chain data*. Be judicious when deciding what data you store on-chain because the blockchain as it exists today is not suitable as a data warehouse. You should store transaction data off-chain (explained next). When you want to rapidly execute large numbers of transactions, you should investigate executing the transactions off-chain.

Off-Chain

The ability to move work off the blockchain and perform it external to the blockchain is known as *off-chain*. Once the off-chain work is performed, the result is moved back on-chain to be committed via consensus to the blockchain. This is reasonable if you want to execute 10,000 rapid transactions, roll them up into one transaction, and then move that one transaction back on-chain to be subjected to consensus and committed to the blockchain. The off-chain transactions can be recorded on what is known as a *side-chain* and maybe via a DLT for fast execution. The Merkle tree of the transactions (shown previously in Figure 1-1) is placed into a single transaction and placed on-chain for consensus and commitment to the primary blockchain.

Scalability

Scalability is one of blockchain's biggest problems. Blockchain employs consensus, and this creates latency in the processing of transactions. Reaching agreement, which is what consensus is all about, takes time. Time is what you need to eliminate if you want to scale. You cannot reach consensus en masse. A lot of research and design work is going into solving this problem.

The finance and insurance sectors have decided to use only DLT, which does not use consensus, as discussed earlier. They can do this because their sectors have an element of trust built in due to being highly regulated industries. For sectors like supply chain, trust needs to exist between parties. This trust has been accomplished by intermediaries. Employing intermediaries carries a significant cost, both in dollars and efficiency. The promise and attraction of blockchain is to eliminate or greatly reduce the need for intermediaries by employing consensus. Scalability is an area of concern that all blockchain projects must plan for in their application design.

Cryptocurrency

Bitcoin is a *cryptocurrency*, or digital asset, designed to be used as money. Hundreds of cryptocurrencies exist. You can think of cryptocurrency as digital cash. That was the inspiration behind its design, but that design has failed to manifest. Instead, it has become an asset like gold, with a devout following and marketplace for daily trading as the price fluctuates.

Few vendors accept cryptocurrency because of its volatility. Fiat money, the currency issued by central banks like the Federal Reserve, is stable for the most part. It, too, could experience a wide variance but is not volatile like cryptocurrency.

Most use cryptocurrency as a high-risk long-term investment, hoping it will appreciate, or as a trading vehicle trying to capitalize on the volatility. Central banks are now looking at moving into the issuance of cryptocurrency and adopting the term *digital cash* because it has many benefits for cross-border and trade finance payments.

Cryptocurrency is supported by blockchain technology and DLT. By using cryptocurrency and blockchain, central banks and governments will be able to extend and control the movement and use of cryptocurrency, which they cannot do with cash.

Enclaves

When you need to sign a transaction, you must use your private key. Anytime you access your private key, you are open to attack and events that may destroy, corrupt, or steal your private key. If something happens to your private key, anything that requires it for access is lost. There may be no way for you to recover your private key, and thus the asset or access granted is lost forever.

You store your keys and anything else digital in an *enclave*, which you use to perform the signing of transactions for you. Enclaves come in two forms: hardware and software. They are like private vaults that allow no entry without a secret password or elaborate ritual. Using an enclave prevents the key from being exposed, thus protecting and safeguarding it. Enclaves can perform their own transactions too, so they can be used to execute routines you want to keep secret.

J.P. Morgan's Quorum blockchain, a modified clone of Ethereum, uses an enclave to perform its cryptographic functions, providing a level of security warranted by a regulated financial institution. The Hyperledger Sawtooth blockchain uses Intel's Software Guard Extensions (SGX), which is a hardware enclave. Sawtooth uses the enclave for executing a secure version of its PoET consensus algorithm.

Oracles

When a blockchain needs external data or verification of internally submitted or generated data, it reaches out to an *oracle*. This is an API, interface, or website that can be scraped for information.

A smart contract that is a betting application, gold futures application, or loan application, for example, needs to know external information. The betting application needs to know who won the game last night, so it scrapes the *USA Today* Sports page or a paid site that offers sports scores for the outcome of the game. The gold futures application accesses the *Wall Street Journal* or a paid brokerage site for the current price of gold. The loan application accesses a site publishing current interest rates.

Oracles can also be other smart contracts. The idea behind the oracle is that it is an external source of valid, trusted information.

DApps

Decentralized applications, or *DApps*, are smart contract–based applications that seek to provide the same type of applications found on the web, from games to financial applications. DApps require fees to operate, unlike web applications. While many DApps exist, few have reached great success, except for a few used to trade virtual goods. The most popular are gambling DApps, which are not allowed in the United States. DApps suffer because of the UX and fees required to operate them.

DApps have not entered the enterprise space but may begin to emerge and transform as enterprises adopt blockchain and as a general-purpose hybrid blockchain is launched and goes viral. A hybrid blockchain spans the enterprise and public space and is architected along a federated design pattern. None exist today.

Virtual Machine

In blockchain, when we talk about a *virtual machine* (*VM*), we are talking about smart contract engines. The first blockchain virtual machine was the Ethereum Virtual Machine (EVM), which established Blockchain 2.0. Since then, it has been cloned, extended, and enhanced by other blockchains. The VM executes the smart contract.

Fork

When a blockchain splits for any reason, it creates a *fork*, which is a diverging chain of blocks, thus creating two versions of the blockchain. This can be seen as a negative or positive event. If all participants agree to the fork and it is managed, then it is positive. This can happen when an update is needed, a severe bug is found in the blockchain software, or a corrupting event has taken place and correction is needed.

Governance

How you manage and control a blockchain is determined by the *governance model* or function. Governance is important for the operation of the blockchain, and without it, a blockchain will not last long. It needs governance to manage the life cycle, which includes upgrades, failures, participant rules, and operational constraints.

Genesis

The first block in a ledger is called the *genesis block*. This special block marks the beginning of the blockchain. It will contain additional data that only the genesis block requires, like metadata describing specific characteristics and attributes about the ledger.

Clients

Transactions are submitted to the blockchain by *clients*. Clients will sign their transaction by using their private key (or keys) and send the signed transactions to a blockchain node. Nodes then replicate the received transactions by sending them to known nodes; eventually, all the nodes have a copy of the client transactions. Clients may host wallets to store their keys and maintain receipts of committed transactions securely.

Summary

This chapter covered a lot of information to help you begin to understand the concept of blockchain. We began with a discussion on the origin of blockchain. Then we discussed several general components of blockchain, followed by its architecture, shared ledger, cryptography, consensus, and smart contract components. We kept the discussion at a high level so you could assimilate the fundamental concepts and formulate your own interpretation based on the knowledge we provided. We hope you research each item in greater detail as your blockchain journey continues and you master smart contract development.

In Part II, we'll discuss the Hyperledger project and tools, followed by the Hyperledger Fabric architecture and components, to provide you with the necessary knowledge for Part III, where we cover smart contract development with Hyperledger Fabric.

Introduction to Hyperledger Projects

Part I introduced and explored the fundamental concepts of the blockchain. Specifically, we surveyed the essential blockchain concepts and terminologies common among all blockchain platforms while briefly touching on concepts related to Hyperledger.

This part consists of two chapters. In Chapter 2, we introduce you to the Hyperledger ecosystem by reviewing its projects, tools, and libraries, and then expand on the Hyperledger terms and concepts discussed in Chapter 1 by explaining them in detail. In Chapter 3, we review the Hyperledger Fabric components—including peer, channel, and chaincodes—that are essential for building blockchain applications and understanding the rest of the chapters. In short, a thorough understanding of all Hyperledger Fabric components is highly recommended for building, deploying, and managing enterprise-level Hyperledger Fabric applications.

Overview of Hyperledger Projects and Tools

The previous chapter introduced you to the concept of blockchain, its main platforms, and terminology. We started with a discussion on the origin of blockchain, and then discussed several of its general components (including shared ledger, cryptography, consensus, and smart contract components), followed by its architecture and supporting technology. This chapter covers the Hyperledger projects and tools, and Chapter 3 covers the Hyperledger Fabric architecture and components. Collectively, Chapters 1 through 3 will provide you with the necessary knowledge for Part III, which delves into smart contract development with Hyperledger Fabric.

This chapter mainly targets those who are relatively new to Hyperledger. The primary goal is to explore projects and tools that are developed under Hyperledger and to equip you with the necessary knowledge and important technical designs of the Hyperledger ecosystem so we can then apply these technologies through real-world use cases. The materials included in this chapter will help you understand Hyperledger as a whole, and you can use this high-level overview as a guideline for making the best of each Hyperledger project.

As a reminder, to design and deploy Hyperledger Fabric blockchain applications, you need not thoroughly understand all tools and projects discussed here. Just use this chapter as your reference for better navigating through the Hyperledger projects. Except for Hyperledger Fabric and a few other projects that we cover in depth (Hyperledger Aries, Hyperledger Grid, Hyperledger Avalon, and Hyperledger Besu), this chapter should not be considered a definitive guide for all Hyperledger projects.

For those who already have a good knowledge of the Hyperledger ecosystem, this chapter would be a good "scratch the surface" review. Or, if you prefer, feel free to jump to the next chapter to explore the Hyperledger Fabric project.

Although we briefly reviewed the history behind blockchain technology in the preceding chapter, in this chapter we will slightly expand on the evolution and phases of blockchain before diving into the Hyperledger family architecture and ecosystem.

This chapter will help you understand the following:

- The four phases in the evolution of blockchain technology
- The architecture and design philosophy behind the Hyperledger family
- Hyperledger distributed ledger technologies like Indy and Sawtooth
- Available tools in the Hyperledger family
- Existing libraries in the Hyperledger family

Evolution and Phases of Blockchain Technology

Since its inception, blockchain technology has incorporated ideas and components like cryptography that are gaining tremendous popularity among businesses. Also, the demand for secure, scalable, and reliable automation practices and solutions are among the major challenges that emerging technologies such as blockchain have to address. Indeed, the traditional business operations in the 21st century are entering into a new phase of automation at the enterprise level. Moreover, at the global level, emerging markets are keen on adopting technologies that have the potential for self-regulation. As a result, the advent of blockchain and its evolution play a prominent role in shaping the landscape of self-governed technologies and automation in the near future.

One way to view the advances of blockchain technology is to categorize its evolution into four generations. Let's briefly survey blockchain generations from 1.0 to 4.0.

Blockchain 1.0

The initial generation of blockchain came into existence with the advent of cryptocurrencies like Bitcoin. The role of blockchain technology was to improve the existing monetary system by allowing people to send transactions relying on cryptography instead of banks. During this generation of blockchain, the network was peer-to-peer, decentralized, anonymous, and at the same time transparent. However, as discussed in Chapter 1, its major drawback was its use of the proof-of-work algorithm, which required lots of mining.

Blockchain 2.0

Blockchain technology turned a corner around 2015 when tech innovators started exploring its trustless feature in addition to monetary transactions. This led to the creation of the Ethereum platform, which brought about two major innovations:

- The use of other digital assets, besides cryptocurrency, as a basis for other decentralized projects.
- The advent of smart contracts (as discussed in Chapter 1) added security to transactions by automatically controlling the execution of all conditions by all actors while automating the transaction processing for all actors in a blockchain.

Blockchain 3.0

The third generation of blockchain focused on improving its flaws and deficiencies while expanding its use cases. For instance, proof-of-stake consensus replaced proof of work. Other features and functionalities were added to boost blockchain performance and make it adoptable by different industries. For example, blockchain architectures such as the consortium or cross-chain transaction processing were invented. Likewise, other changes regarding regulatory compliance and governance, privacy, and smart contracts were introduced.

Blockchain 4.0

Currently, professionals don't agree on the exact features or direction that fourth-generation blockchain technology will take. Some believe that it will merge with other disruptive technologies like the Internet of Things or AI. Others think it should follow the preceding generations by improving its features to make it more efficient, scalable, and accessible to the masses.

Throughout its generations, blockchain has come a long way to establish itself as an emerging technology that transforms many traditional business operations. As such, a good understanding of previous generations or blockchain history will help us foresee its vision and future. Eventually, the technology will find its feet among enterprise application development projects in both the private and public sectors.

The latest trends in blockchain are more often reflected in private blockchain projects, also known as distributed ledger technology. These DLT projects are usually based on three common use cases:

Traceability of assets
> These projects leave a notarized record within the DLT system that makes this information backed up and immutable, to ensure that data that will later be accessible. This data can be displayed publicly to ensure that certain sensitive data flows in; until now, little transparency existed. These projects also can serve

to exploit data internally and improve internal processes in companies. In the end, what you want is to record a series of events that occurred in a physical or digital asset.

Digital identity

This use case is subject to the regulations of each country or region. Many companies and governments want to digitize user credentials to enhance user data security and privacy. This use case has many legal components, and there are different ways to approach it. However, digital identity solutions should be implemented on a private blockchain network using a DLT like Hyperledger Fabric. An increasing number of companies have implementations of self-sovereign digital identities seeking to be accepted by regulation, either by hybridizing existing solutions based on digital certificates or using already developed identity standards. This will be one of the main projects on blockchain.

Digital currency

Digital currency has been one of the main use cases since Ethereum appeared. It is still a project that continues to undergo improvements and evolutions. Companies such as Facebook and Telegram have tried to build their own new payment systems based on digital currency. The end of this new type of currency has not been reached either; we will continue to see new implementations, since both banks and governments will surely end up using this technology for monetary purposes.

Hyperledger Family, Architecture, and Ecosystem

As we covered in the previous chapter, the Hyperledger project was initiated by the nonprofit Linux Foundation as a collaborative (open source) platform for designing and building distributed ledger applications. The platform later gained momentum and popularity as large private companies such as IBM and Accenture endorsed and supported its mission.

Hyperledger's adoption and popularity among private businesses stems from several factors. The most notable are its well-designed architecture for private transactions and its multiledger structure for handling large-scale datasets. With Ethereum, for instance, each node on the network holds the same data, but under Hyperledger Fabric, nodes may carry different data, depending on the nature of the transaction and business requirements. Also, Hyperledger Fabric allows private data sharing among a subset of network members, which is well suited for enterprise business applications. As of this writing, some Hyperledger tools and frameworks are at the incubation stage, whereas others are active.

Hyperledger comes with 16 projects classified into four categories: distributed ledger, tools, libraries, and domain-specific projects. We review these 16 projects in more detail later in this chapter. For a comprehensive review of individual projects and their latest updates or news, visit the Hyperledger project website at *hyperledger.org*.

The Hyperledger Design Philosophy

Before we discuss how the Hyperledger framework works, it would be good to have a basic understanding of the Hyperledger philosophy. Projects under the Hyperledger umbrella have incorporated several principles that are essential for meeting the multitude of business requirements.

Modular architecture

Blockchain applications built with Hyperledger use multiple components such as policies, consensus, and chaincodes. This modular architecture allows these components to communicate with one another efficiently, while making it easy for the developer community to maintain each component independently.

Ultra secure

Since data stored on a blockchain application is immutable, it requires a higher level of security compared with other applications. Also, the enterprise nature of Hyperledger, where multiple ledgers can be stored in its blockchain nodes, requires an ultra level of security. Therefore, Hyperledger was designed and developed with such security considerations in place since its inception. Indeed, the expert team working on Hyperledger security regularly reviews and audits security protocols and procedures to meet the ever-changing requirements of the cybersecurity landscape.

Interoperability

The interoperability feature of Hyperledger is a distinct feature that allows its applications to connect and interact with blockchain applications and networks built on other platforms like Ethereum. Indeed, even within Hyperledger projects, you can use this interoperability to connect one Hyperledger project to another.

Noncryptocurrency architecture

The architecture of Hyperledger does not incorporate cryptocurrency tokens like Bitcoin. Since its inception, Hyperledger was designed to be used for enterprise application development rather than as a place for holding and managing cryptocurrencies.

Application programming interfaces

With current fast-paced developments in the cloud and emerging technologies like artificial intelligence, it is imperative for enterprise blockchain applications to have rich APIs to communicate and exchange data with existing systems. In fact, an API as a bridge between on-chain and off-chain data is common in enterprise blockchain developments. To stay ahead of the game, each project under Hyperledger has embedded rich APIs into its architecture. The API feature alone is advancing the popularity and adoption of Hyperledger among the developer community.

Refer to the official Hyperledger website and publications for more detail about these features. Now let's take a look at how the Hyperledger framework works.

Overview of Hyperledger

Hyperledger comes with several essential components. Here we'll briefly discuss the eight business blockchain components of Hyperledger.

Consensus layer

The consensus layer has undergone various modifications over time in Hyperledger Fabric. First, there was Solo mode, followed by Kafka mode along with Apache Zoo-Keeper to put Fabric networks into production, and now Raft has finally appeared to replace Kafka and ZooKeeper. This latest change has given greater power and simplicity to Fabric deployments and has brought blockchain technology within reach. It is a success for the Hyperledger team.

Smart contract layer

Smart contracts, as with consensus, have evolved within the Hyperledger road map. In the beginning, no clear definition existed of the supported languages within Fabric. The Fabric developer community, for example, removed Java and then included it again. Now developers have also included the TypeScript language. In previous versions of Fabric, the installation of chaincodes was quite centralized. Hyperledger Fabric v2 introduced new governance, allowing for a more decentralized way to perform Fabric installations. We discuss this topic in more detail in Chapter 9, where you'll learn more about new features introduced in v2.

Communication layer

Communication among peers is one of the most sensitive parts in all blockchains, especially to avoid attacks by middlemen. For this reason, it is recommended, in many cases, to use the Transport Layer Security (TLS) configuration that Fabric provides as one more security point in communications.

Data store abstraction

The way data is stored in Fabric is special. We can store data in either Apache CouchDB or by default in LevelDB (you can read more about this in Chapter 9). CouchDB comes with many more features than LevelDB, and supports the following:

- More programming languages, including Ruby and PHP
- APIs and other access methods like RESTful HTTP/JSON API
- Multisource replication and source-replica replication methods

Crypto abstraction

The cryptography that Fabric uses within its operation is quite complex and works perfectly within the entire call flow among network components. Within these cryptographic algorithms, we can find ZKP, which, as discussed in Chapter 1, allows blockchain transactions within the Fabric network to be verified while maintaining user anonymity. Fabric uses another cryptographic protocol called *Identity Mixer* to protect users' privacy when signing, authenticating, and transferring certified attributes.

Identity service

The identity services available with Fabric are based on fairly configurable certificate authority (CA) architectures. Normally, it is advisable to have a root CA, and then intermediate CAs that manage the certificates. And if that were not enough, Hyperledger also allows the management of all these certificates to be carried out with a hardware security module (HSM) connected to the CA.

API

In our opinion, the API is one of the fundamental pieces of Fabric because it is where the use of blockchain data opens up to the outside world. The intuitive and convenient Fabric SDKs are used to interconnect the blockchain with any external digitized system. Fabric has SDKs in both Node.js and Go as well as Java with fairly complete documentation.

Interoperation

Since Fabric is continually evolving, we need interoperability among the multiple versions of Fabric networks. This is a characteristic that Fabric's developers have decided to maintain, and it provides greater continuity to the projects.

Now let's look at how we can utilize the Hyperledger ecosystem to solve real-world business problems. In the next two sections, we cover Hyperledger projects, tools, and libraries.

Overview of Hyperledger Projects

Since Hyperledger is gaining strong support from the open source community, new projects are regularly added to the ecosystem. At the time of this writing, six projects are active and ten others are in the incubation stage. Each project has unique advantages. The Hyperledger projects, as listed in Table 2-1, are categorized into four types: distributed ledger (or framework), libraries, tools, and domain-specific projects.

Table 2-1. Hyperledger projects and types[a]

	Project name	Project type				Status
		Distributed ledger	Libraries	Tools	Domain-specific	
1	Hyperledger Indy	X				Active
2	Hyperledger Fabric	X				Active
3	Hyperledger Aries		X			Active
4	Hyperledger Iroha	X				Active
5	Hyperledger Sawtooth	X				Active
6	Hyperledger Besu	X				Active
7	Hyperledger Quilt		X			Incubation
8	Hyperledger Ursa		X			Incubation
9	Hyperledger Transact		X			Incubation
10	Hyperledger Cactus	X				Incubation
11	Hyperledger Caliper			X		Incubation
12	Hyperledger Cello			X		Incubation
13	Hyperledger Explorer			X		Incubation
14	Hyperledger Grid				X	Incubation
15	Hyperledger Burrow	X				Incubation
16	Hyperledger Avalon			X		Incubation

[a] Based on information available from the Hyperledger website as of August 2021.

This section covers the seven Hyperledger projects that are in the distributed ledger category. Further, we briefly explain Hyperledger Grid, a domain-specific project for building blockchain supply chains. "Overview of Hyperledger Tools and Libraries" on page 37 covers the remaining two Hyperledger project categories.

Distributed Ledger Frameworks

Seven projects are frameworks for building blockchain distributed ledgers with Hyperledger. These framework projects aim to provide platforms for building a variety of distributed ledgers and their components. Each project under the Hyperledger umbrella has an implementation of its own, as briefly discussed in this section.

Hyperledger Indy

A nonprofit group called the Sovrin Foundation originally developed *Hyperledger Indy* as a means for individuals to hold and share their identities with whom they want. With the increasing popularity of identity management, especially among blockchain use cases, Hyperledger Indy gained momentum to become a decentralized platform for managing identities. It comes with tools and features essential for digital wallet management on a blockchain network or other distributed ledger systems. Internet users, for example, can use one single persistent authentication (username and password) stored in Indy for accessing and using all sites on the internet.

Hyperledger Fabric

As covered intensively in this book, *Hyperledger Fabric* is currently the most popular and vastly adopted project under the Hyperledger umbrella. Fabric comes with modular components like peers, smart contracts, and channels that make it suitable for building and managing multiledger enterprise-grade blockchain applications. Its smart contract can be written (as covered in detail in Chapter 4) in multiple languages like Go, JavaScript, and Java.

The architecture of Hyperledger allows for multiple companies to join and conduct transactions as a single consortium. Likewise, as business requirements grow, companies can become members of multiple consortiums at once. Indeed, policies are one of the most powerful components of Fabric; the policies come with configurations that allow both simple (consisting of two members) and complex (consisting of multiple consortiums, each with multiple members) blockchain networks to operate.

Note that since this book is about Hyperledger Fabric, we will cover its framework, architecture, and components in depth in the next chapter.

Hyperledger Iroha

Hyperledger Iroha was originally built by a group of Japanese developers in C++ for a few mobile use cases. Similar to Indy, Iroha manages digital wallets consisting of identities and digital assets. In addition, it offers role-based authentication for accessing and controlling digital credentials.

Hyperledger Sawtooth

Originally developed by Intel, *Hyperledger Sawtooth* has the advanced proof-of-elapsed-time consensus algorithm that can target a large distributed validator population by using the minimum resources possible. Unlike Fabric, Sawtooth has a decentralized ordering service: whereas Fabric has only a centralized orderer node that is responsible for accepting all transactions and adding them to blocks, each node in the Sawtooth network can process and approve transactions and subsequently add them to the blockchain network. Furthermore, Sawtooth supports both private and permissionless networks. Through integration with Hyperledger Burrow, Sawtooth supports the Ethereum Virtual Machine.

Hyperledger Besu

Written in Java, *Hyperledger Besu* runs on both Ethereum public networks and private blockchain networks. One of its main features is its support for multiple consensus algorithms such as proof of work, proof of authority, and Istanbul Byzantine fault tolerance. Its advance permissioning schemes are especially well suited for the large-scale transition processing seen in enterprise consortium applications.

Besu follows the specifications and requirements of the Enterprise Ethereum Alliance (EEA). In a nutshell, EEA regulates the interactions among public and private applications within an Ethereum network. By following EEA guidelines and common interface protocols, Besu makes the communication between private and public blockchain applications within Hyperledger possible. We elaborate on Besu in detail in Chapter 10.

Hyperledger Cactus

Motivated by concerns in the business community concerning the life cycle of an existing blockchain platform and whether companies can perform in an ecosystem in which changing technological environments are inevitable, *Hyperledger Cactus* came into existence. Even though it is still at the incubation stage (as an Apache v2–licensed open source project), Cactus—previously known as the Blockchain Integration Framework—is capable of securely connecting blockchain networks in such a way that the execution of ledger operations is pluggable among multiple blockchain networks at once. Such pluggability, based on its SDK, provides an opportunity for developers from different networks to connect their DLTs to Cactus.

Hyperledger Burrow

Partially based on EVM specifications, *Hyperledger Burrow* was created to provide a permissioned smart contract interpreter to execute EVM and other (for example, WebAssembly) smart contracts on a private virtual machine. Using PoS as its consensus algorithm, Burrow is capable of transaction finality as well as high-transaction throughput. Its two other notable features are on-chain governance, wherein members can vote for self-governed upgrades of smart contracts, and setting code execution permissions at a low level (for example, per account).

Domain-Specific

Now that we reviewed all the framework projects of Hyperledger, we wrap up this section by briefly going over Hyperledger Grid, which is the only domain-specific project.

Hyperledger Grid

As supply chain data is securing its place as a prominent use case of blockchain, it is attracting the attention of the Hyperledger community and blockchain developers to come up with a framework that addresses supply chain solutions. *Hyperledger Grid* brings together technologies, frameworks, and libraries to work in concert while allowing developers to decide which component best fits their industry and market requirements. Grid supports the WebAssembly smart contract engine, which provides internal and external Hyperledger integrations. With regard to supply chain transactions, Grid supports the transformation, exchange, and tracking of assets.

Overview of Hyperledger Tools and Libraries

In the previous section, we briefly reviewed the seven Hyperledger framework projects for building blockchain distributed ledgers. In this section, we continue exploring the remaining projects in two categories: tools and libraries.

Tools

The tool projects provide a set of utilities to make working with blockchain networks easier. These tools handle tasks including performance measurement, on-demand deployment, and building a business network with existing business models. The following are the four key Hyperledger tool projects.

Hyperledger Caliper

Hyperledger Caliper is a benchmarking tool for measuring blockchain performance and is written in JavaScript. Caliper comes with multiple performance indices for measuring transaction throughput like total transactions per second or transaction latency. Using Caliper in conjunction with other Hyperledger distributed ledgers like Fabric is highly recommended, especially for enterprise projects, as it provides developers with objective metrics for system improvements.

Caliper is one of the most important tools to use in Hyperledger projects (even in Quorum or Ethereum projects, since it also supports those types of blockchains). It offers connectors to various blockchains, which gives it great power and usability.

Hyperledger Cello

Hyperledger Cello brings the on-demand deployment model to blockchains and is written in Go. Cello allows blockchain practitioners to manage their blockchains more efficiently. For instance, using Cello, the management of network life cycles can be automated. Likewise, using Cello, system administrators can manage custom configurations of their network. From an implementation perspective, developers can use

Cello to easily build blockchain-service solutions. In short, it is a great resource for all Hyperledger system administrators.

Hyperledger Explorer

Although it is being deprecated, *Hyperledger Explorer* was originally used as a web user interface (UI) dashboard for viewing and managing blockchain transactions as well as network information. Tasks such as querying the block, and invoking or deploying transactions into blocks, were possible. Explorer was popular among non-developers and folks who wanted to manage Hyperledger applications and networks without writing code or using a command-line interface.

Hyperledger Avalon

Previously known as Trusted Compute Framework, *Hyperledger Avalon* addresses issues related to confidentiality and scalability by moving the on-chain processing tasks to off-chain systems whose computational power is enormous. While still at the incubation stage, if implemented in a blockchain, Avalon monitors and tracks off-chain transactions. This will result in better transaction policy enforcement and more transparent transaction audits. Once the power of off-chain computational power is combined with trust, developers can increase production and boost data privacy. One of Avalon's interesting features is its ability to manage the work-order life cycle, from registering workers to submitting and finishing orders. We elaborate on Avalon in Chapter 10.

Libraries

The following are four key Hyperledger libraries.

Hyperledger Aries

Hyperledger Aries is an application (not a blockchain) for managing digital wallets via verifiable credentials so that they can be shared and reused. Its peer-to-peer architecture enables blockchain-based data to be shared and communicated across multiple blockchain networks or distributed ledger technologies. In addition to managing secrets and exchanging verifiable data, Aries allows parties in a blockchain to securely exchange confidential information among themselves by using its peer-to-peer messaging system. Chapter 10 covers Aries in more detail.

Hyperledger Quilt

Although it's at the incubation stage, *Hyperledger Quilt* can act as an intermediary between ledger systems to perform Interledger Protocol (ILP) transactions at the enterprise level. ILP regulates and manages payments across multiple payment networks by connecting distributed ledgers and allowing cross-ledger payment processing. The ILP idea was borrowed from the Internet Protocol, as each node or connector can route packets of money or an asset across independent networks.

Hyperledger Ursa

The main purpose of *Hyperledger Ursa* is to boost blockchain network security by acting as a shared library of cryptographic data, which prevents people from doing redundant cryptographic work. Ursa is currently at the incubation stage; however, it comes with two interesting features. First, Ursa is interoperable across multiple platforms because the cryptographic verification involves a similar protocol on each end of the platforms. Second, Ursa enables modularity through sharing common components across multiple networks, eventually leading to more modular DLT architectures and adoptions.

Hyperledger Transact

Hyperledger Transact is an amazing library for executing transactions with smart contracts regardless of the platform for which that contract is written. If implemented properly, Transact would be able to integrate smart contract technologies like WebAssembly. Although it's at the incubation stage, Transact will bring about a paradigm shift in smart contract development as developers will be able to build a smart contract in one language and deploy it simultaneously on multiple platforms.

Specifically, the capability to execute a smart contract without any dependency on its platform creates lots of avenues for collaboration, ledger implementation, and source code reusability. Smart contracts, which are at the core of a blockchain platform, often consume lots of development time and effort. By using Transact as a unified interface for smart contract execution, companies and developers can reduce their development and product life cycles.

Summary

This chapter started by reviewing the evolution and phases of blockchain and then discussed design philosophy, core components, and the architecture of the Hyperledger ecosystem. You've learned how the various versions, or generations, of blockchain have brought about its adoption in both the private and public sectors. You also learned the eight key components (consensus layer, smart contract layer, communication layer, data store abstraction, crypto abstraction, identity service, API, interoperation) embedded in the Hyperledger architecture, making it the top choice for building enterprise permissioned blockchain applications.

We also briefly reviewed all 16 projects (consisting of six active projects and ten others at the incubation stage) that are part of the Hyperledger ecosystem. Finally, we highlighted all 16 projects' unique advantages and various functionalities by categorizing them into four types: distributed ledger, libraries, tools, and domain-specific projects.

The next chapter expands upon the Hyperledger Fabric architecture and components to prepare you for building Hyperledger Fabric applications in Chapter 4 and onward.

Hyperledger Fabric Architecture and Components

In the previous chapter, we surveyed four generations of blockchain technology, followed by the Hyperledger architecture and its components. We also introduced you to the Hyperledger ecosystem by reviewing its projects, tools, and libraries. This chapter looks deeper into the Hyperledger family by focusing on the Hyperledger Fabric project. Along the way, we will introduce you to all the Hyperledger Fabric components, including peers, channels, and chaincodes, for both building blockchain applications and understanding concepts covered in the rest of the chapters.

This chapter will help you understand the following:

- Major highlights of Fabric versus other blockchain development platforms
- The role of membership service providers, CAs, and identities in a Fabric permissioned network
- The role of the ledger in Fabric
- Main components of the Fabric network
- The roles that a peer plays in a Fabric network
- The mechanisms through which peers process transactions
- The role of private data and data collection in a Fabric permissioned network

Hyperledger Fabric Overview

Hyperledger Fabric started as a codebase project, combining previous work by Digital Asset Holdings (now called Digital Asset), Blockstream's Libconsensus library, and IBM's Open Blockchain platform. Fabric offers a unique elastic and extensible architecture, which performs over and above alternative blockchain platforms. Fabric works very well with other Hyperledger projects, libraries, and tools, allowing it to be a full-fledged blockchain platform. The Fabric network is scalable to meet the needs of enterprise applications.

Fabric is a platform for building distributed ledger solutions. It comes with several handy features, such as a modular architecture that offers high levels of confidentiality, flexibility, and scalability. This modular architecture makes it possible for components like consensus and membership services to act as plug-and-play accessories. Further, Fabric is designed to be resilient to technology changes by catering to the intricacies of the economic ecosystem. Lastly, Fabric is revolutionary because it allows entities to conduct confidential transactions without passing information through a central authority.

Throughout the remainder of this chapter, we will review the various Fabric components to provide a holistic view of its powerful features. By the end of this chapter, you will have a solid understanding of why Fabric is becoming a prominent choice for enterprise blockchain implementation.

Hyperledger Fabric Model

In blockchain application development, developers can build a distributed ledger technology in multiple ways. Hyperledger Fabric, however, is a unique implementation of DLT mainly aimed at enterprises rather than individuals.

Fabric's architecture separates the transaction flow into three main steps while following the execute-order-validate paradigm. In doing so, it lets Fabric execute untrusted codes in an untrusted environment. The execute-order-validate paradigm alone distinguishes Hyperledger from other widely adopted permissionless blockchains like Bitcoin or Ethereum, which have only order-execute models in place. Here's how the steps in the paradigm are executed in a Fabric system:

1. For Fabric to execute a transaction, it first checks the transaction's correctness. Then Fabric produces state updates for the transaction. The nodes that are executing transactions are called endorsers. They are called upon to validate and add a set of state updates produced as the result of a computation. At this stage, multiple transactions can be executed simultaneously. Therefore, state updates may contain a conflict.

2. The Fabric ordering service follows the consensus protocol defined in the Fabric network regardless of transaction semantics. The nodes running the consensus algorithm are called orderers (covered later in this chapter).

3. Fabric validates the transaction to ensure that two conditions are met:

   a. Transactions are executed according to the given transaction logic.

   b. No state conflicts exist among submitted transactions, in which two transactions want to update the same state.

   After transactions are validated, they are added to the ledger by using *committer* nodes. Note that endorsers are also committers.

The execute-order-validate design has several main benefits. First, in an order-execute model, the nodes that are ordering transactions are also executing them. Thus, there will be validation against two assumptions:

- The ordering is correct.
- The computation is carried out properly.

Conversely, trust assumption in Fabric can be treated differently for consensus as compared to transaction execution. This gives Fabric great flexibility, especially when it comes to confidentiality, because only a given subset of the network is called to execute certain transactions and not others.

Secondly, the execute-order-validate design enables the parallel execution of multiple transactions simultaneously by different parts of the network. This is highly beneficial for the system's overall throughput and addresses potential nondeterminism (which prevents the same input from acting differently in different environments). A flexible endorsement policy specifies which peers, or how many of them, should participate in the correct execution of the given business logic.

Fabric has the following six essential capabilities:

Identity management
> The *membership service provider* (*MSP*) handles identity management. Fabric provides a membership identity service that manages user IDs and authenticates all participants on the network. It is a great asset for enterprise applications since they have a huge stock of credentials.

Privacy and confidentiality
> One way to achieve privacy and confidentiality in Fabric is through private channels. To put it simply, *private channels* are restricted message routes that can be used for transactions between specific subsets of network members. These private channels have many practicalities, especially among enterprise consortium

members, as a subset of members may wish to share private data without affecting the rest of the network operation.

Channels deliver their promise as long as the ordering service is trusted, because all transactions must go through ordering, and their content is therefore visible to that service. Fabric offers *private data collections* (PDCs) when the ordering service cannot be trusted for confidentiality. A PDC can be considered a partition of a ledger visible only to a subset of the network. We discuss more on the ordering service and PDC later in this chapter.

Efficient processing

Fabric assigns network roles by node type to provide concurrency and parallelism. Such a feature alone will boost the performance of network operation by allowing transactions to be threaded for faster processing in a Fabric network. In addition, only a subset of the network working on executing certain transactions needs to know the business logic; thus, it frees up resources for the rest of the network. This makes it possible to load the business logic only where it is strictly needed and not make it available to the entire network.

Business logic

The smart contract, or chaincode, defines the business logic that constitutes the execution of a transaction. Business logic can be written in any general-purpose programming language without systemic dependency on a native cryptocurrency. We discuss this more later in this and subsequent chapters.

Governance

Governance models provide another essential capability. In Fabric, these models can be expressed by *policies*. A policy is required to identify the parties that can deploy a chaincode or add an MSP to a channel. They are flexible and can be updated as needed by issuing proper configuration transactions. We discuss more on the role of policies later in this chapter.

Modular architecture

As discussed earlier, Fabric comes with a modular architecture that makes it more resilient to changes while allowing its common parts to be shared with other networks. In other words, once endowed with a modular design, Fabric will result in a universal blockchain architecture that any industry or public domain can adopt.

Blockchain Network

Unlike other blockchain platforms, Fabric comes with a network that offers great flexibility in catering to various project sizes, from a basic two-member layout to a multilayer consortium consisting of multiple consortiums, each with several members. As a whole, networks play a crucial role in the scalability and adaptability of blockchain platforms among enterprises.

The Fabric network may vary depending on the project being implemented. All organizations in a Fabric network will have access to certain components without restrictions, whereas some components are assigned to only a specific organization via an independent node called the *orderer service*. Thus, considering the logical characteristics of Fabric networks, you can begin to understand the multiple components that go into operation within Fabric.

Each organization within the network can deploy as many nodes as it wishes. The trust that Fabric grants as a private and permissioned network is comprehensive, since the identity of all node participants within its network is known.

Identity

The concept of *identity* within Hyperledger Fabric is closely related to the concept of an MSP that we will see later. Each component that is part of the network—such as nodes, computers, administrators, and clients—have certified credentials generated by one or more authorities. These credentials are the identity that accredits them as network operators.

Once an identity is issued, it will act on the network according to its assigned policies. That means it is the job of policies (as discussed later in this chapter) to set several authentication parameters such as who has access to what, and what actions an identity holder can perform in the network. For example, only an identity with specific administrative permissions can install a chaincode on a given peer, or only an identity with write permission can request to append a new transaction to a given ledger.

Fabric does not impose any specific identity infrastructure/technology. This offers great flexibility and allows administrators to deploy Fabric networks in various contexts. Nevertheless, by default, Fabric can be configured to support any *public-key infrastructure (PKI)*. A PKI is a commonly used infrastructure to organize the management of digital identities (from issuance to revocation). A digital identity is usually bound to a cryptographic key pair (public/private keys). In such schemes, digital signatures are generated using a secret key in the possession of the owner of the digital identity, and a public key, available to anybody, is used to verify those signatures.

Last but not least, identities can be revoked. When this happens, an identity loses the ability to operate in the network. The mechanism used to revoke identities depends on the membership service provider used, and therefore, the underlying system used to organize digital identities.

By leveraging the MSP, which we explore in the next section, other ways to organize digital identities can be supported.

Membership Service Provider

The *membership service provider* (*MSP*) provides Fabric a convenient abstraction that hides all the cryptographic mechanisms and protocols behind the definition and validation of identities and authentication. Indeed, an MSP provides a generic notion of identity and the rules to assert its validity. Also, it provides an API for authentication based on the well-defined concept of digital signatures.

Fabric uses one or more MSPs to manage identities and their life cycles in its network. As a result of MSP abstraction, interoperability among different membership standards and architectures becomes a reality. In fact, when a new channel is created, the list of MSPs governing that channel must be included in the genesis block. This list can then subsequently be updated by issuing a proper channel configuration transaction.

On the other hand, an MSP does not prescribe how identities should be issued, only how they should be validated. Indeed, once an identity is issued and assigned to a Fabric entity, this entity can then start interacting with the network. For example, clients use these credentials to authenticate their transactions, and peers use these credentials to authenticate transaction processing results (endorsements).

To be more concrete, let's consider Fabric's default MSP implementation based on the X.509 standard. The *X.509* standard, commonly used on the internet, prescribes how public-key certificates must be formatted and used. These certificates carry public keys and information about the owners of these keys. Each certificate is signed by a certificate authority whose public key is stored in another certificate called the *root certificate*. Intermediate certificates are allowed, forming a chain of certification.

In this context, an X.509-based MSP is defined by a set of root and intermediate certificates identifying the sources of trust for identity certification and a certificate revocation list (CRL). An identity is simply an X.509 certificate. We say that an identity is valid under a given X.509-based MSP if the corresponding certificate has been issued by one of the authorities listed in the MSP and is not in the list of revoked certificates. Keep in mind that certificate authorities typically maintain CRLs. When an authority updates its CRL, the MSP definition must be updated consequently. In Fabric, an MSP definition can be updated by issuing a valid configuration transaction. We talk about this in the coming sections.

To recap, the X.509-based MSP allows Fabric to support almost any PKI whose certificates are issued by the major certificate authorities on the market (the same as normally used in a browser). If needed, a PKI can be put in place by using Hyperledger Fabric CA, a Fabric companion project that implements a certificate authority.

It is worth mentioning that X.509 is not the only technology supported by Fabric. For additional privacy, Fabric is equipped with a technology called *Identity Mixer* (*Idemix*). This cryptographic protocol offers strong authentication while maintaining privacy. This lets a transactor obtain a valid member status for interacting with the network while safeguarding its own identity. Likewise, a transactor can sign multiple transactions without revealing any traces of its signatures. Though the anonymous operation of a transactor is possible, the transaction content can still be used to link multiple transactions and needs to be protected in other ways, such as using private data collections or advanced crypto technologies like ZKPs.

At this point, it should be clear that the permissioned nature of Fabric heavily depends on the MSPs available in a given network. At one extreme, Fabric becomes permissionless as soon as a given network is equipped with an MSP that accepts any public keys like Bitcoin. Under such circumstances, the public parameters of the signature scheme are set in the genesis block. (An exception can still be represented by the orderers whose identities might be fixed in the genesis block.)

As we have seen, the MSP equips Fabric with a well-defined concept of identity on top of which a complex access-control policy can be defined.

Policies

In the previous section, you saw that the MSP gives Fabric the ability to recognize valid identities. Then, *policies* are the tools Fabric provides to reason about these identities. Policies configure the structure for how decisions are made within the network. In other words, these policies configure who can do what and on which element of the network.

Policies are overarching in Fabric, and they are the golden tool used to set the governance of the network. A policy governs who is allowed to access a given ledger, who can deploy a chaincode, and who can upgrade the channel configuration.

The first place where we encounter policies in Fabric is the *system channel*. Each Fabric network must define a system channel that, among other things, contains the MSPs that identify the parties forming the ordering service (also called *ordering organizations*), and the MSPs identifying the identities that can transact in the network (also known as *consortium organizations*). Then, using those MSPs, the system channel identifies who can create application channels (or simply *channels*) via a policy included in the system channel's genesis block.

A channel's *genesis block* is the second place where we come across policies. Indeed, creating a new channel means setting policies to add and remove members, and to approve a chaincode before it is defined and committed to the channel, among others. If policies are not set, they are inherited from the system channel.

Administrators can update a channel's configuration by issuing a proper configuration update transaction. This transaction must be endorsed by enough entities that together can satisfy the specific policy the update is targeting. After the transaction gets committed, the changes are to be considered operational.

The most commonly used form of policy in Fabric is called a *signature policy*. This is simply a monotone Boolean formula. The supported Boolean operators are AND, OR, and NOutOf, and they can be combined with flexibility. Here is an example: OR('Org1.peer', 'Org2.peer'). This policy requires that at least a peer identity, valid under either the MSP named Org1 or the MSP named Org2, provides a signature.

This example also shows another useful tool that Fabric provides, called an *MSP principal*. A principal represents a group of identities that have some common characteristics. For instance, the peer MSP principle identifies all identities that are peers in a Fabric network. Fabric offers a series of handy principles to identify clients, peers, orderers, administrators, and so on.

To summarize, policies are the tools that administrators can use to govern a Fabric network. Policies can be set to configure a network to be permissionless by allowing anyone to perform any operation (again, the ordering service may be an exception) or can be set to restrict access to specific processes.

Nodes

Nodes are the communication entities of the blockchain. A node is just a logical function in the sense that multiple nodes of different types can run on the same physical server. What counts is that the nodes are grouped *into trusted domains* and associated with the logical entities that control them.

A node has an identity, and this identity allows the node to perform certain operations. We can identify the following nodes in a Fabric network:

Clients
    Initiate the life cycle of a transaction in Fabric.

Endorsers
    Responsible for the execution of the business logic encapsulated in programs called *chaincodes*.

Orderers
    Participate in the consensus algorithm to decide the order of transactions.

Committers
    Fetch the ledger from the orderers and apply the validation logic to establish the validity of each ordered transaction. Endorsers are also committers.

Sometimes we will use the word *peer* to mean either an endorser or a committer.

Chaincode

The widely used term *smart contract* is known as *chaincode* in Hyperledger Fabric. A chaincode is a piece of code that implements the application logic and runs during the execution phase. Besides exposing a predefined interface, chaincode developers are free to encode the computation in the best way they find to fit their goals. Fabric, for example, does not require the chaincode to be deterministic.

Chaincode is installed and instantiated in the peers of a channel required to execute it by duly authorized members and through a *Fabric chaincode life cycle*. A chaincode can be updated as well using a similar process.

Each chaincode must define an *endorsement policy* that is evaluated by the committers in the validation phase. A typical endorsement policy lets the chaincode specify the endorsers for a transaction in the form of a set of peers necessary for endorsement. It represents the trust assumption for the correct execution of the specific business logic encoded in the chaincode.

A chaincode must expose two functions: Init and Invoke. Init is used to initialize any data structure the chaincode might need and is invoked only once, at initialization time. Invoke is the entry point to the business logic offered by the chaincode. A chaincode receives arguments, and on these, the chaincode decides what operation to execute.

A chaincode can be thought of as a namespace inside the ledger that groups a set of key-value pairs managed by that chaincode. Those pairs are subject to change by completing a Fabric transaction life cycle. Let's review this life cycle. The following steps are required to successfully commit a transaction:

1. Propose the transaction. A client prepares and sends a transaction proposal to the endorsers of the chaincode the proposal is targeting. The transaction proposal specifies the chaincode and the arguments for the chaincode invocation.

2. Execute the transaction proposal. The endorsers that receive the proposal execute, or simulate, the chaincode with the arguments provided in the proposal (the Invoke function is invoked). The result of the simulation consists of a return value and a read/write set.

   The *read/write set* is a data structure that captures the updates to and the dependencies on the world state (more on this in "Ledger" on page 50). The *read set* contains a list of unique keys and their current version numbers (the value does not need to be added because it is already known to the network). On the other hand, the *write set* contains the updated list of unique keys. In this case, the new values assigned to the keys must be included. Finally, a marker can be used to say that a key is deleted and should not be available anymore in the world state.

We call the execution of the chaincode a *simulation* because the world state does not change at this stage. These are only proposed changes to the world state that need to be validated later. All peers that execute the chaincode sign the output of the execution and send it back to the application. This signature is called an *endorsement*.

3. Assemble the transaction. The client bundles all endorsers' responses (the endorsements) into a transaction (an endorser transaction) and sends it to the ordering service.

4. Order the transaction. The ordering service collects incoming transactions and assembles them into blocks based on a consensus algorithm. Once a block is complete, the ordering service sends it to the committing peers.

5. Validate the transaction. When the committing peers receive a new block, they append it to the ledger and validate every transaction in that block. Validation consists of ensuring that two requirements are satisfied: the endorsements of a transaction satisfy the endorsement policy for that chaincode, and the read/write set does not conflict with concurrent updates that were committed before. Only if a transaction is valid, the world state is updated by applying the changes in the read/write set.

6. Decide transaction finality. As a nonmandatory step, the client can contact a selected number of peers in the network to ask about the finality of the transaction.

A chaincode can also be invoked to retrieve state information as a result of a computation or just a lookup in the world state (e.g., the value of a certain key). This operation is sometimes called a *query*. In this case, steps 3 to 6 can be avoided. The client is just retrieving information, not updating. Suppose the client decides to assemble a transaction with the received endorsements and submits that transaction for ordering. In that case, the client is making a *strong query* because the result is timestamped on the ledger and can be verified by anyone.

Long story short, the endorsers do not differentiate between an invocation or a query. The entry point is always the Invoke function.

Ledger

The *ledger* is one of the fundamental pieces within the entire blockchain and in Hyperledger Fabric as well. The ledger is stored as identical copies in each of the nodes that make up the network. Thus, each Fabric channel is bound to a ledger. Notice that a Fabric network can contain multiple channels, and in this sense, a channel can be seen as a way to partition data in multiple shards.

When we talk about a ledger, we refer to two key concepts: the world state and the blockchain. The *world state* is a part of the blockchain that refers to key-value pairs containing the latest data recorded within it. It is an easier way to access stored data. And then the *blockchain* is something bigger. It is all the records stored within the blockchain, in the form of transactions. These transactions are stored in blocks to be consulted later.

Because of the execute-order-validate model used by Fabric, the ledger can be distinguished as a *raw ledger* or *validated ledger*. The former represents the sequence of transactions ordered by the ordering service; the latter represents the sequence of valid transactions. It is from the validated ledger that the world state is constructed.

The Ordering Service

The orderers run the *ordering service*—a communication that provides a guarantee of delivery. The ordering service can be implemented in various ways: from a centralized service (used, for example, in development and testing) to distributed protocols that target different networks and different types of nodes.

The ordering service provides a shared communication channel to the nodes of a Fabric network, offering a broadcast service for messages containing transactions. Clients connect to the ordering service and can broadcast messages on a given channel, as long as the client has permissions to do that, which are then delivered to all peers. The channel broadcasts the same messages to all connected peers and sends them to all peers in the same logical order. The communicated messages are the candidate transactions for inclusion in the blockchain state.

In short, a defined group of nodes orders transactions in blocks and broadcasts them to all connected peers. Some peers can interact directly with the ordering service to broadcast blocks in the network to make the block delivery fast. Such a dissemination process is done via a gossip protocol, which is particularly useful by preventing each peer from connecting to the ordering service.

Private Collections of Data

Among the evolutions of Hyperledger Fabric technology, one of the largest was the creation of *private data collections (PDCs)*. The two primary use cases of a PDC are as follows:

- When the ordering service cannot be trusted for confidentiality
- When data in a single ledger or Fabric channel must be partitioned and made visible only to certain parties

Each PDC is attached to a list of organizations and properties that define how private data should be disseminated and endorsed. With Fabric v2+, PDC definitions are part of the chaincode definition. The chaincode developer can use a specific API to manipulate those collections.

A PDC can then be thought of as a subnamespace defined in the chaincode's namespace. It consists of a private part and a public part. The private part contains data disseminated via a peer-to-peer protocol among the organizations' peers belonging to the PDC. The public part contains hashes of the private data that are endorsed and committed to the ledger. By default, these hashes are not salted; therefore, they can be susceptible to dictionary attacks. The chaincode developers should use proper strategies to avoid that.

Summary

In this chapter, you learned about the features and components of Hyperledger Fabric. We started by reviewing its key features, such as assets, privacy, and consensus. We then discussed the following important elements of the blockchain network: identities, membership service providers, policies, peers, smart contracts and chaincode, ledgers, the ordering service, and private data collections. Understanding the Fabric network and how its components interact with one another is essential for building blockchain applications in Hyperledger Fabric.

We hope that you have developed a good foundation for building your first blockchain application in Fabric by now. Indeed, this chapter gave you a high-level review of all parts that usually work in conjunction with one another in an enterprise Fabric blockchain application.

In brief, in all previous chapters, we moved from a high-level hierarchy to a lower one by covering the concepts of blockchain, the Hyperledger family, and Hyperledger Fabric step by step. Now that we have covered all practical concepts, we will proceed with coding. We will start doing hands-on coding in the next chapter by building the first chaincode, or Fabric smart contract.

Developing Smart Contracts with Hyperledger Fabric

Part III is divided into Chapters 4, 5, and 6. Chapter 4 covers the coding of smart contracts and the API libraries provided by Hyperledger Fabric for smart contract development. Chapter 5 applies that content to the invocation of smart contracts. Finally, Chapter 6 brings it all together as we explore maintaining and testing smart contracts.

## CHAPTER 4

Smart Contract Development

In this chapter, you will learn about Fabric smart contract development by examining a simple smart contract and the Fabric APIs used to implement Fabric smart contracts. Once you understand the basics of coding a smart contract and the APIs, we can move on to Chapter 5, where we will take the content from this chapter and apply it to invoking smart contracts. To get started, we first need to download the Hyperledger Fabric development tools. They provide a rapid start to developing Fabric smart contracts by encapsulating a complete two-organization Fabric runtime with scripts to bring it up and take it down.

We are going to use the Hyperledger-provided binaries and sample projects from the Fabric project. These binaries and sample projects will help us start a Fabric test network, and the sample projects provide several example smart contracts from which to learn how to develop your own. This chapter examines an example smart contract from a sample project called Fabcar. The binaries we use have the same name on all supported operating systems.

This chapter will help you achieve the following practical goals:

- Writing a Fabric smart contract by using the JavaScript programming language
- Installing and instantiating a Fabric smart contract
- Validating and sanitizing inputs and arguments in a smart contract
- Creating and running simple or complex queries
- Working with a private data collection in Fabric

Installing Prerequisites and Setting Up Hyperledger Fabric

Before we can develop Fabric smart contracts, we need to download and install the software required to download Hyperledger Fabric. To download and set up Hyperledger Fabric for developing Fabric smart contracts, we will execute a script that requires certain software to exist on the platform you are developing on—Windows, Linux, or Mac. We need to install Git, cURL, Node.js, npm, Docker and Docker Compose, and the Fabric installation script.

Git

Git is used to clone the *fabric-samples* repository from GitHub to your local machine. If you don't have Git installed, you can download it from *https://git-scm.com/down loads*. Once you download and install it, verify Git installation with the following command:

```
$ git --version
git version 2.26.2
```

cURL

We use cURL to download the Fabric binaries from the web. You can download cURL from *https://curl.haxx.se/download.html*. Once it's downloaded and installed, verify the installation by executing the following command:

```
$ curl -V
curl 7.54.0 (x86_64-apple-darwin18.0) libcurl/7.54.0 LibreSSL/2.6.5 zlib/1.2.11
nghttp2/1.24.1
Protocols: dict file ftp ftps gopher http https imap imaps ldap ldaps pop3
pop3s rtsp smb smbs smtp smtps
telnet tftp
Features: AsynchDNS IPv6 Largefile GSS-API Kerberos SPNEGO NTLM NTLM_WB SSL
libz HTTP2 UnixSockets HTTPS-
proxy
```

Node.js and npm

We will be using JavaScript for developing our Fabric smart contracts. Fabric uses Node.js and npm for processing smart contracts. The supported versions of Node.js are 10.15.3 and higher, and 12.13.1 and higher. The supported versions of npm are 6 and higher. Node.js includes npm in the installation. You can download Node.js from *https://nodejs.org/en/download*. You can verify the installation of Node.js and npm by executing the following commands:

```
$ node -v
v10.15.3

$ npm -v
6.11.2
```

Docker and Docker Compose

Hyperledger Fabric consists of several components, each of which operates as a separate executable service, so Fabric maintains Docker images of each component. The images are hosted on the official Docker Hub website. At minimum, you need Docker version 17.06.2-ce. You can get the latest version of Docker at *https:// www.docker.com/get-started*. When Docker is installed, Docker Compose is also installed. You can verify the Docker version by executing the following command:

```
$ docker -v
Docker version 19.03.13, build 4484c46d9d
```

Then verify your Docker Compose version by executing this:

```
$ docker-compose --version
docker-compose version 1.27.4, build 40524192
```

Before proceeding, start Docker, because Docker needs to be running to complete the installation of the Fabric installation script.

Fabric Installation Script

Create and change to the directory you will use to install the Fabric binaries and sample projects. Docker must be running because the script requires Docker to download the Fabric images.

The script will do the following:

1. Download the Fabric binaries
2. Clone *fabric-samples* from the GitHub repo
3. Download the Hyperledger Fabric Docker images

Here is the command to execute the script:

```
curl -sSL https://bit.ly/2ysbOFE | bash -s
```

But we are not going to execute this command yet. First, we are going to save the command output, so we can examine it. Make sure you are in the directory you have created to install the Fabric binaries and sample projects, and then execute the following command:

```
curl -sSL https://bit.ly/2ysbOFE > FabricDevInstall.sh
```

Now you can open *FabricDevInstall.sh* in your favorite editor and examine the script to see how it clones *fabric-samples* from GitHub, downloads the Fabric binaries, and downloads the Docker images. Understanding the operation of this script may help you later if you want to customize your Fabric development environment or optimize it based on your workflow.

After you finish examining the script, open a shell and change *FabricDevInstall.sh* to an executable by executing the following command:

```
$ chmod +x FabricDevInstall.sh
```

Now let's execute *FabricDevInstall.sh* with the following command:

```
FabricDevInstall.sh
```

Once the script completes execution, we should be all set. The *fabric-samples* directory, Docker images, and Fabric binaries are installed in the *fabric-samples/bin* directory. In the directory where you ran the command, there should now be a directory called *fabric-samples*. Everything we need is in *fabric-samples*. First, we will dig into the Fabcar sample smart contract, which you can find in the *fabric-samples* directory.

Fundamental Requirements of a Smart Contract

The Fabcar example smart contract is a valid, functional example of a basic smart contract. We have much more to add before it would be ready for production, including security, error management, reporting, monitoring, and testing. We want to remember several important points from this example smart contract. Let's go through them:

Contract *class*
> Smart contracts extend the `Contract` class. This is a simple class with few functions. We will look at this class later in the chapter.

Transaction context
> All smart contract transaction functions pass a transaction context object as their first argument. This transaction context object is a `Context` class. When we look at the `Contract` class, we will look at this class too.

Constructor
> All smart contracts must have a constructor. The constructor argument is optional and represents the name of the contract. If not passed, the class name will be used. We recommend you pass a unique name and think of this in terms of a namespace, like a reverse domain name structure.

Transaction function
> A transaction function to initialize a smart contract can be created and called prior to client requests. You can use this to set up and execute your smart

contract with any required resources. These resources could be tables or maps of data used for lookups, translations, decoding, validating, enriching, security, and so forth.

World state

We can query the world state in multiple ways. The *simple query* is a key lookup, and a *range query* gets a set. There is another called a *rich query*. We look at world state in Chapter 5.

`putState`

To write data to the ledger, we use the `putState` function. It takes as arguments a key and `value`. The `value` is a byte array, so the ledger can store any data. Typically, we will store the equivalent of business objects that are marshaled into byte arrays prior to being passed as the `value` argument.

`ChaincodeStub`

The `ChaincodeStub` class contains several functions used to interact with the ledger and world state. All smart contracts get an implementation of this class as the `stub` object contained and exposed by the `Context` class implementation called `ctx`, which all transaction functions receive as their first argument.

Read/write transactions

An update in a smart contract is executed in three steps: a read transaction, an update to the in-memory data returned from the read transaction, followed by a write transaction. This creates a new world state for the key while maintaining the history of the key in the immutable file-based ledger.

This point is important to remember: *you cannot update (or write to) the ledger and read back what you wrote in the same transaction*. It does not matter how many other transaction functions you call from a transaction function. You need to think about the data flow of a transaction request. Clients submit transaction requests to peers, which endorse the request transaction (this is where the smart contract executes); the endorsements with read and write sets are sent back to clients; and endorsed requests are sent to an orderer, which orders the transactions and creates blocks. The orderer sends the ordered requests to commit peers, which validate the read and write sets prior to committing the writes to the ledger and updating the world state.

In the simplest form, a smart contract is a wrapper around `ChaincodeStub`, because smart contracts must use the interface exposed through this class to interact with the ledger and world state. This is an important point to remember. You should consider implementing business logic in a modular design, treating your `Contract` subclass like a datasource. This will facilitate evolving your code over time and partitioning logic into functional components that can be shared and reused. In Chapter 5, we look into design in the context of packaging and deploying, and in Chapter 6, we delve into modular design and implementation to facilitate maintenance and testing.

Multiple peers, the endorsing peers, will be executing your smart contracts. Today the architecture places the smart contracts behind a gateway, which is middleware in the smart contract SDK. The gateway receives smart contract requests, processes them, and dispatches them to one or more peers. The peers instantiate the chaincode for execution.

SDK

Fabric provides an SDK implemented in Go, Java, and Node.js (JavaScript) for developing smart contracts. We are interested in the Hyperledger Fabric smart contract development SDK for Node.js, which is called *fabric-chaincode-node*. While you do not need to download it for smart contract development, you can download or clone *fabric-chaincode-node* from GitHub (*https://oreil.ly/GKM7g*).

The *fabric-chaincode-node* SDK has a lot going on. We are interested in a few components that are central to developing smart contracts. The remaining files are low-level interfaces, support artifacts, tools, and more required to implement the Contract interface with Node.js. This SDK helps developers like us by providing a high-level API so we can learn fast and focus on our smart contract business logic and design.

The first API we are interested in is *fabric-contract-api*. It is located under the *apis* subdirectory of *fabric-chaincode-node*. The other API you see, *fabric-shim-api*, is the type definition and pure interface for the *fabric-shim* library, which we look at later in this chapter.

When we start our smart contract project and execute npm install, which we will do in Chapter 5, npm will download *fabric-contract-api* as a module from the npm public repository as well as *fabric-shim*. This download happens because we have two explicit smart contract dependencies for developing Hyperledger Fabric smart contracts. These are displayed in this excerpt from the *package.json* file of the Fabcar smart contract:

```
"dependencies": {
    "fabric-contract-api": "^2.0.0",
    "fabric-shim": "^2.0.0"
},
```

fabric-contract-api and *fabric-shim* are the only modules we need to develop our smart contracts. *fabric-contract-api* contains the *contract.js* and *context.js* files, which implement the Contract and Context classes.

Contract class

Contract is a simple class. Beyond the constructor are utility functions that you can override to implement logic before and after transactions:

```
constructor(name) {
    this.__isContract = true;
    if (typeof name === 'undefined' || name === null) {
        this.name = this.constructor.name;
    } else {
        this.name = name.trim();
    }
    logger.info('Creating new Contract', name);
}
```

The `beforeTransaction` function is called before any contract transaction functions are invoked. You can override this method to implement your own custom logic:

```
async beforeTransaction(ctx) {
// default implementation is do nothing
}
```

The `afterTransaction` function is called after any contract transaction functions are invoked. You can override this method to implement your own custom logic:

```
async afterTransaction(ctx, result) {
    // default implementation is do nothing
}
```

The `getName` function is a getter that returns the contract name:

```
getName() {
    return this.name;
}
```

And the `createContext` function creates a custom transaction context:

```
createContext() {
    return new Context();
}
```

Transaction context

You can create a custom transaction context to store your own objects that your functions can access through the `ctx` object, which all transaction functions receive as their first argument. Here is an example of creating a custom context:

```
const AssetList = require('./assetlist.js');

class MyContext extends Context {
    constructor() {
        super();
        this.assetList = new AssetList(this);
    }

}

class AssetContract extends Contract {
    constructor() {
```

```
        super('org.my.asset');
    }

    createContext() {
        return new MyContext();
    }
}
```

With the custom context MyContext, transactions can access *assetList* as *ctx.assetList*.

As you can see, creating a simple, smart contract is easy. You import Contract from *fabric-contract-api* and extend it. Then create a no-argument constructor and export our contract. That's it.

Context class

OK, that's the Contract class, but what about the Context class? You just learned how to create a custom transaction context, but what does the Context class contain? As you have learned, every transaction function gets a Context object called ctx as its first argument. This is the transaction context. It contains two important objects: stub and clientIdentity. The stub is a ChaincodeStub class implementation, and clientIdentity is a ClientIdentity class implementation. We discuss these classes next.

ChaincodeStub has all the functions we need to interact with the ledger and world state. It is our API for the ledger and world state. It is contained in the *fabric-shim* module under the *lib* directory and implemented in the *stub.js* file. The two primary functions are getState and putState. Several additional functions are available. Most can be grouped into the following categories:

- State related
- Query related
- Transaction related
- Private data related

These four groups represent most of the functions. The *state-related functions* are used to read from and write to the ledger. They use or involve the use of a key.

The *query-related functions* are two rich query functions, one with pagination. *Rich queries* are string queries native to the database. To use rich queries, you need to use CouchDB for the database. We will do this in Chapter 5, where you'll learn about invoking smart contracts. Another unique query function is getHistoryForKey, which takes a key and returns the history for it. This can be used to audit changes and find transactions that failed.

Hyperledger has five *transaction-related functions*:

- getTxID(): *string*;
- getChannelID(): *string*;
- getCreator(): SerializedIdentity;
- getMspID(): *string*;
- getTransient(): Map<*string, Uint8Array*>;

Use getTxID to retrieve the transaction ID, getChannelID for the channel's ID, get Creator for the client, getMspID for the organization the client belongs to, and get Transient for private data. We will execute each of these in the next two chapters.

Hyperledger has nine *private data–related functions*:

- getPrivateData(collection: *string*, key: *string*): Promise <*Uint8Array*>;
- getPrivateDataHash(collection: *string*, key: *string*): Promise <*Uint8Array*>;
- putPrivateData(collection: *string*, key: *string*, value: *Uint8Array*): Promise<void>;
- deletePrivateData(collection: *string*, key: *string*): Promise<void>;
- setPrivateDataValidationParameter(collection: *string*, key: *string*, ep: *Uint8Array*): Promise<void>;
- getPrivateDataValidationParameter(collection: *string*, key: *string*): Promise<*Uint8Array*>;
- getPrivateDataByRange(collection: *string*, startKey: *string*, endKey: *string*): Promise<Iterators.StateQueryIterator> & AsyncIterable<Iterators.KV>;
- getPrivateDataByPartialCompositeKey(collection: *string*, objectType: *string*, attributes: *string[]*): Promise<Iterators.StateQueryIterator> & AsyncIterable<Iterators.KV>;
- getPrivateDataQueryResult(collection: *string*, query: *string*): Promise<Iterators.StateQueryIterator> & AsyncIterable<Iterators.KV>;

These nine private data functions provide the ability to read and write to a private data collection, get a private data hash, delete from private data, set and get an endorsement policy for private data validation, and get private data by range, partial composite key, or rich query. We will execute some of these in Chapters 5 and 6 when we employ the use of private data with our smart contract transactions.

Now that you have a good idea of what sort of functionality is available through the stub object we get from the ctx object, let's look at ClientIdentity, the other object in the transaction context.

The clientIdentity object contained in the transaction context as ctx.clientIdentity is the implementation of the ClientIdentity class, which is a small class with only five functions:

- assertAttributeValue(attrName: *string*, attrValue: *string*): boolean;
- getAttributeValue(attrName: *string*): *string* | null;
- getID(): *string*;
- getIDBytes(): *Uint8Array*;
- getMSPID(): *string*;

The assertAttributeValue and getAttributeValue functions operate on the client certificate. Using these functions, granular security can be implemented by employing the certificate attribute values. The getID and getIDBytes functions retrieve the client's identity, and getMSPID is used to get the organization the client belongs to. Using these functions, you can implement a wide range of authentication and authorization design patterns.

Transaction functions

Transaction functions are the smart contract functions that clients call. These are the business functions you design and implement in your smart contracts. Here is an example of three transaction functions from the Fabcar smart contract. We will define them in "Defining a Smart Contract" on page 67:

```
async queryCar(ctx, carNumber)
async createCar(ctx, carNumber, make, model, color, owner)
async queryAllCars(ctx)
```

All transaction functions receive as the first argument the transaction context, the ctx object. Transaction functions use this object to reference the stub and clientIdentity objects—for example, ctx.stub and ctx.clientIdentity. The stub is an instance of ChaincodeStub. The clientIdentity is an implementation of ClientIdentity and exposes functions for getting the transaction ID, client ID, any client attributes, and the organization ID. These functions can be used for application- and transaction-specific authentication and authorization.

It is common for most transaction functions to contain a call to the ledger or world state. The stub provides the functions for reading from the world state and writing to the ledger, which updates the world state.

The way you design your transaction functions is completely under your control. You can group them, mix them, create libraries, and more. Remember, for transactions that write, all of the designated endorsing peers must execute your smart contracts.

Endorsement policies determine whether a transaction gets committed. For example, an endorsement policy might state that three out of four peers must endorse the transaction. If, for some reason, fewer than three peers can endorse the transaction, then the transaction will not get committed, meaning the data will not be available on the ledger.

A point to remember is that even though a write transaction may fail, it will be flagged as invalid and written to the ledger. An invalid transaction will not be part of the world state.

As a best practice, Fabric smart contracts demand deterministic code. Many peers need to execute the code, and they all need to arrive at the same result. Therefore, the inputs must always return the same result. It must not matter what peer executes the code. Given the same inputs, the peer should return the same results. This should happen no matter the number of times the code is executed.

The code should have a beginning and an end. It should never depend on dynamic data or long random executions. The code should be fast and efficient, with clear logic flows that are not circular. For example:

```
async CreateAsset(ctx, id, amount, owner) {
        const asset = {
            ID: id,
            Amount: amount,
            Owner: owner
        };
        return ctx.stub.putState(id,Buffer.from(
            JSON.stringify(asset)));
    }
```

When creating an asset, we will expect the asset ID, amount, and owner as inputs.

Validate and sanitize arguments

Transactions must validate and sanitize their arguments. This is not unique to smart contracts. It is a wise default practice if you want to ensure the integrity and availability of your smart contract.

Employ known techniques for validating your arguments and preventing any data that may harm your smart contract. You also want to sanitize your arguments and ensure the quality of the data you expect. You want to limit unnecessary processing of data that will later in your logic cause a failure or edge case not covered. Here is an example that checks whether the function is Process; if it is not, we will throw an exception:

```
func (c *Asset) Invoke(stub shim.ChaincodeStubInterface) pb.Response {
    function, args := stub.GetFunctionAndParameters()
    if function == "Process" {
        return c.Process(stub, args)
    }
    return shim.Error("Invalid function name")
}
```

Simple state interaction (get, put, delete)

Fabric smart contracts at the core are state machines that evolve over time, keeping an immutable history of all prior states. The three primary stub functions you will use are the following:

```
getState(key: string): Promise<Uint8Array>;
putState(key: string, value: Uint8Array): Promise<void>;
deleteState(key: string): Promise<void>;
```

The stub functions provide your smart contracts the functionality to read from the world state, write to the ledger, and delete from the world state.

The ledger and world state are key-value data stores. This keeps it simple and easy but allows rich data to be stored on the ledger, queried, and viewed by the world state, a document, or NoSQL database. Currently, LevelDB and CouchDB are supported. LevelDB is a simple key-value data store, while CouchDB is a rich and robust NoSQL document database. This means you can read and write simple to complex JSON data structures to the ledger and query the world state database for rich data. Several functions are available for queries.

Create and Execute Queries

Smart contracts often need to look up or query data from the world state while processing a transaction. Remember the update to our Fabcar sample smart contract? To perform an update, a smart contract typically must find and load the existing object to update. Then it updates the in-memory data and writes the updated data to the ledger—remember putState to write and getState to read.

Unlike a relational database in which we can update a field without selecting the row first, with Fabric smart contracts, we must load the value of a key and update the value. That may be a single field in a very large and complex JSON data structure, or it may be a simple object with one field, the field we are updating. Why is this? Because all data is tied to a unique key. If a key's associated value is an object with four fields, we think of each field as a value—but to the ledger, it is all just one value object identified by a single unique key.

Here are the available `stub` functions you can use for finding data:

- `getState(key: `*`string`*`): Promise<`*`Uint8Array`*`>;`

- `getStateByRange(startKey: `*`string`*`, endKey: `*`string`*`): Promise<Iterators.StateQueryIterator> & AsyncIterable<Iterators.KV>;`

- `getStateByRangeWithPagination(startKey: `*`string`*`, endKey: `*`string`*`, pageSize: `*`number`*`, bookmark?: `*`string`*`): Promise<StateQueryResponse<Iterators.StateQueryIterator>> & AsyncIterable<Iterators.KV>;`

- `getQueryResult(query: `*`string`*`): Promise<Iterators.StateQueryIterator> & AsyncIterable<Iterators.KV>;`

- `getQueryResultWithPagination(query: `*`string`*`, pageSize: `*`number`*`, bookmark?: `*`string`*`): Promise<StateQueryResponse<Iterators.StateQueryIterator>> & AsyncIterable<Iterators.KV>;`

- `getHistoryForKey(key: `*`string`*`): Promise<Iterators.HistoryQueryIterator> & AsyncIterable<Iterators.KeyModification>;`

We discuss these in Chapter 5, when we use them in a smart contract and invoke them from a client.

Defining a Smart Contract

Let's start with the simple Fabcar smart contract. In the *fabric-samples* directory, locate the *chaincode* directory. In the *chaincode* directory, locate the *fabcar* directory. In the *fabcar* directory, locate the *javascript* directory. Change to this directory in your shell and execute the following command:

```
$ npm install
```

This will create the *node_modules* directory and install the dependent modules defined in *package.json*. We did this because we depend on the *fabric-contract-api* and *fabric-shim* modules. These are the two modules we use when developing Fabric smart contracts in JavaScript. We will look at these after we examine the Fabcar smart contract.

Now let's examine the Fabcar smart contract. This simple smart contract is a great example for learning Fabric smart contract development because it contains necessary details to form a foundation from which we can move on to more advanced smart contracts. It is located in the *lib* directory in the current directory, which should be the *fabric-samples/chaincode/fabcar/javascript* directory. Open *fabcar.js* in your favorite editor; Example 4-1 shows the source code.

Example 4-1. fabcar.js

```
/*
 * Copyright IBM Corp. All Rights Reserved.
 *
 * SPDX-License-Identifier: Apache-2.0
 */
'use strict';
const { Contract } = require('fabric-contract-api'); ❶
class FabCar extends Contract { ❷
    async initLedger(ctx) { ❸
        console.info('============= START : Initialize Ledger ===========');

        const cars = [ ❹
            {
                color: 'blue',
                make: 'Toyota',
                model: 'Prius',
                owner: 'Tomoko',
            },
...
        ];
        for (let i = 0; i < cars.length; i++) { ❺
            cars[i].docType = 'car';
            await ctx.stub.putState('CAR' + i,
                Buffer.from(JSON.stringify(cars[i]))); ❻
        }
    }
    async queryCar(ctx, carNumber) { ❼
        const carAsBytes = await ctx.stub.getState(
        carNumber); // get the car from chaincode state ❽
        if (!carAsBytes || carAsBytes.length === 0) {
            throw new Error(`${carNumber} does not exist`);
        return carAsBytes.toString();
    }
    async createCar(ctx, carNumber, make, model, color, owner) { ❾
        console.info('============= START : Create Car ===========');
        const car = {color, docType: 'car',make, model, owner}

        await ctx.stub.putState(carNumber, Buffer.from(
        JSON.stringify(car))); ❿
    }
    async queryAllCars(ctx) { ⓫
        const startKey = '';
        const endKey = '';
        const allResults = [];
        for await (const {key, value} of ctx.stub.getStateByRange(
            startKey, endKey)) { ⓬
            const strValue = Buffer.from(value).toString('utf8');

            let record;
            try {
```

```
            record = JSON.parse(strValue);
        } catch (err) {
            record = strValue;
        }
        allResults.push({ Key: key, Record: record });
    }
    return JSON.stringify(allResults);
    }
    async changeCarOwner(ctx, carNumber, newOwner) { ⓭
```

```
const carAsBytes = await ctx.stub.getState(carNumber); ⓮
if (!carAsBytes || carAsBytes.length === 0) {
        throw new Error(`${carNumber} does not exist`);
    }
    const car = JSON.parse(carAsBytes.toString());
    car.owner = newOwner;
    await ctx.stub.putState(carNumber, Buffer.from(
JSON.stringify(car))); ⓯
    }
}
module.exports = FabCar; ⓰
```

❶ We start by importing the *fabric-contract-api* module.

❷ All Fabric smart contracts extend the Contract class. We get the Contract class
    from the *fabric-contract-api* module we imported in line 1.

❸ Smart contracts can use transactions to initialize them prior to processing client
    application requests. This line is the beginning of the function that initializes the
    smart contract. All smart contract functions receive a transaction context object
    as an argument, called by convention ctx.

❹ In this example, the initLedger function is creating an array of objects called
    cars. Each array object contains key-value pairs. You can think of the array of
    objects as records of assets, and the object key-value pairs as the fields. This func-
    tion effectively preloads an array of car objects for exercising the transaction
    functions in the smart contract.

❺ Next, the initLedger function is iterating through the array of car asset objects
    and adding a field called docType to each object, and assigning the string value
    car to each object.

❻ This line is the first use of the ctx object (Context class) passed as the first func-
    tion argument to all Contract class transaction functions. The ctx object con-
    tains the stub object, which is a ChaincodeStub class. The ChaincodeStub class

implements an API to access the ledger. This line calls the `putState` function, which writes the key and value to the ledger and world state.

 Hyperledger Fabric implements the blockchain ledger in two components: a file-based component and a database component. The *file-based component* is the low-level immutable data structure implementing the ledger, and the *database component* exposes the current state of the file-based ledger. The database component is called the *world state* because it represents the current state of the ledger. The file-based component maintains the perpetual immutable ledger. The *fabric-contact-api* accesses the world state. Lower-level APIs access the file-based ledger.

❼ The first transaction function comes next. As stated earlier, the first argument of all smart contract transaction functions is the `ctx` object, which represents the transaction context and is a `Context` class. Any other arguments are optional.

❽ The `queryCars` function is a read transaction. Using the `ctx` object, it calls the stub's `getState` function, which will read from the world state—the database. The `stub` is an implementation of the `ChaincodeStub` class, which we will cover later. For this function, the argument called `carNumber` is the key passed to the `getState` function, which will search the world state database for the key and return the associated value stored for it. The remainder of the function checks whether data was returned and, if so, converts the byte array returned into a string and returns the string that represents the value of the key stored in the world state. Remember, the world state is a representation of the perpetual immutable file-based ledger's current state for any key-value pair stored in the ledger. While the database may be mutable, the file-based ledger is not. So even when a key-value pair is deleted from the database or world state, the key-value pair is still in the file-based ledger where all history is maintained in the perpetual immutable ledger.

❾ Then we have the second transaction function. It passes the values required to create a new `car` record object, which we will add to the ledger.

❿ With the `car` record object built from the function arguments, we call the `Chain codeStub` API function implemented by `stub`, called `putState`, which will write the key and value to the ledger and update the current world state. The first two arguments that pass to the `putState` function are a key and a value, respectively. We need to change the `value`, the `car` record object, into a byte array, which `ChaincodeStub` APIs require.

⑪ The next transaction function, called queryAllCars, is a read transaction and demonstrates a range query. A range query, like all queries, is executed by the peer that receives the request. A range query takes two arguments: the beginning key and the ending key. These two keys represent the beginning and end of the range. All keys that fall into the range are returned along with their associated values. You can pass an empty string for both keys to retrieve all keys and values.

⑫ A for loop is executed, which stores all the keys and associated values returned from the ChaincodeStub API function getStateByRange.

⑬ The last transaction function, changeCarOwner, combines both read and write tasks to change the world state. The business logic here is a transfer of ownership. In addition to the ctx argument, two arguments are passed: a key called carNumber, and a value object called newOwner.

⑭ Next, we need to retrieve the record object from the world state, which represents the current key and value for this record. The key is carNumber. We use it to execute the ChaincodeStub API getState. Once we retrieve the current car record object for carNumber, we change the owner field to newOwner.

⑮ After retrieving the ledger data representing the world state and updating the retrieved data, we update the ledger for this car record object by executing the ChaincodeStub API putState. This writes a new key and value to the ledger that represents the world state. If the car record object is now retrieved, the ledger will not show the new owner until the record object is committed to the ledger. It is important to understand that once committed, the ledger is appended, and the database state will be changed (the world state will be updated). You can think of the ledger as an ever-growing stack of objects, each with a unique identifier called the *key*. There can be many keys with the same value, but only one represents the current or world state. This is how the database implements the view of the world state, while the file-based ledger implements the immutable history of all keys in timestamp order.

 The file-based ledger stores all write transactions. Both successful and unsuccessful write transactions are part of the file-based immutable ledger. Flags control the validity of transactions stored in the immutable file-based ledger. This facilitates an audit of all submitted write transactions.

⑯ This line is Node.js specific. We discuss exporting smart contract modules in Chapter 5, when we cover smart contract execution, including project structure, packaging, and deployment.

This completes this simple smart contract. We will now discuss it, in summary, to point out the fundamental requirements to develop a smart contract. From this basic smart contract, complex smart contract applications can be designed and developed.

Define Assets by Using Key-Value Pairs

When designing smart contracts, you may need to think in terms of assets. *Assets* are generic and can represent many things, including tangible and intangible objects. They could be machine parts, dog food, currency, or green derivatives. We use name-value pairs, or key-value pairs, depending on how you want to think about it, to create our data structures. Here is an example we can discuss:

```
const assets = [
    {
        color: 'blue',
        make: 'Honda',
        model: 'Accord',
        owner: 'Jones',
    },
    {
        color: 'red',
        make: 'Ford',
        model: 'Mustang',
        owner: 'Smith',
    },
];
for (let i = 0; i < assets.length; i++) {
    assets[i].docType = 'asset';
    await ctx.stub.putState('ASSET' + i,
        Buffer.from(JSON.stringify(assets[i])));
}
```

We've seen this before in the Fabcar example. It is a good example of basic processing, from which you can advance based on your unique use case. This example creates an array of objects that represent assets. The key-value pairs define the attributes, or characteristics, of each asset. The array acts as a simple database of assets. Each asset is written to the ledger by calling `ctx.stub.putState`, which takes a key and value. The value must be a byte array, so we convert the JSON object to a string and then convert the string to the byte array. You will do this a lot and may want to simplify it and start building a utility or library. This particular code was used to initialize the smart contract.

We can also define assets by using a smart contract transaction. The `createAsset` transaction function shown next illustrates how simple it is to create an asset and write it to the ledger. This function would be called by a client. The client could be a user or process. What's important to remember is the asset will not be available until the transaction is committed to the ledger. So you can't write a bunch of assets to the ledger and later in your smart contract expect to read and use their data to continue processing. This disconnected state is something to think about when you begin designing and brainstorming. Here's the `createAsset` transaction function:

```
async createAsset(ctx, assetNumber, make, model, color, owner) {
        const asset = {
        color,
        docType: 'asset',
        make,
        model,
        owner,
        };
    await  ctx.stub.putState(assetNumber, Buffer.from(JSON.stringify(asset)));
}
```

Collect Private Data

The *private data collection (PDC)* is a partition of ledger data belonging to an organization that stores private data and keeps data private from other organizations on that channel. This includes private data and the hash value of private data. Chapter 9 provides more details. The need to keep specific data private is important to developing smart contracts. Many smart contracts need to be compliant with privacy and security requirements. Fabric supports private data for transaction functions and smart contracts.

The private data can be shared or kept isolated and secure. We can expire the private data after a number of blocks are created or on demand. The data placed into the PDCs remains separate from the public data, and PDCs are local and protected. The world state can be used in conjunction with PDCs by the use of hashes as well as public keys.

Table 4-1 lists several functions that are available from `stub`.

Table 4-1. Commands for working with private data

API	Note
getPrivateData(collection: *string*, key: *string*): Promise<*Uint8Array*>	Returns the endorsement policy from the collection name and the specified key.
putPrivateData(collection: *string*, key: *string*, value: *Uint8Array*): Promise<void>	Puts the collection name and the specified key and value into the transaction's private writeSet.
deletePrivateData(collection: *string*, key: *string*): Promise<void>	Deletes the endorsement policy by providing the collection name and private data variable key.
setPrivateDataValidationParameter(collection: *string*, key: *string*, ep: *Uint8Array*): Promise<void>	Sets the endorsement policy by providing the collection name and private data variable key.

API	Note
`getPrivateDataValidationParameter(collection: string, key: string): Promise<Uint8Array>`	Returns the endorsement policy by providing the collection name and private data variable key.
`getPrivateDataByRange(collection: string, startKey: string, endKey: string): Promise<Iterators.StateQueryIterator> & AsyncIterable<Iterators.KV>`	Returns the endorsement policy from the collection name and the private data variable key.
`getPrivateDataByPartialCompositeKey(collection: string, objectType: string, attributes: string[]): Promise<Iterators.StateQueryIterator> & AsyncIterable<Iterators.KV>`	Queries the endorsement policy in a given collection name and a given partial composite key.
`getPrivateDataQueryResult(collection: string, query: string): Promise<Iterators.StateQueryIterator> & AsyncIterable<Iterators.KV>`	Performs a rich query against a given private collection. It is supported for state databases that can run a rich query (e.g., CouchDB).

Employing private data can be tricky, and patterns exist for using it under differing circumstances. We will cover most of these functions in Chapter 5, when we implement private data functions to invoke, and again in Chapter 6, when we use them in maintenance and testing.

Set Attribute-Based Access Control

Eventually, you will need a way to implement granular authentication and authorization. Clients have an identity that controls access. The identities must belong to authorized organizations, and organizations belong to channels that host chaincode. A certificate represents the client's identity. It supports attributes that can be used to implement transactions and smart-contract-level authentication control and authorization policies.

You access this information from the `clientIdentity` object contained in the transaction context. This object has two functions related to attribute values:

```
assertAttributeValue(attrName: string, attrValue: string): boolean;
getAttributeValue(attrName: string): string | null;
```

Use `assertAttributeValue` to check for the presence of an attribute and use `getAttributeValue` to retrieve a specific attribute. It is good practice to assert the attribute before retrieving it. In Chapters 5 and 6, we will employ attributes for security and other purposes.

Initialize the Ledger State

The initialization of the ledger is often a required task. The following example from the Fabcar code we looked at earlier illustrates how to initialize your smart contract state. You will initialize it right after it has been committed. After that, you can start to submit transactions and query ledger data by invoking smart contract methods.

You create a function that you will call to execute your initialization; here, it is called `initLedger`. In the `initLedger` function, you can perform what you need to do to initialize. In this example, we create an array of business objects, loop through the `cars` array, and then add an additional attribute `docType` to each `car` object in the `cars` array. Here is the `initLedger` logic:

```
async initLedger(ctx) {
    const cars = [
        {
            color: 'blue',
            make: 'Toyota',
            model: 'Prius',
            owner: 'Tomoko',
        },
        .
        .
        .
        {
            color: 'brown',
            make: 'Holden',
            model: 'Barina',
            owner: 'Shotaro',
        },
    ];
    for (let i = 0; i < cars.length; i++) {
        cars[i].docType = 'car';
        await ctx.stub.putState('CAR' + i,
        Buffer.from(JSON.stringify(cars[i])));
        console.info('Added <--> ', cars[i]);
    }
}
```

The `initLedger` function writes the array objects to the ledger by using the `putState` function. To execute the `initLedger` function, we need to invoke the smart contract. We can use the `peer` CLI invoke command. Let's take a look at how we can call `initLedger` through the `invoke` command.

Chaincode invoke init

To execute a transaction function on our smart contract, we can use the invoke command provided by the *peer* binary. This binary offers many commands, several of which you will learn in Chapters 5 and 6. Here we use it to invoke our initLedger function:

 We have printed the following command on multiple lines for readability. When you type in the command, it must be on one line, or it will fail to execute.

```
peer chaincode invoke
-o localhost:7050
--ordererTLSHostnameOverride orderer.example.com
--tls true
--cafile /OReilly/fabric-samples/test-network/organizations/ordererOrganizations
/example.com/orderers/orderer.example.com/msp/tlscacerts/tls/
ca.example.com-cert.pem
-C mychannel
-n fabcar
--peerAddresses localhost:7051
--tlsRootCertFiles /OReilly/fabric-samples/test-network/organizations
/peerOrganizations/org1.example.com/peers/peer0.org1.example.com/tls/ca.crt
--isInit
-c '{"function":"initLedger","Args":[]}'

[chaincodeCmd] chaincodeInvokeOrQuery -> INFO 001 Chaincode invoke successful.
result: status:200
```

The invoke command executes the command object following the -c command argument flag. The command object specifies the function to execute and any function arguments. Here we are executing the initLedger function, and there are no function arguments.

We can test the results of the initLedger function. We expect to return the contents of the array written to the ledger. We will use the query command; let's look at how we can query ledger data.

Chaincode query

Using the peer's query command, we can execute one of our smart contract query functions. In this case, we set the -c command flag to execute queryAllCars:

```
peer chaincode query
-C mychannel
-n fabcar
-c '{"Args":["queryAllCars"]}'
```

Here is the return output:

```
[{"Key":"CAR0","Record":{"color":"blue","docType":"car",
"make":"Toyota","model":"Prius","owner":"Tomoko"}},
.
.
.
{"Key":"CAR9","Record":{"color":"brown","docType":"car","make":"Holden",
"model":"Barina","owner":"Shotaro"}}]
```

The result shows the `initLedger` function executed, and our smart contract is initialized.

Installing and Instantiating a Smart Contract

In preparation for Chapter 5, let's go over what we need to do once we finish coding our smart contract. This section discusses several steps that we need to perform to reach a point where we can invoke our smart contract either from the command line or from a smart contract client. These steps are as follows:

1. Package the chaincode.

2. Install the chaincode.

3. Query the installation.

4. Approve the package.

5. Check commit readiness.

6. Commit the chaincode definition.

7. Query whether the chaincode is committed.

8. Initialize the contract.

9. Execute a query.

Chapter 5 covers these steps in more detail. They contain example command-line code, and some have output. The following `peer` commands can be referenced in the Hyperledger Fabric documentation. (*https://oreil.ly/baQSm*)

Package the Chaincode

The first thing we need to do is package our code. As you can see from the following command, we use the `peer` CLI to perform this step and all remaining steps.

To prepare our smart contract, we use the following `peer` package command:

```
peer lifecycle chaincode package fabcar.tar.gz \
        --path ../chaincode/fabcar/javascript/ \
        --lang node \
        --label fabcar_1
```

Once this command completes, we have a *tar.gz* file containing our smart contract. Next, we need to install this package.

Install the Chaincode

After we have packaged our smart contract, we can install it. If several organizations are collaborating, there is no need for all organizations to package smart contracts separately. One smart contract package can be used by all organizations. Once an organization receives the package, it is installed on their endorsing peers. Chapter 9 covers this in more detail.

Here is the installation command, which shows a successful output message:

```
peer lifecycle chaincode install fabcar.tar.gz

[cli.lifecycle.chaincode] submitInstallProposal -> INFO 001 Installed
```

Once the contract is installed, you may want to verify it.

Query the Installation

You can execute the following command to get the details of the latest chaincode installed:

```
peer lifecycle chaincode queryinstalled

Installed chaincodes on peer:
Package ID: fabcar_1:5a00a40697…330bf5de39,
Label: fabcar_1
```

You may receive many package IDs, depending on the number of installed packages. You can use a script to filter the output if you need to automate a task that is dependent on a particular package being installed or not installed. Once a chaincode package is installed, it must be approved.

Approve the Package

After installing a package, an organization must approve it before it can be committed and accessed. This command has a lot of parameters. The one of most interest, for our purposes, is –package-id. We can get it from the output of the preceding queryinstalled command. package-id is used as the identifier for the chaincode installation package:

```
peer lifecycle chaincode approveformyorg
-o localhost:7050
--ordererTLSHostnameOverride orderer.example.com
--tls true
--cafile /OReilly/fabric-samples/test-network/organizations/ordererOrganizations
/example.com/orderers/orderer.example.com/msp/tlscacerts/
```

```
tlsca.example.com-cert.pem
--channelID mychannel
--name fabcar
--version 1
--init-required
--package-id fab-
car_1:5a00a406972168ac5856857b5867f51d5244208b876206b7e0e418330bf5de39
--sequence 1
```

Once the approve command completes, we are ready to determine whether we can commit it. We use the `checkcommitreadiness` command.

Check Commit Readiness

A number of organizations must approve the chaincode package before it can be committed. The number depends on the policy, which could demand that all organizations or a subset of organizations approve. Ideally, you want all organizations to approve. We can use the `checkcommitreadiness` command to determine whether we can commit the package. In this case, we cannot because Org2 has not approved yet. Once it does, this command will show `true` for `Org1` and `true` for `Org2`:

```
peer lifecycle chaincode checkcommitreadiness
--channelID mychannel
--name fabcar
--version 1
--sequence 1
--output json
--init-required

{
    "approvals": {
        "Org1MSP": true,
        "Org2MSP": false
    }
}
```

In a Hyperledger configuration, we can define different types of life-cycle endorsement policies. The default is `MAJORITY Endorsement`. This requires a majority of the peers to endorse a chaincode transaction for validation and execution in the channel and commit the transaction to the ledger. Chapter 9 covers this in more detail. Once all approvals are true, we can commit the chaincode package.

Commit the Chaincode Definition

Once all organizations or subsets of the organization have been approved to satisfy the policies mentioned, the chaincode can be committed to the ledger. To commit the chaincode, we use the commit command shown here:

```
peer lifecycle chaincode commit
-o localhost:7050
--ordererTLSHostnameOverride orderer.example.com
--tls true
--cafile /OReilly/fabric-samples/test-network/organizations/ordererOrganizations
/example.com/orderers/orderer.example.com/msp/tlscacerts/
tlsca.example.com-cert.pem
--channelID mychannel
--name fabcar
--peerAddresses localhost:7051
--tlsRootCertFiles /OReilly/fabric-samples/test-network/organizations
/peerOrganizations/org1.example.com/peers/peer0.org1.example.com/tls/ca.crt
--version 1
--sequence 1
--init-required
```

Here is the output after the command runs:

```
[chaincodeCmd] ClientWait -> INFO 001 txid
[ef59101c320469be3242daa9ebe262771fc8cc8bd5cd0854c6424e1d2a0c61c2] committed
with status (VALID) at
localhost:9051
```

Next, we can check whether the chaincode is committed with querycommitted.

Query Whether the Chaincode Is Committed

Chaincode must be committed before it can be invoked. To determine whether chaincode is committed, use the querycommitted chaincode command:

```
peer lifecycle chaincode querycommitted
--channelID mychannel
--name fabcar
```

Here is the output:

```
Committed chaincode definition for chaincode 'fabcar' on channel 'mychannel':
Version: 1, Sequence: 1, Endorsement Plugin: escc, Validation Plugin: vscc,
Approvals: [Org1MSP: true,
Org2MSP: true]
```

Running the querycommitted command tells us our chaincode is ready. This chaincode contains a smart contract that needs initialization. To initialize it, we will invoke
it.

Initialize the Contract

We can finally initialize our smart contract because the chaincode is approved and
committed. We can use the invoke command to execute smart contract transactions:

```
peer chaincode invoke
-o localhost:7050
--ordererTLSHostnameOverride orderer.example.com
```

```
--tls true
--cafile /OReilly/fabric-samples/test-network/organizations/ordererOrganizations
/example.com/orderers/orderer.example.com/msp/tlscacerts/
tlsca.example.com-cert.pem
-C mychannel
-n fabcar
--peerAddresses localhost:7051
--tlsRootCertFiles /OReilly/fabric-samples/test-
network/organizations/peerOrganizations/org1.example.com/peers
/peer0.org1.example.com/tls/ca.crt
--peerAddresses localhost:9051
--tlsRootCertFiles /OReilly/fabric-samples/test-network/organizations
/peerOrganizations/org2.example.com/peers/peer0.org2.example.com/tls/ca.crt
--isInit
-c '{"function":"initLedger","Args":[]}'
```

After executing the invoke command, we will see the following output; it returns a
200 response status if chaincode invocation is successful:

```
[chaincodeCmd] chaincodeInvokeOrQuery -> INFO 001 Chaincode invoke successful.
result: status:200
```

At the bottom of the invoke command, we see the -c command flag and command
object, which contains the function key and value initLedger with no arguments.
This means the smart contract transaction function initLedger will be executed. The
output shows a successful result. Our smart contract is now initialized and ready for
clients. We can test our smart contract now by executing a query.

Execute a Query

We have gone through the steps to take your smart contract source-code project and
instantiate it. We can test it by executing a query like this one:

```
peer chaincode query
-C mychannel
-n fabcar
-c '{"Args":["queryAllCars"]}'
```

Here is the output after executing the queryAllCars command:

```
[{"Key":"CAR0","Record":{"color":"blue","docType":"car",
"make":"Toyota","model":"Prius","owner":"Tomoko"}},
.
.
.
{"Key":"CAR9","Record":{"color":"brown","docType":"car",
"make":"Holden","model":"Barina","owner":"Shotaro"}}]
```

This query executes the smart contract transaction function called queryAllCars.
Writes get committed and thus require endorsing, which involves several peers. A
query should not have to task more than one peer for execution. This is what the

client-side code does for us. This example illustrates how a transaction function wraps a `ChaincodeStub` function, in this case a `rangeQuery` abstracted as `queryAll Cars`.

Summary

We began by setting up our Hyperledger Fabric development environment in preparation for Chapters 5 and 6 and using it to explore and examine a simple but complete smart contract called Fabcar. The code we write for Fabric smart contracts depends on the APIs provided by the SDKs. We covered the Fabcar code because it is small and simple to learn. This allowed us to focus on the code of smart contracts, the classes and interfaces employed, and the Fabric smart contract APIs we depend on.

Fabric smart contract SDKs are available for JavaScript, Java, and Go, with more coming. We used the JavaScript Fabric smart contract SDK for Node.js. Using it allowed us to explore *fabric-contract-api*, and the core classes and objects we need to develop Fabric smart contracts.

With knowledge of the API, we covered how to create a smart contract and what smart contract transaction functions are. Functions execute our smart contract transactions, so it was important to introduce several important topics like validating and sanitizing function arguments, initializing smart contracts, and interacting with the ledger. The Fabric contract API provides the interface to the ledger, which you learned how to access in our smart contracts through the transaction context every transaction receives. There was a lot to cover, but we tried to keep it simple yet provide you with exposure to the *fabric-contract-api*, which contains the interfaces you need to design and implement robust smart contracts.

Once the smart contract code is written, we need to package and deploy it to the Fabric network. This requires several steps to accomplish. Step by step, we went through each one. It is important to know these steps to take our smart contracts from source code to instantiated chaincode. We can execute only instantiated code.

In Chapters 5 and 6, we'll package and instantiate the smart contracts we create by using the knowledge you learned in this chapter. Now we can move on to Chapter 5 and focus on the invocation of smart contracts.

Smart Contract Invocation

This chapter equips you with the knowledge you need to invoke smart contracts. We'll use the prerequisites installed in Chapter 4. Then, using a script, we'll start and stop a local Fabric test network and deploy the Fabcar smart contract.

Since we are leveraging Fabcar and the Fabric test network, we start with a review of *fabric-samples*, the Fabcar smart contract, and the Fabric test network. We'll then start our test network and deploy the Fabcar smart contract. Next, we'll go through the steps executed by the script. Once our test network is up and running with the Fabcar smart contract deployed, we'll invoke Fabcar smart contract functions. We'll use the peer invoke command as well as a command-line Node.js application to execute a Fabcar smart contract function. The Node.js application will use the Fabric Client SDK for Node.js.

This chapter will help you achieve the following practical goals:

- Invoking smart contracts via the command-line interface
- Evaluating transaction functions for queries
- Submitting transactions and query transaction history
- Creating and issuing an application contract

Overview of fabric-samples, Fabcar, and the Test Network

In this section, you'll learn how to start, deploy, and invoke a smart contract on the Hyperledger Fabric test network. We'll first look at the structure and components of *fabric-samples*. Then we'll walk through the essential steps for deploying our sample smart contract, Fabcar. Once Fabric is set up and running, we will start invoking the Fabric smart contract through the peer command and Node.js methods. The Fabric test network is a great place for experimenting and running essential operations on smart contracts before moving your Fabric application to production.

fabric-samples

Installing the prerequisites in Chapter 4 included *fabric-samples*, which is Hyperledger Fabric's project for helping developers learn Fabric smart contract development. It contains many smart contract samples and tools for the rapid development of Fabric smart contracts. Included is a complete development Fabric network comprising two organizations. Each organization has a peer and CA. The network is containerized using Docker, which makes it easy and fast to launch and manage.

If you followed the instructions in Chapter 4 to install the prerequisites, you should have the *fabric-samples* directory. We will use the *bin*, *test-network*, *chaincode*, and *fabcar* subdirectories with this chapter and Chapter 6.

Hyperledger Fabric has shown firm support for *fabric-samples*. Fabric continues to introduce new functionality, improve existing code, and advance tools that together make *fabric-samples* the primary project for Hyperledger Fabric smart contract developers.

The *bin* subdirectory contains the peer executable, which we will use as the first method to invoke the Fabcar smart contract. The *chaincode* subdirectory contains the Fabcar smart contract, and the *fabcar* directory contains the command-line client for the Fabcar smart contract. We will use *test-network* to deploy the *fabcar* smart contract. Once the contract is deployed, we can invoke it.

In this chapter, we will launch a test network for Fabcar with the help of the *fabcar* script. Every Fabric smart contract needs a Fabric network. You can continue to advance your skills by leveraging the test network and apply what you learn in this chapter to the additional smart contracts in *fabric-samples*.

Fabcar

The Fabric smart contract, Fabcar, is one the earliest and simplest sample smart contracts in *fabric-samples*. It is great for learning the basics of Fabric smart contract operation and development. Getting hands-on with Fabric smart contract development is easy and fast with Fabcar because it is mature, stable, and simple in design, but fully functional. It implements the core functionality we need to understand and develop Fabric smart contracts.

Fabcar has two parts. The first part is the Fabcar smart contract, which we examined in Chapter 4. The other part is the Fabcar client. The client invokes the smart contract.

Fabcar client

As you can see in Figure 5-1, the Fabcar client has multiple implementations. We are interested in the JavaScript implementation.

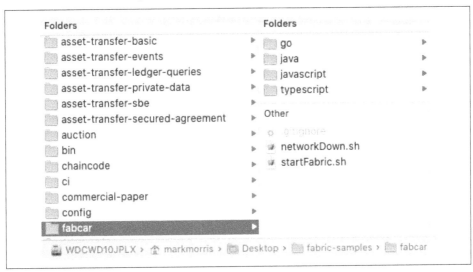

Figure 5-1. Fabcar client implementations

Provided are two shell scripts, *startFabric.sh* and *networkDown.sh,* to start and stop our Fabcar test network. The *startFabric.sh* script prepares and runs a new environment; then it deploys and initializes our Fabcar smart contract. The *networkDown.sh* script shuts down all Docker containers, removes them, and cleans up the environment.

 When the Fabric network restarts, it typically cleans all of the data. If you need to persist any work that's in a container that's part of your Fabcar test network, you need to persist your data prior to starting or stopping the test network. Typically, you need to mount a volume for the directory */var/hyperledger/production* in the orderer and peer Docker containers.

The Fabcar client is implemented as four Node.js command-line applications, highlighted in Figure 5-2. Two of the applications, *enrollAdmin.js* and *registerUser.js,* handle enrolling an administrator and registering an application user. The other two Node.js applications, *invoke.js* and *query.js,* handle an invoke transaction and a query evaluation, respectively.

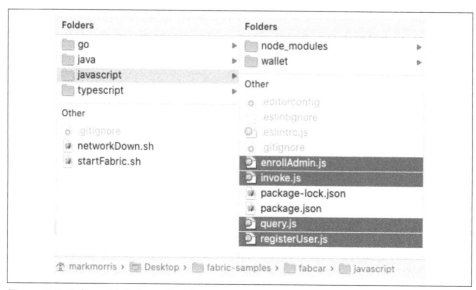

Figure 5-2. Fabcar Node.js applications

These are the four Node.js applications we will examine and execute to invoke the Fabcar smart contract. In Chapter 6, we will refactor and incorporate them into a new Node.js Express web application we develop, called Fabcar UI.

Fabric smart contract clients use a language-specific version of the Fabric Client SDK. Clients developed in JavaScript can use the Fabric Client SDK for Node.js (*https:// oreil.ly/HKK42*) to incorporate the Fabric smart contract functionality to authenticate, submit transactions, and evaluate queries. Because of these Node.js package dependencies from the *package.json* file, npm installs the four Node.js modules highlighted in Figure 5-3:

```
"dependencies": {
    "fabric-ca-client": "^2.1.0",
    "fabric-network": "^2.1.0"
},
```

The two packages we will directly use are *fabric-ca-client*, which handles the interaction with the authority to enroll, register, and administrate identities, and *fabric-network*, which provides `gateway`, `network` (channel), and `contract` objects to interact with the Fabric smart contract.

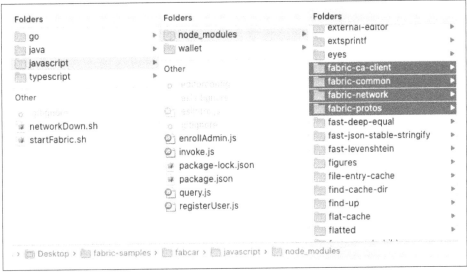

Figure 5-3. Fabcar client Fabric SDK for Node.js modules

Fabcar smart contract

The Fabcar smart contract, *fabcar.js*, like the client, is implemented in several languages; we discussed its implementation in Chapter 4. The *chaincode/fabcar/javascript* subdirectory with the *lib* subdirectory should be selected. The Fabcar smart contract that we will deploy and invoke in this chapter is in the *lib* subdirectory.

The Node,js smart contract has dependencies:

```
"dependencies": {
    "fabric-contract-api": "^2.0.0",
    "fabric-shim": "^2.0.0"
},
```

These two dependencies, *fabric-contract-api* and *fabric-shim*, result in the Node.js packages being imported into the project. Only one import is required for Fabric smart contracts, *fabcar.js*:

```
const { Contract } = require('fabric-contract-api');
```

The package *fabric-shim* is a low-level interface to the chaincode, and *fabric-shim-api* is used by both *fabric-shim* and *fabric-contract-api* to provide type definitions.

Fabric Test Network

The Fabric test network will launch a working Fabric network that can be used for smart contract deployment. The *network.sh* script is used indirectly when we use the Fabcar scripts *startFabric.sh* and *networkDown.sh* to start and stop the test network, respectively. This script is modular and can be refactored into a set of granular tools, suitable to your workflow and style. It can also serve as a good example for learning how to develop a script or scripts to launch and manage your own custom Fabric network. For our development, it is a quick start and takes the pain out of designing, configuring, and managing all the resources required to implement a functional Fabric network.

Once you develop a production-ready smart contract, you can package and promote it to production. The process of deploying it is dependent on the network it is being deployed to. Each production network will be different, but the functioning of your smart contract will be consistent across each network. In Chapter 9, we discuss test networks for Hyperledger Fabric v2. As applications grow in complexity, you will need to architect new custom networks to suit your specific requirements. The Fabric test network is a minimal network, but fully functional. It is designed with two organizations, and each runs a peer. Each organization has a CA to issue X.509 certificates to the members of the organization.

Docker Container and CouchDB databases

The test network configuration for Fabcar in the Docker Dashboard has the following servers running in Docker containers:

ca_org2
: The credential authority for organization 2

ca_orderer
: The credential authority for the network orderer

ca_org1
: The credential authority for organization 1

couchdb1
: The world state database for organization 2

orderer.example.com
: The network orderer that creates blocks and sends them for commit

couchdb0
: The world state database for organization 1

peer0.org2.example.com
    The peer for organization 2

peer0.org1.example.com
    The peer for organization 1

The two top containers are the smart contract runtime containers for each organization's peer.

The world state database for the organizations in our test network is CouchDB. We can access CouchDB with our browser by using the Fauxton web application, which is part of CouchDB. Open your browser and go to the following CouchDB URL: *docs.couchdb.org/en/latest/intro/tour.html*.

You will receive a page to log in to CouchDB. You can enter `admin` for username, and `adminpw` for the password, which are the defaults. These would be changed and secured with limited access in production, but for development, this works well. Also, the username and password will be part of network configurations and will be available in your *.yaml* file.

After the login, you will receive the page displaying the *couchdb0* databases for organization 1. The ninth row displays *mychannel_fabcar*. This is our Fabcar world state database. *mychannel* is the name of the Fabcar Fabric channel, and *fabcar* is the name of our chaincode.

Each CouchDB instance in our test network can be accessed by changing the port number in the URL to the port number displayed in the Docker Dashboard list of Fabric containers, which shows port 5984 is *couchdb0*, and port 7984 is *couchdb1*. So changing the port to **7984** in the CouchDB URL gives us access to *couchdb1*, the world state database for organization 2. Notice they are identical, as they should be, since they represent the world state for Fabcar.

Here is a summary of key takeaway points:

- Every organization in a Fabric network can have one or multiple channels.
- Each channel will have a world state (like a database) per smart contract.
- The world state database (and likely its contents) will be different for each channel.
- Each instance of a smart contract will run simultaneously on all channels in a Fabric network.

Now that you understand the basics of *fabric-samples*, *fabcar*, and *test-network*, we're ready to launch a Fabcar test network and deploy the Fabcar smart contract.

Deploying a Smart Contract

We need a Fabric network to deploy our Fabcar smart contract. For development, it is convenient to use *test-network*, part of *fabric-samples*. While you can execute *test-network's network.sh* to start a default network, we use *startFabric.sh* to start *test-network* and *networkDown.sh* to stop *test-network*.

When *startFabric.sh* is executed, the first thing it does, besides setting the default implementation language, is stop the network. This is to prevent runtime issues relating to resources and their runtime states.

 The test network has no persistence, and each execution brings up a new network.

Understand the startFabric.sh Anatomy

Before we execute *startFabric.sh*, let's examine it. The default implementation language is Go. This line from the script sets the default implementation to Go:

```
CC_SRC_LANGUAGE=${1:-"go"}
```

You can choose another supported implementation language, like JavaScript, by supplying a supported argument as shown here:

```
$ ./startFabric.sh javascript
```

After setting the implementation language, run the following command:

```
# clean out any old identities in the wallets
rm -rf javascript/wallet/*
rm -rf java/wallet/*
rm -rf typescript/wallet/*
rm -rf go/wallet/*
```

As you can see, all implementations have their *wallet* subdirectory contents removed. We will discuss wallets when we execute the Fabcar client applications.

Finally, the script executes:

```
./network.sh down
./network.sh up createChannel -ca -s couchdb
./network.sh deployCC -ccn fabcar -ccv 1 -cci initLedger
-ccl ${CC_SRC_LANGUAGE} -ccp ${CC_SRC_PATH}
```

As you see, *startFabric.sh* calls the *network.sh* script three times, supplying various arguments. The first call instructs *network.sh* to shut down the network. It does not matter if the network is not running; no errors are generated. It always runs and is a safety measure to ensure that a new error-free network is launched.

The second execution, or `createChannel` command, brings up the network, creates a channel (network), and sets the world state database to CouchDB. After this command completes, the network is up and running.

The third execution deploys the Fabcar chaincode (smart contract) to the network. The network provides many default *.sh* scripts—for example, the channel name, which is *mychannel*. Once completed, the Fabcar network is up and running, and our Fabcar smart contract is deployed and initialized.

Execute startFabric.sh

Now that we have looked at the *startFabric.sh* script and understand what it does, let's execute it and briefly review the output. It's verbose but informative, so becoming familiar with it will help us better understand what the *network.sh* script is accomplishing for us.

Open a shell and make sure Docker is running. You can check whether Docker is running by executing the following:

```
$ docker -v
Docker version 19.03.13, build 4484c46d9d
```

Change to the *fabric-samples/fabcar* directory located where you installed the prerequisites described in Chapter 4 and execute this:

```
$ ./startFabric.sh javascript
```

Your console will begin scrolling text output and continue to completion. The script will take a few minutes to complete. Once it's completed, you can save the text output for use and study. It contains the step-by-step sequence used to bring up the network. We are interested in the last command and the sequence of commands used to deploy the Fabcar smart contract.

Before we look at the smart contract deployment, let's take a quick look at the first part of the output, because it provides useful information, including the channel name and versions:

```
Start network command
Creating channel 'mychannel'.

If network is not up, starting nodes with CLI timeout of '5' tries
and CLI delay of '3' seconds and using database
'couchdb with crypto from 'Certificate Authorities'

Bringing up network
LOCAL_VERSION=2.3.0
DOCKER_IMAGE_VERSION=2.3.0
CA_LOCAL_VERSION=1.4.9
CA_DOCKER_IMAGE_VERSION=1.4.9
```

We see our channel name is *mychannel*, and the Fabric version is 2.3.0, indicated by `LOCAL_VERSION` and `DOCKER_IMAGE_VERSION`. The credential authority is version 1.4.9.

Generate Fabric Certificate Authorities

Next, we are informed the script is going to generate certificates for CAs, create the network, and create Docker containers for organization 1, organization 2, and the orderer credential authorities (as shown in the following output). Credential authorities play an important role in managing identities for each organization and the orderer:

```
Generate certificates using Fabric CA's

Creating network "net_test" with the default driver

Creating ca_org2    ... done
Creating ca_org1    ... done
Creating ca_orderer ... done
```

Then we are informed that the script is going to create the identities for organization 1. This will take several commands to accomplish. The script repeats these steps for organization 2 and the orderer.

Create Org1 Identities

We can use this output to capture commands and have a record of their expected result. You can use a simple pattern to make this easy. First, the script employs descriptive and informative text to guide the reader. Second, the script commands are clearly identified by a leading + sign. For example, the following informative text tells us the action is to enroll the CA admin, and it is followed by the + character and command on the next line. The command to perform this action is `fabric-ca-client`. The command is followed by command output:

```
Enroll the CA admin
+ fabric-ca-client enroll -u https://admin:adminpw@localhost:7054
--caname ca-org1 --tls.certfiles
/markmorris/Desktop/fabric-samples/test-network/organizations/fabric-ca/org1/
tls-cert.pem
2021/02/14 17:26:55 [INFO] Created a default configuration file at /markmorris/
Desktop/fabric-
samples/test-network/organizations/peerOrganizations/org1.example.com/
fabric-ca-client-config.yaml
2021/02/14 17:26:55 [INFO] TLS Enabled
2021/02/14 17:26:55 [INFO] generating key: &{A:ecdsa S:256}
2021/02/14 17:26:55 [INFO] encoded CSR
2021/02/14 17:26:55 [INFO] Stored client certificate at /markmorris/Desktop/
fabric-samples/test-network/organizations/peerOrganizations/org1.example.com/
msp/signcerts/cert.pem
2021/02/14 17:26:55 [INFO] Stored root CA certificate at /markmorris/Desktop/
```

```
fabric-samples/test-network/organizations/peerOrganizations/org1.example.com/
msp/cacerts/localhost-7054-ca-org1.pem
2021/02/14 17:26:55 [INFO] Stored Issuer public key at /markmorris/Desktop/
fabric-samples/test-network/organizations/peerOrganizations/org1.example.com/
msp/IssuerPublicKey
2021/02/14 17:26:55 [INFO] Stored Issuer revocation public key at /markmorris/
Desktop/fabric-samples/test-network/organizations/peerOrganizations/
org1.example.com/msp/IssuerRevocationPublicKey
```

The commands the script executes, including `fabric-ca-client`, are contained in the *bin* subdirectory of *fabric-samples*. This means we can execute these commands by using this output as a model or guide. This pattern repeats for each command and group of commands. The script groups repeatable sequences; for example, we use a common sequence to create org1 identities, create org2 identities, and create orderer identities but supply different arguments.

Invoke the Peer Chaincode

We will discuss the smart contract deployment after we look at the last command executed by the script, which is `peer chaincode invoke`. We use this last command to initialize the Fabcar smart contract:

```
+ peer chaincode invoke -o localhost:7050 --ordererTLSHostnameOverride
orderer.example.com --tls
--cafile /markmorris/Desktop/fabric-samples/test-network/organizations/
ordererOrganizations/example.com/orderers/orderer.example.com/msp/
tlscacerts/tlsca.
example.com-cert.pem -C mychannel -n fabcar --peerAddresses localhost:7051
--tlsRootCertFiles/markmorris/Desktop/fabric-samples/test-
network/organizations/peerOrganizations/org1.example.com/peers/
peer0.org1.example.com/tls/ca.crt --peerAddresses localhost:9051
--tlsRootCertFiles /markmorris/Desktop/fabric-samples/test-network/
organizations/peerOrganizations/org2.example.com/peers/
peer0.org2.example.com/tls/ca.crt --isInit
-c '{"function":"initLedger","Args":[]}'
```

The peer command has many subcommands, and one we are interested in is `peer chaincode invoke`. The `invoke` subcommand can invoke smart contract functions, which we will do shortly. The last parameter switch is `-c`. It is followed by an argument that designates the smart contract function to execute and any optional arguments. We will use this command as one method to invoke a smart contract transaction and evaluate a query.

Our primary purpose for this script is to start up our fully functional Fabric network, so we can develop Fabric smart contracts. The secondary purpose is to capture and leverage the script output. Toward this secondary purpose, we already have a command we can use to invoke our smart contract and query it. Next, we can leverage the script output's smart contract deployment section in maintenance and testing, which we'll discuss in Chapter 6.

When developing smart contracts, we want a fast iteration cycle. When we need to deploy or redeploy smart contracts repeatedly, starting and stopping the network will not work, so we need to customize the script and customize how we execute our deployment to facilitate fast iterations. Hyperledger Fabric v2 comes with external builders and launchers, which allow chaincodes to be deployed and executed independently (Chapter 9 covers this in more detail). First, we can examine the script output at the point where it deploys the smart contract, in order to capture the steps that show us how to deploy it.

To locate the deployment section of the script output, go to the end of the output and scroll up to the beginning of the last command:

```
+ peer chaincode invoke...
```

From there, scroll up until you see this:

```
Query chaincode definition successful on peer0.org2 on channel 'mychannel'
```

This is the end of the script output's deployment section. To locate the start of the script output's deployment section, scroll up until you see this:

```
deploying chaincode on channel 'mychannel'
```

This is the beginning of the script output's deployment section. In Chapter 6, we will look at the commands we need, and use the script output to help us deploy for maintenance and testing. Right now, let's look at the six-step deployment sequence the script executed:

1. Chaincode is packaged on *peer0.org1*.
2. Chaincode is installed on *peer0.org1*.
3. Chaincode is installed on *peer0.org2*.
4. Chaincode definition is approved on *peer0.org1* on channel *mychannel*.
5. Chaincode definition is approved on *peer0.org2* on channel *mychannel*.
6. Chaincode definition is committed on channel *mychannel*.

These six steps are the required actions we need to perform to deploy our smart contracts so we can invoke them. We do not include the checks or queries the script executed because they are only informative on status. From the six actions, we can derive four groups of actions we need to execute for deployment:

1. Package
2. Install
3. Approve
4. Commit

We need to do the package action only once—in this case, on *peer0.org1*. We can then distribute the package as needed to organizations (*peer0.org2*). The install action must be executed for every peer that endorses. The approve action must be performed by all organizations as stated in policies, and the commit action is executed once but includes all organizations' endorsing peers in the command. In Chapter 7, we provide script files to execute all these commands.

With the successful completion of *startFabric.sh*, the Fabcar test network is up and running. You can generate this output anytime you need an example of a command or need to verify changes you may make.

Our Fabcar smart contract is deployed and initialized. The script executed a command that invoked Fabcar. We can also use the command to invoke Fabcar, which we will see next. But before we leave, we should appreciate the utility of this output. It maps out the commands and command responses for creating from scratch a Fabric network with an orderer, orderer credential authority, and two organizations, each with a peer, a database, and a credential authority. The *network.sh* script responsible for the output is a resource we can put to good use as our needs change. For now, all we need is provided by this script. It has launched our test network, deployed the Fabcar smart contract, and initialized it.

We can now invoke the smart contract functions of Fabcar.

Invoking Smart Contract Transactions

The `peer chaincode invoke` command is the first method we will look at and execute to invoke our Fabcar smart contract functions. The next method we will look at and use incorporates the Hyperledger Fabric SDK for Node.js, which can be used for developing smart contract clients.

By using the Hyperledger Fabric SDK for Node.js, you can develop both command-line Fabric smart contract clients, like Fabcar, and Fabric smart contract clients that incorporate a UI into the design of the Fabric smart contract client application. We discuss a UI version of the command-line Fabcar smart contract client in Chapter 6. Let's now look at and execute the `peer chaincode invoke` method.

Peer Command

The `peer` command is a Hyperledger Fabric core binary. When you installed the pre-requisites, the *peer* binary along with several other binaries were downloaded and placed into the *bin* subdirectory of *fabric-samples*. This binary has five functions, or subcommands, it performs:

```
peer chaincode [option] [flags]
peer channel   [option] [flags]
peer node      [option] [flags]
peer version   [option] [flags]
```

The `peer node` command is the subcommand used to function as a Fabric node or Fabric peer:

```
Creating peer0.org1.example.com ... done
Creating peer0.org2.example.com ... done
```

Examining *docker-compose-test-net.yaml* in the *docker* subdirectory of *test-network*, you see the startup command executed to start the node:

```
command: peer node start
```

The `peer` subcommand we are interested in is the `chaincode` subcommand. This sub-command also has several subcommands:

```
install
instantiate
invoke
list
package
query
signpackage
upgrade
```

We want to use the `invoke` subcommand. Some other `peer chaincode` subcom-mands were used in the script that launches the test network and can be found by searching the output text we saved from the launch.

Using the `peer` command involves many parameters, so in a practice environment, we use variables to minimize the length of the resulting peer command-line text. We will use environment variables so we can execute `peer chaincode invoke` against our Fabcar test network.

When we executed *startFabric.sh*, we were in the *fabric-samples/fabcar* subdirectory. The script executes a change directory command while saving the current directory, which is *fabric-samples/fabcar*. The script changes to *fabric-samples/test-network*. This makes *fabric-samples/test-network* the current directory for the execution of the script. This is important to us because we are going to reuse the `peer chaincode invoke` command from the script to execute our `invoke` command. For this to work,

---

we need to open a shell and change the directory to *fabric-samples/test-network*. Then execute these export commands to configure your environment to find the *peer* binary in the *bin* subdirectory, the created *test-network* configuration in *fabric-samples/config*, and additional information peer needs to find in order to execute correctly:

```
export PATH=${PWD}/../bin:$PATH
export FABRIC_CFG_PATH=$PWD/../config/
export CORE_PEER_TLS_ENABLED=true
export CORE_PEER_LOCALMSPID="Org1MSP"
export
CORE_PEER_TLS_ROOTCERT_FILE=${PWD}/organizations/peerOrganizations/
org1.example.com/peers/peer0.org1.example.com/tls/ca.crt
export
CORE_PEER_MSPCONFIGPATH=${PWD}/organizations/peerOrganizations/org1.example.com/
users/Admin@org1.example.
com/msp
export CORE_PEER_ADDRESS=localhost:7051
```

Once you execute these, your environment is configured to execute peer. To test this, execute the following:

```
peer version
```

Your versions may be different, but you should see a result like this:

```
peer:
 Version: 2.3.0
 Commit SHA: ec81f3e74
 Go version: go1.14.12
 OS/Arch: darwin/amd64
 Chaincode:
  Base Docker Label: org.hyperledger.fabric
  Docker Namespace: hyperledger
```

Locate the peer chaincode invoke command that initializes the Fabcar smart contract and copy it to your editor, so we can refactor it. Remember, it is at the last command executed in the launch script output and looks like this, except your paths will be different:

```
peer chaincode invoke -o localhost:7050 --ordererTLSHostnameOverride
orderer.example.com --tls --cafile /Volumes/WDCWD10JPLX/markmorris/Desktop/
v2.3.0/fabric-samples/
test-network/organizations/ordererOrganizations/example.com/orderers/
orderer.example.com/msp/tlscacerts/tlsca.
example.com-cert.pem -C mychannel -n fabcar --peerAddresses localhost:7051
--tlsRootCertFiles
/Volumes/WDCWD10JPLX/markmorris/Desktop/v2.3.0/fabric-samples/
test-network/organizations/peerOrganizations/org1.example.com/peers/
peer0.org1.example.com/tls/ca.crt
--peerAddresses localhost:9051 --tlsRootCertFiles /Volumes/WDCWD10JPLX/
markmorris/Desktop/v2.3.0/fabric-samples/test-network/organizations/
```

```
peerOrganizations/org2.example.com/peers/peer0.org2.example.com/tls/ca.crt
--isInit -c '{"function":"initLedger","Args":[]}'
```

We want to modify the text

```
--isInit -c '{"function":"initLedger","Args":[]}'
```

at the end of the command into this:

```
-c '{"Args":["queryAllCars"]}'
```

Make sure you delete the --isInit switch. Since we removed the command to be executed for initialization, it will fail and error, because this switch is informing the peer to perform an initialization.

Once you modify the command text, it should look like this:

```
peer chaincode invoke -o localhost:7050 --ordererTLSHostnameOverride
orderer.example.com --tls--cafile
/Volumes/WDCWD10JPLX/markmorris/Desktop/v2.3.0/fabric-samples/test-
network/organizations/ordererOrganizations/example.com/orderers/
orderer.example.com/msp/tlscacerts/tlsca.example.com-cert.pem
-C mychannel -n fabcar --peerAddresses localhost:7051 --tlsRootCertFiles
/Volumes/WDCWD10JPLX/markmorris/Desktop/v2.3.0/fabric-samples/test-network/
organizations/
peerOrganizations/org1.example.com/peers/peer0.org1.example.com/tls/ca.crt
--peerAddresses localhost:9051 --tlsRootCertFiles /Volumes/
WDCWD10JPLX/markmorris/Desktop/v2.3.0/fabric-samples/test-
network/organizations/peerOrganizations/org2.example.com/
peers/peer0.org2.example.com/tls/ca.crt -c
'{"Args":["queryAllCars"]}'
```

Now copy the command to your shell and execute it. The output will look like this:

```
[chaincodeCmd] chaincodeInvokeOrQuery -> INFO 001 Chaincode invoke successful.
result: status:200
payload:"[
{\"Key\":\"CAR0\",\"Record\":{\"color\":\"blue\",\"docType\":\"car\",\"make\":
\"Toyota\", \"model\":\"Prius\",\"owner\":\"Tomoko\"}},
{\"Key\":\"CAR1\",\"Record\":{\"color\":\"red\", \"docType\":\"car\",\"make\":
\"Ford\",\"model\":\"Mustang\",\"owner\":\"Brad\"}},
{\"Key\":\"CAR2\",\"Record\":{\"color\":\"green\",\"docType\":\"car\",\"make\":
\"Hyundai\",\"model\":\"Tucson\",\"owner\":\"JinSoo\"}},
{\"Key\":\"CAR3\",\"Record\":{\"color\":\"yellow\",\"docType\":\"car\",\"make\":
\"Volkswagen\",\"model\":\"Passat\",\"owner\":\"Max\"}},
{\"Key\":\"CAR4\",\"Record\":{\"color\":\"black\",\"docType\":\"car\",\"make\":
\"Tesla\",\"model\":\"S\",\"owner\":\"Adriana\"}},
{\"Key\":\"CAR5\",\"Record\":{\"color\"\":\"purple\",\"docType\":\"car\",\"make
\":\"Peugeot\",\"model\":\"205\",\"owner\":\"Michel\"\"}},
{\"Key\":\"CAR6\",\"Record\":{\"color\":\"white\",\"docType\":\"car\",\"make\":
\"Chery\",\"model\":\"S22L\",\"owner\":\"Aarav\"}},
{\"Key\":\"CAR7\",\"Record\":{\"color\":\"violet\",\"docType\":\"car\",\"make\":
\"Fiat\",\"model\":\"Punto\",\"owner\":\"Pari\"}},
{\"Key\":\"CAR8\",\"Record\":{\"color\":\"indigo\",\"docType\":\"car\",\"make
```

```
\":\"Tata\",\"model\":\"Nano\",\"owner\":\"Valeria\"}},
{\"Key\":\"CAR9\",\"Record\":{\"color\":\"brown\",\"docType\":\"car\",\"make\"":
\"\"Holden\",\"model\":\"Barina\",\"owner\":\"Shotaro\"}}]"
```

We just invoked the Fabcar smart contract. What we invoked was a query, which is a read transaction. When we invoke, we execute either a write or a read transaction. The read transactions are not committed to the ledger; only write transactions are committed, provided they get properly endorsed and validated.

The Fabcar smart contract transaction we invoked was the queryAllCars transaction. Looking at *fabcar.js*, this Fabcar transaction is calling getStateByRange with the arguments set to an empty string. This will return all data for a specific car key, which we see in the result:

```
ctx.stub.getStateByRange(startKey, endKey)
```

Remember, the ctx object is the first argument passed to every smart contract transaction.

It provides access to the stub object, which instantiates a ChaincodeStub class (an implementation of IChaincodeStub), and the clientIdentity object, which instantiates a ClientIdentity class (which implements IClientIdentity):

```
export class Context {
    stub: ChaincodeStub;
    clientIdentity: ClientIdentity;
```

These two classes, ChaincodeStub and ClientIdentity, are part of the *fabric-shim* package, a Node.js module. We do not directly use the *fabric-shim* module, because we use the *fabric-contract-api* package, which provides the Contract object for our use:

```
const { Contract } = require('fabric-contract-api');
```

The Contract object provides access to both ChaincodeStub and ClientIdentity via the Context object ctx, which all smart contract functions receive as their first argument. The Contract object also provides functions we can use as interceptors before and after an invoked transaction. We look at these in the next chapter, when we discuss maintenance and testing.

Now let's use peer chaincode invoke to invoke a Fabcar write transaction. We can use the same command we used for the query. All we need to do is change the argument to the -c switch. Let's execute changeCarOwner:

```
-c '{"Args":["changeCarOwner", "CAR0", "Mark"]}'
```

After you change the -c switch argument, you should have a command like this:

```
peer chaincode invoke -o localhost:7050 --ordererTLSHostnameOverride
orderer.example.com --tls --cafile
/Volumes/WDCWD10JPLX/markmorris/Desktop/v2.3.0/fabric-samples/test-
```

```
network/organizations/ordererOrganizations/example.com/orderers/
orderer.example.com/msp/tlscacerts/tlsca.
example.com-cert.pem -C mychannel -n fabcar --peerAddresses localhost:7051
--tlsRootCertFiles/Volumes/WDCWD10JPLX/markmorris/Desktop/v2.3.0/fabric-samples/
test-network/organizations/peerOrganizations/org1.example.com/peers/
peer0.org1.example.com/tls/ca.crt --peerAddresses localhost:9051
--tlsRootCertFiles
/Volumes/WDCWD10JPLX/markmorris/Desktop/v2.3.0/fabric-samples/test-
network/organizations/peerOrganizations/org2.example.com/peers/
peer0.org2.example.com/tls/ca.crt -c
'{"Args":["changeCarOwner", "CAR0", "Mark"]}'
```

Now execute it and see this for the result:

```
[chaincodeCmd] chaincodeInvokeOrQuery -> INFO 001 Chaincode invoke successful.
result: status:200
```

This shows the transaction executed successfully. Since we change the owner of CAR0, let's check it with another query, but this time for specific data. Again using the same peer command, we just need to change the -c switch argument:

```
-c '{"Args":["queryCar", "CAR0"]}'
```

After executing, you should see this:

```
[chaincodeCmd] chaincodeInvokeOrQuery -> INFO 001 Chaincode invoke successful.
result: status:200
payload:"{\"color\":\"blue\",\"docType\":\"car\",\"make\":\"Toyota\",\"model\":
\"Prius\",\"owner\":\"Mark\"}"
```

It worked! We changed the owner. Later you will see how to get the history of transactions that are associated with the same key. The key for our write transaction, changeCarOwner, is CAR0. Remember, the ledger has two parts: the world state and the blockchain ledger (a file-based implementation of an immutable linked list, in simple terms). The world state is the current state of the blockchain for a given key. Our world state is implemented by CouchDB for our Fabcar test network.

We can see our change by using the CouchDB browser interface we discussed earlier in the chapter. Let's view our change in the world state database. As we have already discussed accessing CouchDB earlier in this chapter, open your browser and log in to CouchDB with the username **admin** and password **adminpw**:

http://127.0.0.1:5984/_utils/#login

Then go to this URL in CouchDB:

http://127.0.0.1:5984/_utils/#database/mychannel_fabcar/CAR0

You should see that the owner of CAR0 is Mark, as displayed in Figure 5-4.

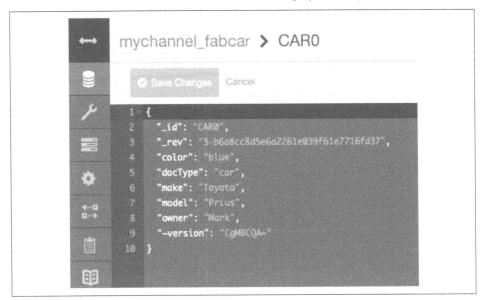

Figure 5-4. CAR0 record in CouchDB

We'll use the peer chaincode invoke command for more advanced purposes in the next chapter. Now let's look at the Fabcar client and see how it invokes the Fabcar smart contract.

Fabric SDK for Node.js Command-Line Application

In Chapter 4, we examined the Fabcar smart contract in depth. Now we are going to examine the Fabcar smart contract client and use it to invoke the contract. The Fabcar smart contract client, as discussed earlier in this chapter, is a group of four Node.js JavaScript command-line applications: *enrollAdmin.js, invoke.js, query.js,* and *registerUser.js.*

We will execute each one and look at how they work to invoke the Fabcar smart contract. To begin, open a shell and change to the directory *fabric-samples/fabcar/java-script.* The Fabcar client is a Node.js command-line application, so we need to execute the following:

```
npm install
```

This command will install project dependencies into our Fabcar project. When the command completes, you should have a *node_modules* subdirectory. This is where the dependencies listed here are placed:

```
"dependencies": {
    "fabric-ca-client": "^2.1.0",
    "fabric-network": "^2.1.0"
},
```

If we look in the *node_modules* subdirectory for installed Fabric modules, we find the Fabric modules listed here:

```
fabric-ca-client
fabric-common
fabric-network
fabric-protos
```

These modules, which represent the Hyperledger Fabric SDK for Node.js, can be found in the Fabric GitHub repo *fabric-sdk-node* (*https://oreil.ly/HKK42*). The *fabric-protos* module implements the Protocol Buffers protocol, which is a binary encoded communication protocol. We don't have to worry about this module, and we don't directly use it. The *fabric-common* module contains code used by both the *fabric-ca-client* and *fabric-network* modules. The *fabric-ca-client* module is used by the Fabcar client, but is not required for a Fabric smart contract client. You need to import and use *fabric-ca-client* only if your smart contract client needs to interact with Fabric CA to manage the life cycle of user certificates. This includes the ability to enroll, register, renew, and revoke users. If your smart contract client does not perform any of these functions, you do not need *fabric-ca-client*.

The *fabric-network* module is the only Fabric module required for a Fabric smart contract client. It connects your client to the network and provides the ability to invoke transactions, including writing to the ledger and querying the world state and ledger.

Now that our dependencies are installed, we can perform the following:

- Enroll our application administrator.
- Register our application user.
- Invoke a write transaction.
- Query the world state.

We first need to enroll an application admin to create an admin-level wallet. Then we can register users in an application with an assigned user wallet to secure network access.

Enroll our application administrator

To enroll our administrator, we execute the *enrollAdmin.js* application:

```
node ./enrollAdmin.js
```

You should see the following result:

```
Successfully enrolled admin user "admin" and imported it into the wallet
```

Now we can execute *registerUser.js* to register our user:

```
node ./registerUser.js
```

You should see the following result:

```
Successfully registered and enrolled admin user "appUser" and imported it into
the wallet
```

Great! We can now invoke our smart contract by using the user identity we just registered. But first let's look at what happened here. We need to understand what's going on with these two applications to invoke transactions, because we use identities when we invoke our transactions.

The identities associate us with an organization as a member and permit us to perform transactions. Let's start with the *enrollAdmin.js* application because it must be executed first. Open *enrollAdmin.js* in your editor. We are not going to parse every line but rather focus on the important ones. The imports are first:

```
const FabricCAServices = require('fabric-ca-client');
const { Wallets } = require('fabric-network');
```

We can see the imports from *fabric-ca-client* and *fabric-network*. We import all of *fabric-ca-client* and only *Wallets* from *fabric-network*. This is a Node.js command-line application, so we have a main function that executes all the application logic. This will come in handy when we look at the Fabcar UI, which we ported Fabcar to. Now the main logic begins:

```
// load the network configuration
const ccpPath = path.resolve(__dirname, '..', '..', 'test-network',
'organizations', 'peerOrganizations',
'org1.example.com', 'connection-org1.json');
const ccp = JSON.parse(fs.readFileSync(ccpPath, 'utf8'));

// Create a new CA client for interacting with the CA.
const caInfo = ccp.certificateAuthorities['ca.org1.example.com'];
const caTLSCACerts = caInfo.tlsCACerts.pem;
const ca = new FabricCAServices(caInfo.url, { trustedRoots: caTLSCACerts,
verify: false },
caInfo.caName);
```

First, the filesystem path to the connection profile for organization 1 is assembled and read. This path typically uses the *ccp-template.json* and *ccp-template.yaml* files as templates, passing organization name, peer port, CA port, and CA Privacy Enhanced Mail (PEM) certificates to generate organization connection files. Chapter 7 discusses this in more detail. This defines the network configuration to the client.

Once the connection profile is loaded, the certificate authority info and certificate authority TLS certificate are set. Using the CA information and TLS certificate, the CA object is created. We are using self-signed certificates, so we set the `verify` parameter to `false`.

After we have created our CA, we create our wallet:

```
// Create a new filesystem-based wallet for managing identities.
const walletPath = path.join(process.cwd(), 'wallet');
const wallet = await Wallets.newFileSystemWallet(walletPath);
console.log(`Wallet path: ${walletPath}`);
```

First, we create a path. The code is using the current path, which should be where our *fabric-samples/fabcar/javascript* subdirectory is located. The code appends to the path *wallet*. This is the *wallet* subdirectory in our *fabric-samples/fabcar/javascript* subdirectory. Using the full path as an argument to the `Wallets.newFileSystemWallet` function, we create a wallet object that we will use to store identities. Next, we check whether the `admin` is already enrolled:

```
// Check to see if we've already enrolled the admin user.
const identity = await wallet.get('admin');
if (identity) {
    console.log('An identity for the admin user "admin" already exists in the
wallet');
    return;
}
```

We can enroll only once by design. If the `admin` is not enrolled, we continue and enroll the admin:

```
// Enroll the admin user, and import the new identity into the wallet.
const enrollment = await ca.enroll({ enrollmentID: 'admin', enrollmentSecret:
'adminpw' });
const x509Identity = {
    credentials: {
        certificate: enrollment.certificate,
        privateKey: enrollment.key.toBytes(),
    },
    mspId: 'Org1MSP',
    type: 'X.509',
};
await wallet.put('admin', x509Identity);
console.log('Successfully enrolled admin user "admin" and imported it into the
wallet');
```

The CA we created is now used to execute the enroll function. We can see it takes the user ID and password for our `admin` as the `enrollmentID` and `enrollmentSecret`. Then we create an `x509Identity` object by using the enrollment object we just created. We are creating an `x509Identity` that contains the credentials—an object containing the certificate and private key, both of which were created and returned by the CA enroll function.

Along with the credentials, we add object metadata that identifies the organization this identity belongs to and the type of identity. Here `x509Identity` indicates a certificate containing a public key paired with a private key. With the identity created, we pass it to the wallet we created, which will store it.

You should see a file called *admin.id* in the *wallet* subdirectory. If you view it, you can see the data structure we just went over. This is it for the *enrollAdmin.js* application. Its purpose is to enroll the admin. To accomplish this, it requires a CA and a wallet. The CA comes from *fabric-ca-client*, and the wallet comes from *fabric-network*. This sequence is specific to the admin. Now let's look at *registerUser.js* and see what's different.

Register our application user

The beginning of *registerUser.js* contains the same imports as *enrollAdmin.js*, but in a different order, which does not matter. Like *enrollAdmin.js,* its logic is contained in a `main` function. The `main` logic starts off as in *enrollAdmin.js,* loading the network configuration, creating the certificate authority, and creating a wallet. We can see a pattern:

- Load the network configuration.
- Create the certificate authority.
- Create the wallet.

What then follows is a check to determine whether the user has an identity in the wallet, which indicates the user is already registered and enrolled:

```
const userIdentity = await wallet.get('appUser');
```

We return if the user is already in the wallet. This will happen if you execute *startFabric.sh* and the *wallet* subdirectory contains these identities. At this point, these identities do not exist in the Fabcar test network. The Fabcar application is not designed for multiple enrollments by a user. When this happens, you need to delete the contents of the *wallet* subdirectory and try the client again. The *wallet* subdirectory is then checked for the `admin` identity, which should exist because we always execute *enrollAdmin.js* first. If the `admin` is not found, we return. At this point in the code, *registerUser.js* and *enrollAdmin.js* differ. They differ because building the identity for the user differs from building the `admin` identity.

To build the user identity, we begin by using *wallet* to get a `provider` of the x509 type and use it to create a `User` object from the `admin` identity. We will use this identity to authenticate to the CA when we register our application user:

```
const provider = wallet.getProviderRegistry().getProvider(adminIdentity.type);
const adminUser = await provider.getUserContext(adminIdentity, 'admin');
```

Next we register our application user with the CA, providing our organization, our ID, and our role. We supply the `admin` user we created with the x509 `provider`. The CA registers our application user and returns an enrollment secret:

```
const secret = await ca.register({
    affiliation: 'org1.department1',
    enrollmentID: 'appUser',
    role: 'client'
}, adminUser);
```

From this point on, the logic is the same as in *enrollAdmin.js,*, except *enrollAdmin.js* used the `admin` password for the enrollment secret, and *registerUser.js* will use the secret we got back from the CA when we registered using the `admin` user to authenticate to the certificate authority. Therefore, we need the `admin` identity because it is used to register users. The application user secret is like a password, except the user will not know it and does not care to know. They have an identity, which in this implementation is type x509, and it is stored in the wallet, which is a filesystem-based store. We are now ready to execute *invoke.js* and then *query.js* and compare the two.

Invoke a write transaction

The *invoke.js* application has a main function, and all logic is contained within the main function. The application imports from only *fabric-network*:

```
const { Gateway, Wallets } = require('fabric-network');
```

This means it requires no interaction with the CA to invoke transactions. Similar to *enrollAdmin.js* and *registerUser.js,* it also makes use of *Wallets* from *fabric-network*. This makes sense because we need an identity to submit requests to the network, and identities for a client are stored in a *wallet*.

A user can have several identities, each with a unique name and purpose, like a driver's license, school ID, passport, and so forth.

The `Gateway` from *fabric-network* is our means to connect to the network, as we will see shortly.

The logic begins with familiar-looking code we saw in *enrollAdmin.js* and *registerUser.js* to load the network configuration, which contains the information for connecting to the network, creating the wallet, and checking for an identity. We are seeing boilerplate code here that cross-cuts applications and is something we would want to pull out and place in common code:

```
// load the network configuration
const ccpPath = path.resolve(__dirname, '..', '..', 'test-network',
'organizations', 'peerOrganizations',
'org1.example.com', 'connection-org1.json');
let ccp = JSON.parse(fs.readFileSync(ccpPath, 'utf8'));

// Create a new filesystem-based wallet for managing identities.
const walletPath = path.join(process.cwd(), 'wallet');
const wallet = await Wallets.newFileSystemWallet(walletPath);
console.log(`Wallet path: ${walletPath}`);

// Check to see if we've already enrolled the user.
const identity = await wallet.get('appUser');
if (!identity) {
    console.log('An identity for the user "appUser" does not exist in the
wallet');
    console.log('Run the registerUser.js application before retrying');
    return;
}
```

We need the user identity to exist so the gateway can find it; if it does not we return. To connect to the network, we use the `Gateway` we imported from *fabric-network* to create a `gateway` object and use it to connect. The arguments we pass to the `connect` function are the connection information, the wallet, the name of the identity to use, and some discovery options used to locate peers:

```
// Create a new gateway for connecting to our peer node.
const gateway = new Gateway();
await gateway.connect(ccp, { wallet, identity: 'appUser', discovery: { enabled:
true, asLocalhost: true }
});
```

After connecting, we use the gateway to get the network, which is our channel identified by our channel name:

```
// Get the network (channel) our contract is deployed to.
const network = await gateway.getNetwork('mychannel');
```

With the `network` object, we get a connection to our Fabcar smart contract:

```
// Get the contract from the network.
const contract = network.getContract('fabcar');
```

Finally, we get to invoke our smart contract. We are performing a transaction that will change the ledger, so this is a write transaction, and we expect it to be committed.

The `contract` API function we want to use is `submitTransaction`. This will call our `createCar` smart contract function with these arguments:

```
// Submit the specified transaction.
// createCar transaction - requires 5 argument, ex: ('createCar', 'CAR12',
'Honda', 'Accord', 'Black', 'Tom')
// changeCarOwner transaction - requires 2 args , ex: ('changeCarOwner',
'CAR12', 'Dave')
await contract.submitTransaction('createCar', 'CAR12', 'Honda', 'Accord',
'Black', 'Tom');
console.log('Transaction has been submitted');
```

As you can see, we invoke our smart contract indirectly through the `contract` API. This design pattern is powerful but also risky if mitigations are not implemented to prevent unwanted side effects from unexpected character or binary data. The best industry practices should be implemented to validate and protect data integrity.

At the end, the gateway is disconnected, and the application exits:

```
// Disconnect from the gateway.
await gateway.disconnect();
```

Now let's execute *invoke.js*:

```
node ./invoke.js
```

You should see the following result:

```
Transaction has been submitted
```

Did you notice the time to process and return? There is a large difference in the processing time to commit versus query, as we will see next when we execute *query.js* and return the results of our committed transaction, which created a new car.

Query the world state

Let's execute *query.js* and compare its logic to *invoke.js* to see any differences and commonalities between them:

```
node ./query.js
```

You should see the following result:

```
Transaction has been evaluated, result is:
[{"Key":"CAR0","Record":{"color":"blue","doc-
Type":"car","make":"Toyota","model":"Prius","owner":"Tomoko"}},
{"Key":"CAR1","Record":{"color":"red","doc-
Type":"car","make":"Ford","model":"Mustang","owner":"Brad"}},
{"Key":"CAR12","Record":{"color":"Black","doc-
Type":"car","make":"Honda","model":"Accord", "owner":"Tom"}},
{"Key":"CAR2","Record":{"color":"green","docType":"car","make":"Hyun-
dai","model":"Tucson", "owner":"JinSoo"}},
{"Key":"CAR3","Record":{"color":"yellow","docType":"car","make":"Volkswa-
gen","model":"Passat","owner":"Max"}},
```

```
{"Key":"CAR4","Record":{"color":"black","doc-
Type":"car","make":"Tesla","model":"S", "owner":"Adriana"}},
{"Key":"CAR5","Record":{"color":"purple","docType":"car","make":"Peu-
geot","model":"205","owner":"Michel"}},
{"Key":"CAR6","Record":{"color":"white","doc-
Type":"car","make":"Chery","model":"S22L","owner":"Aarav"}},
{"Key":"CAR7","Record":{"color":"violet","doc-
Type":"car","make":"Fiat","model":"Punto","owner":"Pari"}},
{"Key":"CAR8","Record":{"color":"indigo","doc-
Type":"car","make":"Tata","model":"Nano","owner":"Valeria"}},
{"Key":"CAR9","Record":{"color":"brown","docType":"car","make":"Holden",
"model":"Barina","owner":"Shotaro"}}]
```

Can you find the car we created, CAR12? It's the third one right after CAR1. Great, our submitTransaction was committed. If we looked in CouchDB, we would see this data in our world state database: *mychannel_fabcar.*

Let's look at the code. The code is the same except for the contract API function called:

```
const result = await contract.evaluateTransaction('queryAllCars');
```

For the query, we use evaluateTransaction because a query transaction is not committed to the ledger. A query does not follow the same processing path as a write transaction, which will use submitTransaction, so the transaction is processed for committing to the ledger.

Did you notice the difference in processing speed compared to *invoke.js*? Queries are much faster and can get cached, making them even faster because they do not access the database. Writes are much longer and may never be committed. As a Fabric smart contract developer, you will need to design for this long latency and for no guarantee of being committed. In Chapter 6, we will look at how events can help with these operating constraints.

We have executed the four applications that make up the Fabcar smart contract client. We saw the differences and common code they use. Each performs one application function, and has dependencies that determine the order they are executed. You learned we need to first enroll an application administrator, and then use the administrator to register and enroll application users. Once we have a user identity, we can submit transactions to commit data to the ledger and query the world state. These applications serve as good examples for solutions that are best implemented with a command-line application, like batch jobs or serverless commands.

Summary

In this chapter, you learned how to invoke a Fabric smart contract. We began with a review of the Hyperledger *fabric-samples*, Fabcar smart contract, and Fabric test network. This provided you with the background needed to understand the resources used for this chapter and the next.

We then launched our Fabric test network and discussed the launch script and its output to gain an understanding of what it takes to stand up a Fabric network for developing Fabric smart contracts. Besides launching the test network, the script also deployed the Fabcar smart contract. We went through the steps used by the script to deploy a smart contract, which will help you to understand and perform the deployment task for your own smart contracts.

Next, we executed each of the four Fabcar client's Node.js command-line applications that together make up the Fabcar smart contract client. At the same time, we examined each Fabcar application's code, noting the common code and differences in the applications, and their use of the Fabric SDK for Node.js. The Fabcar applications use the SDK to call the Fabric APIs for interacting with Fabric smart contracts, credential authorities, and wallets as well as for invoking smart contracts.

In the next chapter, we will take these four applications and refactor them into Node.js modules we can import into a Node.js and Express.js web application called Fabcar UI. This application mirrors the functionality of the four command-line Fabcar applications, but with a UI. You'll continue to learn more about the Fabric SDK for Node.js and the API available to Fabric smart contract developers.

## CHAPTER 6

Testing and Maintenance

Welcome to the final chapter in Part III. The life cycle for smart contracts is the same as for other software. Once the software is developed, tested, and deployed, our attention transitions to maintenance.

Many activities are performed to test and maintain software throughout its life cycle. These activities are grouped into two broad categories: technical and nontechnical. Our concern is with the technical activities that modify the software. Under maintenance, the modifications are generally either fixing something or adding something new. When bugs are discovered, they need to be corrected, so a maintenance task is created to fix the bug. When new features or capabilities are demanded, a maintenance task is created to add one or more new features to the software. Sometimes significant modifications can result in a release of a new version of software. This applies also to the clients of smart contracts. These activities continue until the software is retired. The majority of the software life cycle is consumed by maintenance. When fixing bugs or adding new features, testing is critical to success.

Throughout the entire life cycle, including both development and maintenance, the activity of testing is relied upon to ensure that the software is working as expected and meets the functional and nonfunctional requirements. Testing can be executed in many ways, and several schools of thought exist on how to approach and implement testing. Whichever school you adhere to will work well for smart contract development and maintenance. Testing can be formal, not formal, or a combination of both. The choice is yours.

This chapter is divided into four distinct sections. The first section presents a smart contract maintenance task, which adds a web UI to the Fabcar smart contract. We provide the code, which gives you a working example of a web UI client application. *fabric-samples* and SDKs do not offer any web UI samples. Instead, command-line clients are provided. We provide you with a web UI smart contract client to jump-start your smart contract client development and serve as an example of a smart contract maintenance task. With a web UI client, you can perform end-to-end testing of your smart contract. Most smart contracts you develop will require one or more web UI clients. You test smart contract web UI clients just as you would any other web UI client. Testing smart contracts can be slow and difficult, using *test-network*. When testing smart contracts, especially prior to system or integration testing, you will want a way to iterate quickly as you build out your smart contract API, represented by your smart contract functions or transactions.

The second section walks you through a setup for rapidly testing smart contracts. This setup has a lot of steps, but delivers a way to rapidly and iteratively test smart contracts without the need to launch the test network and go through the time-consuming stop-deploy-start development cycle. With the method you will learn in this section, testing your smart contract functions is fast and easy. However, other system components (such as the peers, orderers, and databases) support your smart contract functions, and testing these components can be problematic. You will need to access these components' log files to view and understand their output while you test your smart contract functions.

In the third section, you'll learn about the available logs provided by the various components. You can use these logs, provided by Hyperledger Fabric, to help support your development, maintenance, and testing activities. In the fourth and final section, you'll learn about unit testing, which is essential for maintaining code quality.

This chapter will help you achieve the following practical goals:

- Handling errors and processing responses in Fabric applications
- Testing and debugging a Fabric smart contract
- Running unit tests on Fabric smart contracts
- Following best practices for identifying and reviewing logs

Creating a Fabcar UI Client

The Fabcar smart contract has no web UI client, so for an example maintenance exercise, we added one. We have already created the client for you by consolidating the Fabcar command-line executables into a web UI application client. You can download the client code from *https://myhsts.org/hyperledger-fabric-boo/* (*https://myhsts.org/hyperledger-fabric-book*). Then follow along as we go through the code in this section to show you how easy it is to add a web client to a smart contract. Before we dive into the code, let's discuss handling error responses.

Error Response Handling

Fabric can be deployed on premises or to the cloud, or in a hybrid architecture. Where Fabric is deployed should not change the expected error or success responses. If misconfigurations exist, error responses will be received. We will see some error and success responses later in this section.

The same best practices for handling error and success responses in web and software development should be practiced. Catch your errors, augment them with additional information if available, and present the error or response to the user in a readable and understandable format. Errors should be logged for analysis and correction.

Most of the error handling for smart contracts is transparent and encapsulated in the SDKs and middleware that together form a cohesive distributed network and application architecture. This distributed architecture can be constructed with virtual technology like Docker, which provides flexibility in designing, operating, and managing the application and the way the responses behave. Fabric provides a virtualized architecture and operating environment suitable for developing smart contracts on a single laptop, cloud environment, or custom environment. The approach you choose and the tools you decide to use will vary with your personal preferences and provided resources, but the expected responses should be consistent across all environments.

We used JavaScript and Node.js to implement the web UI application, which we named *fabcar-ui*. Regardless of the client framework, responses will be the same across SDKs. The language selected for the smart contract development is independent from the language selected for the smart contract client and should not change the responses.

By designing enterprise application APIs, we can establish contract interfaces between our smart contracts and clients, providing a blueprint for what responses should look like and how to handle error responses. We can even extend this effort to the design of smart contract–specific APIs packaged into application libraries to be used by new and existing enterprise applications defining the expected error and success responses. This makes maintenance and testing much easier, consistent, and repeatable. This type of standardization supports the ability to extend the smart contract response to existing applications as well.

Fabcar UI Web Pages

The interface of the Fabcar UI is focused on simplicity. It takes the Fabcar smart contract client application executables and wraps them in a web GUI. We did not want to change any of the functional code and wanted to keep the separation of the executable's function. We wanted to end up with a simple web app that you can extend, experiment with, and potentially use as a test harness, as well as provide you with an example of a simple smart contract web application.

With Node.js as our client platform, we selected the popular and easy-to-use Express framework. Express makes it easy to create small web applications. For a production application, frameworks like Angular, React, or Vue.js will work too. Applications can leverage the smart contract service via an enterprise published API. This allows for controlled maintenance and testing to ensure quality control. Let's take a look at the Fabcar UI web pages. Figure 6-1 shows the main page.

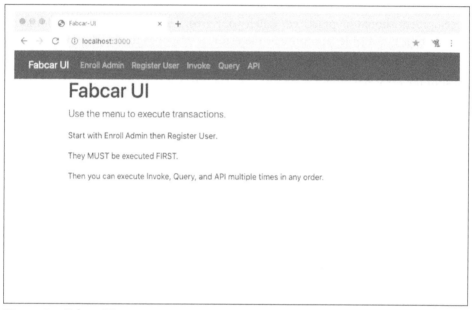

Figure 6-1. Fabcar UI main page

This simple web page displays the application menu and instructions for using the Fabcar UI. Looking at the menu bar, you can see a menu item for each of the Fabcar smart contract command-line applications we explored in Chapter 5.

On the far right is a menu item labeled API. We called it API to be generic, because it loads a page for calling our new smart contract function, callApi. We will implement this new function in a bit, but before we do, we will use the Fabcar UI to call the non-existent function and see the error response returned. Then we will implement it and see the successful response.

Reading the instructions displayed on the main page, you can see that the Fabcar smart contract sequence of execution is retained and mandatory, as it was in the command-line version. The goal of the Fabcar UI web app is to mirror the command-line app, but with a web UI, and keep it simple, so the separation between the web application code and the code specific to the Fabcar smart contract is clean. This design facilitates the ability to quickly iterate and add new functions and features, potentially becoming a test harness.

The UI interface of *fabcar-ui* is responsive and will work on any device capable of running a modern browser. All of the web pages are designed with the same layout: a menu, a button, and text display for instructions and responses. The responses are displayed in text without any formatting. Let's review each page, starting with Enroll Admin. We will not display all the pages because they are similar.

Enroll Admin

We add the Enroll Admin page to our *fabcar-ui*. Clicking the Enroll Admin button will execute the `enroll` transaction request. The other pages—Register User, Invoke, Query, and API—look and function similar to the Enroll Admin page.

Register User

The Register User page functions like the Enroll Admin page. Clicking the Register User button executes the `register` function, which uses `Admin` to register the user. This is why we need to execute the Enroll Admin page first. Here is the successful response displayed after clicking the button:

```
The returned result was: Successfully registered user "appUser" and imported
user into the wallet
```

Invoke

Now with the `Admin` and `User` identities in the `wallet`, we can execute the `invoke` and `query` functions.

When we click the Invoke button, we execute the `invoke` request. This request will call the Fabcar smart contract `invoke` transaction. This transaction adds a record to the ledger. Here is the successful response displayed:

```
The returned result was: Transaction has been submitted
```

The `invoke` function can be executed multiple times.

Query

The Query page will display the records from the ledger, which contain the records added by `invoke`. Clicking the Query button will display the records.

The `invoke` function on the client side generates a random number and appends it to the string `CAR0.`, so we can exercise the `invoke` transaction multiple times and see a unique response.

API

The final page is the API page. It too has a button and displays a text response. When the button is clicked, the `callApi` request is executed, which calls the `callApi` smart contract transaction. We have not added the `callApi` transaction to the Fabcar smart contract, so we will get an error response when we click the API button.

Now that we have looked at the web pages of the Fabcar UI web application, let's review the code.

Fabcar UI Code

We won't review all the code in detail because we covered the smart contract–related code in Chapter 5. What we want to focus on is the new code, so you can modify or extend it to learn or for your own purpose.

We developed the Fabcar UI web application with Node.js, Express, and Jade, a templating tool. The main file is *app.js*, which is executed with Node.js like this:

```
node app
```

This starts up a web server and listens on localhost and port 3000. Once it's started, you can open a browser and go to *http://localhost:3000* to display the Fabcar UI main page. The main file, *app.js*, contains the Express setup, the application `views`, which are the pages we reviewed, and the `actions`, which are executed by the buttons. The buttons call the `actions`, and the `actions` map to `handlers` that execute the smart contract client code. Let's take a look at *app.js*.

The code begins by importing the `handlers`—one for each function. Each function is the code from the Fabcar client command-line version. Following the imports, we set up Express to point to our `views` that represent our pages and to our public directory that contains public resources like Bootstrap and CSS files. Here is the code that loads the `handlers` and sets up Express:

```
// Fabcar command-line client for enrolling and Admin
var enrollAdmin = require("./handlers/enrollAdmin");
var registerUser = require("./handlers/registerUser");
var invoke = require("./handlers/invoke");
var query = require("./handlers/query");
var api = require("./handlers/api");

///////////////////////////////////////////////
// Express setup
var express = require("express");
var app = express();
app.set("views", "./views");
app.use(express.static("public"));
```

Next we have the views. With Express, one easy way to handle requests is to map them to a view and then render the view when the request is received. We implemented our views in a templating language called Jade. It's a simple text-based markup language to simplify and reduce the verbosity of HTML. The page is responsive and uses Bootstrap with CSS to facilitate our visual style and menu. Here is the code that maps a request to a view that is rendered as a web page:

```
/////////////////////////////////////////
// VIEWS
app.get('/', function (req, res){
    res.render("index.jade")
});
app.get('/enroll', function (req, res){
    res.render("enroll.jade")
});
app.get('/register', function (req, res){
    res.render("register.jade")
});
app.get('/invoke', function (req, res){
    res.render("invoke.jade")
});
app.get('/query', function (req, res){
    res.render("query.jade")
});
app.get('/api', function (req, res){
    res.render("api.jade")
});
app.get('/test', function (req, res){
    res.render("test.jade", {title: "TEST"})
});
```

After the views, we mapped the actions by using the same simple design pattern. The actions call the handlers, which encapsulate the code from the command-line Fabcar smart contract client. These actions carry out an asynchronous design pattern. The request is received from the view when a user clicks a view button and then calls the smart contract and renders the response from the smart contract. Here is the code implementing the actions, which call the smart contract and render the response:

```
/////////////////////////////////////////
// ACTIONS
app.get('/actionEnrollAdmin', function (req, res){
    //var promiseEnrollAdmin = enrollAdmin.log();
    var promiseEnrollAdmin = enrollAdmin.enroll();
    var promiseValue = async () => {
        const value = await promiseEnrollAdmin;
        console.log(value);
        res.render("enroll.jade", {data: value});
    };
    promiseValue();
```

```
});
app.get('/actionRegisterUser', function (req, res){
    //var promiseRegisterUser = registerUser.log();
    var promiseRegisterUser = registerUser.register();
    var promiseValue = async () => {
        const value = await promiseRegisterUser;
        console.log(value);
        res.render("register.jade", {data: value});
    };
    promiseValue();
});
app.get('/actionInvoke', function (req, res){
    //ar promiseInvoke = invoke.log();
    var promiseInvoke = invoke.invokeTransaction();
    var promiseValue = async () => {
        const value = await promiseInvoke;
        console.log(value);
        res.render("invoke.jade", {data: value});
    };
    promiseValue();
});
app.get('/actionQuery', function (req, res){
    //var promiseQuery = query.log();
    var promiseQuery = query.queryTransaction();
    var promiseValue = async () => {
        const value = await promiseQuery;
        console.log(value);
        res.render("query.jade", {data: value});
    };
    promiseValue();
});
app.get('/actionApi', function (req, res){
    var promiseApi = api.callApi();
    //var promiseApi = api.log();
    var promiseValue = async () => {
        const value = await promiseApi;
        console.log(value);
        res.render("api.jade", {data: value});
    };
    promiseValue();
});
```

The *app.js* code ends by setting the port for the server to listen on, printing a message to the console, and exiting:

```
app.listen(3000,function (){
    console.log('fabcar-ui listening on port 3000');
});
```

A `view` file is displayed when a page request is received. The view is rendered, and when a button is clicked, a request for an `action` is sent by the page and received by *app.js*, where it is processed by one of the `handler` files. The `handler` files encapsulate the code from the command-line Fabcar smart contract client.

All the `view` files use the same code template as shown here but vary their data where appropriate (for example, in `h1` or `href`):

```
extends layout
block content
    h1 Fabcar UI - Enroll Admin
    #data
        if data != undefined && data.length > 0
            p.lead The returned result was: #{data}
        else
            a.btn.btn-lg.btn-primary(href='/actionEnrollAdmin') Enroll Admin
script(src='/bootstrap/js/bootstrap.bundle.js')
```

When a `view` button is clicked, the `action` is called. The link is mapped in the *app.js* file to a `handler` that implements the `action`, which is one of the functions the command-line Fabcar smart contract client executed. Each executable has been taken from the Fabcar smart contract command-line client and refactored to a Node.js module, which can be imported and provides functions to call.

The same techniques were used for each handler. The main function was replaced and refactored to a module. This provides the module name as a reference to this function, which is called in *app.js* when the request is received as a result of clicking the button in the view. A variable was added, called `result`, to hold the response returned to the client.

We set the `result` variable with the success response we will return to the client. We commented out `process.exit(1)`, because we don't want to exit the process, which is our web server. Then we set an error response to return to the client when an error occurs. Lastly, we replace the `main` function with the return `result`. Now the executable is a Node.js module that we can import to call the function. We performed these tasks for all executables, turning each into a module. This was easy because the executables were self-contained and independent.

This completes the code review portion. The separation of functions is clean. The handlers are where the smart contract–related code is implemented. These could be mocked and developed independently of the smart contract. As with the command-line Fabcar smart contract client, the *package.json* file contains the two Fabric SDK dependencies:

```
"fabric-ca-client": "^2.2.4",
"fabric-network": "^2.2.4"
```

The *wallet* subdirectory works the same as it does in the command-line Fabcar smart contract client. When you execute `Enroll Admin`, an `Admin` identity is created and placed in the *wallet* subdirectory. When you execute `Register User`, an `appUser` identity is created and placed in the *wallet* subdirectory. Each time you start the test network, you must ensure that these identities are removed from the *wallet* subdirectory. If either identity is found, the client will print an error response to the console:

```
Wallet path: /fabric-samples/fabcar-ui/wallet
An identity for the admin user "admin" already exists in the wallet

Wallet path: /fabric-samples/fabcar-ui/wallet
An identity for the user "appUser" already exists in the wallet
```

This completes our coverage of Fabcar UI web pages and code. Now let's execute *fabcar-ui* and look at responses we can receive.

Fabcar UI Execution

If you have a test network up, we want to shut it down for this task. To shut down the test network, execute *networkDown.sh* located in the *fabcar* subdirectory. Keep the terminal open, because we will start the test network after looking at the error responses we will receive when it's shut down. Open another terminal, go to the *fabcar-ui* subdirectory, and execute this:

```
npm install
```

When this finishes, execute the following:

```
node app
```

You should see the following output:

```
fabcar-ui listening on port 3000
```

Now open your browser and go to the following:

```
http://localhost:3000
```

You should see the Fabcar UI main page. Click the API menu item and then click the API button. You should see the failed response shown in Figure 6-2.

Figure 6-2. Fabcar UI `callApi` error response page

In the console, you should see the following result:

```
Failed to evaluate transaction: Error: ENOENT: no such file or directory, open
'/fabric-samples/test-network/organizations/peerOrganizations/org1.example.com/
connection-org1.json'
Failed to enroll admin user "admin": Error: ENOENT: no such file or directory,
open '/fabric-samples/test-network/organizations/peerOrganizations/
org1.example.com/connection-org1.json'
```

This is an indication the test network is not up. Now in the terminal where you shut down *test-network*, make sure you are in the *fabcar* client subdirectory and start the test network by executing the following:

```
startFabric.sh javascript
```

Once the test network is up and running, let's perform the same test: click the API menu item and then the API button. Figure 6-3 shows the result.

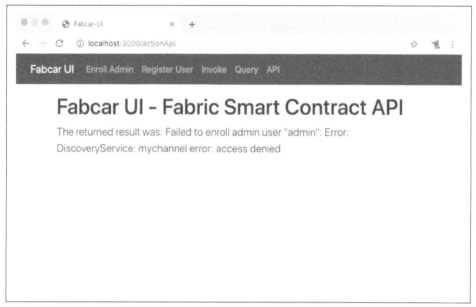

Figure 6-3. Fabcar UI failed `enroll admin` page

You should see this in your console:

```
Wallet path: /fabric-samples/fabcar-ui/wallet
2021-02-20T05:01:01.222Z - error: [DiscoveryService]: send[mychannel]
- Channel:mychannel received
discovery error:access denied
Failed to evaluate transaction: Error: DiscoveryService: mychannel error:
access denied
Failed to enroll admin user "admin": Error: DiscoveryService: mychannel error:
access denied
```

This indicates a problem with the `admin` identity. We receive this because we started a test network that removes all prior artifacts, so the identities we have in our client wallet are not valid. Delete the two identities in the Fabcar UI *wallet* subdirectory and then execute the Enroll Admin and Register User requests. Then try the API request again. Figure 6-4 shows the response.

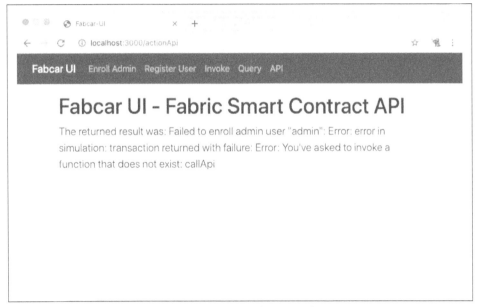

Figure 6-4. Fabcar UI page indicating callApi function does not exist

In your console, you should see the following:

```
Wallet path: /fabric-samples/fabcar-ui/wallet
callApi will be called
Failed to evaluate transaction: Error: error in simulation: transaction
returned with failure: Error:
You've asked to invoke a function that does not exist: callApi
Failed to enroll admin user "admin": Error: error in simulation: transaction
returned with failure:
Error: You've asked to invoke a function that does not exist: callApi
```

This response indicates that the Fabcar smart contract has no function by the name callApi.

We need to implement it in the Fabcar smart contract. This is the type of error response you will receive when a client calls a transaction that does not exist.

Since we are going to extend the Fabcar smart contract with a new function named callApi, it would be great if we had a way to quickly test the new function without requiring the test network to be stopped and started with each iteration, or the need to go through the deployment process discussed in earlier chapters. Well, there is a way, and it will allow quick iteration. Several setup steps are required, but in the end it is well worth the effort. Let's get started.

Performing Rapid Smart Contract Testing

Hyperledger Fabric v2 provides the test network. It includes all of the basic required components—for example, all Docker files, organization-related configuration, and scripts to install and deploy smart contracts. Developers can create applications and test smart contracts by using the test network, but using it can be slow. In this section, you'll learn how to create an alternative development environment for rapidly testing the smart contract.

Setting Up

First, shut down the test network because we will get port conflicts if we do not. Remember, you use *networkdown.sh* in the *fabcar* client subdirectory to shut down the test network. Once it is shut down, create a new directory in *fabric-samples* called *fabcar-debug* and change to that directory. Then download Fabric version 2.3 (or the version you are working with) from *https://github.com/hyperledger/fabric*, and unzip it and copy it to *fabcar-debug*. All of our commands will be executed from this subdirectory, so keep this in mind as we progress through the several steps required to set up our smart contract testing and debugging environment.

Start the orderer

From the subdirectory in *fabcar-debug* that contains the downloaded Fabric code, execute the following:

```
make orderer peer configtxgen
```

When this command completes, there will be a new *build/bin* subdirectory. It contains the binaries we just built. We want to place this subdirectory on our path, so execute this:

```
export PATH=$(pwd)/build/bin:$PATH
```

A sample configuration is provided that we can leverage, so we want to set an environment variable so the tools can locate that configuration. Execute this command to set the environment variable:

```
export FABRIC_CFG_PATH=$(pwd)/sampleconfig
```

Now we need to generate a genesis block. It will be used by the orderer we will start next. To generate the genesis block, execute this command, all on one line:

```
configtxgen
-profile SampleDevModeSolo
-channelID syschannel
-outputBlock genesisblock
-configPath $FABRIC_CFG_PATH
-outputBlock $(pwd)/sampleconfig/genesisblock
```

You should see this at the end of the output:

```
doOutputBlock -> Writing genesis block
```

Now we are almost ready to start the orderer. But first, we need to create the *hyperledger* subdirectory in the *var* subdirectory. This is a location Fabric uses. To create the *hyperledger* subdirectory, execute these commands, replacing the question marks with your username:

```
sudo mkdir /var/hyperledger
sudo chown ????? /var/hyperledger
```

Now we can start the orderer:

```
ORDERER_GENERAL_GENESISPROFILE=SampleDevModeSolo orderer
```

You should see this:

```
[orderer.common.server] Main -> Beginning to serve requests
```

If you get port conflicts, you can execute this command:

```
netstat -n -a -p tcp
```

This will list the TCP ports in use. The two ports you may have conflicts with are 8443 and 9443. If you do, just change the port in conflict to 19443 or 18443 in the *orderer.yaml* file located in the *sampleconfig* subdirectory. Look for ListenAddress in the Operations and Admin sections of the file to find the port. With the orderer running, it's time to start our peer.

Start the peer

We need to start our peer in another terminal. Open another terminal and change to the Fabric subdirectory we are working in. Just as with the orderer, we need to set up our environment, so execute the commands to set the PATH and FABRIC_CFG_PATH:

```
oilil
export FABRIC_CFG_PATH=$(pwd)/sampleconfig
```

Now start the peer by executing, on one line, the following command:

```
FABRIC_LOGGING_SPEC=chaincode=debug
CORE_PEER_CHAINCODELISTENADDRESS=0.0.0.0:7052
peer node start --peer-chaincodedev=true
```

You may get this error:

```
Error: failed to initialize operations subsystem: listen tcp 127.0.0.1:9443:
bind: address already in use
```

You can fix it by changing the port to 19443 in the *core.yaml* file located in the *sampleconfig* subdirectory. Look for the Operations section and ListenAddress to find the port.

When the peer is started, you should see this message near the end of the output:

```
serve -> Started peer with ID=[jdoe], network ID=[dev],
address=[192.168.86.37:7051]
```

Create a channel and join the peer

With the orderer and peer running, we need to open a third terminal and execute some deployment commands. So open a third terminal, change to the Fabric subdirectory we are working in, and set our two environment variables:

```
export PATH=$(pwd)/build/bin:$PATH
export FABRIC_CFG_PATH=$(pwd)/sampleconfig
```

Then we can execute the next step, which is to create our channel and join the peer. Execute this command, all on one line, which generates the create channel transaction:

```
configtxgen
-channelID ch1
-outputCreateChannelTx ch1.tx
-profile SampleSingleMSPChannel
-configPath $FABRIC_CFG_PATH
```

You should see this at the end of the output:

```
[common.tools.configtxgen] doOutputChannelCreateTx -> Writing new channel tx
```

Then execute this command, which will create the channel:

```
peer channel create -o 127.0.0.1:7050 -c ch1 -f ch1.tx
```

You should see this at the end of the output:

```
[cli.common] readBlock -> Received block: 0
```

Next, we join the peer by executing this command:

```
peer channel join -b ch1.block
```

You should see at the end of the output:

```
[channelCmd] executeJoin -> Successfully submitted proposal to join channel
```

The peer is now a member of the channel.

Build and run the chaincode

At this point, we can build our chaincode, start it, approve it, and commit it. Once we execute these final steps, we can stop and start a smart contract, and invoke its transactions.

To build the chaincode used to make this setup work, execute this command:

```
go build -o simpleChaincode ./integration/chaincode/simple/cmd
```

When the command finishes, start the chaincode by executing this command, all on one line:

```
CORE_CHAINCODE_LOGLEVEL=debug
CORE_PEER_TLS_ENABLED=false
CORE_CHAINCODE_ID_NAME=mycc:1.0
./simpleChaincode -peer.address 127.0.0.1:7052
```

Approve and commit the chaincode

Leave the chaincode running and open a fourth terminal that we will use to approve, commit, and execute the chaincode. In the fourth terminal, set our two environment variables:

```
export PATH=$(pwd)/build/bin:$PATH
export FABRIC_CFG_PATH=$(pwd)/sampleconfig
```

Now execute the three following commands, each on one line, that will approve, check the commit readiness of, and commit the chaincode:

```
peer lifecycle chaincode approveformyorg
-o 127.0.0.1:7050
--channelID ch1
--name mycc
--version 1.0
--sequence 1
--init-required
--signature-policy "OR ('SampleOrg.member')"
--package-id mycc:1.0

peer lifecycle chaincode checkcommitreadiness
-o 127.0.0.1:7050
--channelID ch1
--name mycc
--version 1.0
--sequence 1
--init-required
--signature-policy "OR ('SampleOrg.member')"

peer lifecycle chaincode commit
-o 127.0.0.1:7050
--channelID ch1
--name mycc
--version 1.0
--sequence 1
--init-required
--signature-policy "OR ('SampleOrg.member')"
--peerAddresses 127.0.0.1:7051
```

All of these steps need to be executed only once. We can now execute transactions, stop and start smart contracts, and stop and start the orderer and peer. We can close and open new terminals. But for each new terminal, we need to set the PATH and FAB

RIC_CFG_PATH environment variables to point to the *build/bin* directory and the *sampleconfig* configuration directory. Using absolute paths and setting these in your shell configuration eliminates the need to set these each time a terminal is opened for use in this task. The directory used to set this up contains the created artifacts that let you reuse this setup when you need to.

This configuration and setup will let us start and stop any smart contract and let us debug it, but don't expect advanced APIs to function correctly. There is no security, and the configuration is limited, but for fast debugging and experimentation, this is a good setup that's much faster than executing the deployment steps (which take time and do not work well when needing to iterate quickly on a smart contract).

Test the deployed chaincode

We can run and debug only one smart contract at a time with this setup. Before we stop the running chaincode we started in the third terminal, let's make sure everything is working. This smart contract needs to be initialized, so in this fourth terminal, execute this command, all on one line:

```
CORE_PEER_ADDRESS=127.0.0.1:7051 peer chaincode invoke
-o 127.0.0.1:7050
-C ch1
-n mycc
-c '{"Args":["init","a","100","b","200"]}'
--isInit
```

You should see output like this:

```
INFO 001 Chaincode invoke successful. result: status:200
```

Now that the contract is initialized, we can invoke a transaction that moves 10 units from A to B by using this command, entered on one line:

```
CORE_PEER_ADDRESS=127.0.0.1:7051 peer chaincode invoke
-o 127.0.0.1:7050
-C ch1
-n mycc
-c '{"Args":["invoke","a","b","10"]}'
```

You should see a successful response:

```
INFO 001 Chaincode invoke successful. result: status:200
```

And finally, we can query to see whether a has the value 90, as expected, with this command, entered on one line:

```
CORE_PEER_ADDRESS=127.0.0.1:7051 peer chaincode invoke
-o 127.0.0.1:7050
-C ch1
-n mycc
-c '{"Args":["query","a"]}'
```

And you should see the response we expect:

```
INFO 001 Chaincode invoke successful. result: status:200 payload:"90"
```

Our smart contract debugging setup is complete and working. We can now stop the running smart contract in the third terminal we opened and close the third terminal. We will use the current terminal we are in, the fourth terminal, to invoke transactions on the Fabcar smart contract after we prepare it for this local testing and debug setup.

Preparing the Fabcar Smart Contract for Testing and Debugging

Now open a fifth terminal and change to the *fabric-samples/chaincode/fabcar/java-script* subdirectory. Before we can start the Fabcar smart contract or any other Node.js JavaScript smart contract, we need to install the dependencies and modify the start command in the *package.json* file. When we deploy to a network like *test-network*, we don't need to install the dependencies. The runtime will perform this for us in the deployed container before executing the app with Node.js. In a production environment, this may be an issue because npm will access the internet to pull down the dependencies, and this may be a security risk.

To install the dependencies, execute the following:

```
npm install
```

This command creates a new subdirectory called *node_modules*. It contains our dependencies. Now we need to edit *package.json* and modify the start command, so open *package.json* in your editor. Change the start command to this single-line command and save the file:

```
"start": "fabric-chaincode-node start
--peer.address localhost:7052
--chaincode-id-name \"mycc:1.0\""
```

Now back in the fifth terminal where we just executed the npm install command, execute this:

```
npm run start
```

You should see this at the end of the output:

```
Successfully established communication with peer node. State transferred to
"ready"
```

The Fabcar smart contract is now running, and we can invoke it from terminal 4.

We have gone through a lot of terminals to get to this point. So let's review what we have running:

- Terminal 1 with orderer running.
- Terminal 2 with peer running.

- We closed the third terminal—we used it to run a sample Go smart contract to test that the setup is working.
- Terminal 4, which we use to submit requests to test our smart contracts.
- Terminal 5, with the Fabcar smart contract running.

Now from the fourth terminal, enter this command, all on one line, to initialize the Fabcar smart contract:

```
peer chaincode invoke
-o 127.0.0.1:7050
-C ch1
-n mycc
-c '{"Args":["initLedger"]}'
```

You should see the following:

```
INFO [chaincodeCmd] chaincodeInvokeOrQuery -> Chaincode invoke successful.
result: status:200
```

Now enter this command, all on one line, to query all cars:

```
peer chaincode invoke
-o 127.0.0.1:7050
-C ch1
-n mycc
-c '{"Args":["queryAllCars"]}'
```

You should see this output response:

```
INFO [chaincodeCmd] chaincodeInvokeOrQuery -> Chaincode invoke successful.
result: status:200 payload:"[
{\"Key\":\"CAR0\",\"Record\":{\"color\":\"blue\",\"make\":\"Toyota\",\"model\":
\"Prius\",\"owner\":\"Tomoko\",\"docType\":\"car\"}},
{\"Key\":\"CAR1\",\"Record\":{\"color\":\"red\",\"make\":\"Ford\",\"model\":
\"Mustang\",\"owner\":\"Brad\",\"docType\":\"car\"}},
{\"Key\":\"CAR2\",\"Record\":{\"color\":\"green\",\"make\":\"Hyundai\",\"model
\":\"Tucson\",\"owner\":\"JinSoo\",\"docType\":\"car\"}},
{\"Key\":\"CAR3\",\"Record\":{\"color\":\"yellow\",\"make\":\"Volkswagen\",
\"model\":\"Passat\",\"owner\":\"Max\",\"docType\":\"car\"}},
{\"Key\":\"CAR4\",\"Record\":{\"color\":\"black\",\"make\":\"Tesla\",\"model\":
\"S\",\"owner\":\"Adriana\",\"docType\":\"car\"}},
{\"Key\":\"CAR5\",\"Record\":{\"color\":\"purple\",\"make\":\"Peugeot\",\"model
\":\"205\",\"owner\":\"Michel\",\"docType\":\"car\"}},
{\"Key\":\"CAR6\",\"Record\":{\"color\":\"white\",\"make\":\"Chery\",\"model\":
\"S22L\",\"owner\":\"Aarav\",\"docType\":\"car\"}},
{\"Key\":\"CAR7\",\"Record\":{\"color\":\"violet\",\"make\":\"Fiat\",\"model\":
\"Punto\",\"owner\":\"Pari\",\"docType\":\"car\"}},
{\"Key\":\"CAR8\",\"Record\":{\"color\":\"indigo\",\"make\":\"Tata\",\"model\":
\"Nano\",\"owner\":\"Valeria\",\"docType\":\"car\"}},
{\"Key\":\"CAR9\",\"Record\":{\"color\":\"brown\",\"make\":\"Holden\",\"model\":
\"Barina\",\"owner\":\"Shotaro\",\"docType\":\"car\"}},
{\"Key\":\"a\",\"Record\":70},{\"Key\":\"b\",\"Record\":230}]"
```

Great! We can now run Fabcar in our smart contract testing and debugging setup. This means we can rapidly test and debug it and any other smart contract too. Using this setup, let's add a new transaction to the Fabcar smart contract and then test and debug it.

Performing Fabcar Testing and Debugging

First, we need to stop the running Fabcar smart contract in terminal 5 by pressing Ctrl-C. Then we need to load the Fabcar project into our editor or IDE.

With the chaincode Fabcar JavaScript project loaded in your editor or IDE, let's add the following `callApi` function right after the `changeCarOwner` function at the bottom of the *fabcar.js* file:

```
async callApi(ctx, apiRequest) {
    console.info('======== START : callApiRequest ========');
    console.info(apiRequest);
    // ClientIdentity
    let id = await ctx.clientIdentity.getID();
    let idBytes = await ctx.clientIdentity.getIDBytes();
    let mspid = await ctx.clientIdentity.getMSPID();
    let clientIdentity =  'id: ' + id + ', ' +
        'idBytes: ' + idBytes + ', ' +
        'mspid: ' + mspid + ' '
    ;
    console.info======== END : callApiRequest ========
    return '*** ClientIdentity *** ' + clientIdentity;
}
```

Save the file and start Fabcar. You can start it through your IDE or from the command line in terminal 5 as we did previously. Then in terminal 4, use this command to test the new transaction by invoking the `callApi` transaction via the `peer` command:

```
peer chaincode invoke -o 127.0.0.1:7050 -C ch1 -n mycc -c '{"Args":["callApi"]}'
```

You should see the following output:

```
Error: endorsement failure during invoke. response: status:500
message:"error in simulation: transaction returned with failure:
Error: Expected 1 parameters, but 0 have been supplied"
```

The error response is telling us we need to supply an argument. This is an example of the help the middleware provides for testing and debugging. Let's correct this by executing this command:

```
peer chaincode invoke
-o 127.0.0.1:7050
-C ch1
-n mycc
-c '{"Args":["callApi", "dummy"]}'
```

```
INFO [chaincodeCmd] chaincodeInvokeOrQuery -> Chaincode invoke successful.
result: status:200
payload:"*** ClientIdentity *** id: x509::/C=US/ST=California/L=San
Francisco/OU=COP/CN=peer0.org1.example.com::/C=US/ST=California/L=San
Francisco/O=org1.example.com/OU=COP/CN=ca.org1.example.com, idBytes:
-----BEGIN CERTIFICATE-----
\nMIICNjCCAd2gAwIBAgIRAMnf9/dmV9RvCCVw9pZQUfUwCgYIKoZIzj0EAwIwgYEx
\nCzAJBgNVBAYTAlVTMRMwEQYDVQQIEwpDYWxpZm9ybmlhMRYwFAYDVQQHEw1TYW4g
\nRnJhbmNpc2NvMRkwFwYDVQQKExBvcmcxLmV4YW1wbGUuY29tMQwwCgYDVQQLEwND
\nT1AxHDAaBgNVBAMTE2NhLm9yZzEuZXhhbXBsZS5jb20wHhcNMTcxMTEyMTM0MTEx
\nWhcNMjcxMTEwMTM0MTExWjBpMQswCQYDVQQGEwJVUzETMBEGA1UECBMKQ2FsaWZv
\ncm5pYTEWMBQGA1UEBxMNU2FuIEZyYW5jaXNjbzEMMAoGA1UECxMDQ09QMR8wHQYD
\nVQQDExZwZWVyMC5vcmcxLmV4YW1wbGUuY29tMFkwEwYHKoZIzj0CAQYIKoZIzj0D
\nAQcDQgAEZ8S4V71OBJpyMIVZdwYdFXAckItrpvSrCf0HQg40WW9XSoOO0076I+Umf
\nEkmTlIJXP7/AyRRSRU38oI8Ivtu4M6NNMEswDgYDVR0PAQH/BAQDAgeAMAwGA1Ud
\nEwEB/wQCMAAwKwYDVR0jBCQwIoAginORIhnPEFZUhXm6eWBkm7K7Zc8R4z7LW4H
\nossDlCswCgYIKoZIzj0EAwIDRwAwRAIgVikIUZzgfuFsGLQHWJUVJCU7pDaETkaz
\nPzFgsCiLxUACICgzJYlW7nvZxP7b6tbeu3t8mrhMXQs956mD4+BoKuNI
\n-----END CERTIFICATE-----
\n,mspid: SampleOrg "
```

We loaded the smart contract code in an editor, modified it, ran it, and tested it. This was a fast iteration. Using this procedure for development is robust even if we do not have the tooling to load the code in an IDE and debug it.

Let's take a quick look at debugging. Remember, this setup we just went through is awesome because with it you can treat Fabric smart contracts just like regular Node.js JavaScript. With the setup up and running, we can almost forget about it. When we use the special `start` command to start our smart contracts, they run as a node process but are known to the peer, orderer, and channel—so we get the basic chaincode functionality we need to develop smart contracts, but without all the network overhead and chaincode deployment requirements. This `start` command can be reused and applied to any chaincode smart contract we want to run and test or debug:

```
"start": "fabric-chaincode-node start
--peer.address localhost:7052
--chaincode-id-name \"mycc:1.0\""
```

With this setup, you easily run the sample smart contracts in *fabric-samples* without the need to go through the deployment process. Just load the project in your IDE, install the dependencies, modify the `start` command, and then start or debug the smart contract. It will load and run, enabling you to submit requests by using the `peer` command, as we have demonstrated throughout this section.

This quick look at debugging uses WebStorm. After loading the chaincode Fabcar smart contract in WebStorm, all we need to do is click the start command in the *package.json* file and select the debug option.

Then WebStorm starts the app and attaches a debugger, as shown here:

```
/node/12.3.1/bin/node /node/12.3.1/lib/node_modules/npm/bin/npm-cli.js run
start --scripts-prepend-
node-path=auto

Debugger listening on ws://127.0.0.1:56883/44db63ca-f74a-46bd-9995-350abb82cf2d
For help, see: https://nodejs.org/en/docs/inspector
Debugger attached.

> fabcar@1.0.0 start /fabric-samples/chaincode/fabcar/javascript
> fabric-chaincode-node start --peer.address localhost:7052 --chaincode-id-name
"mycc:1.0"

Debugger listening on ws://127.0.0.1:56886/947e10eb-8b5a-4b2a-8793-3131ce74efa5
For help, see: https://nodejs.org/en/docs/inspector
Debugger attached.
```

Now we can set breakpoints in the Fabcar code or even dive into *node_modules* and set breakpoints on the Fabric SDK modules, which let us step through and learn how they operate and which functions are called as a result of our code. This can be a wonderful way to learn how the smart contracts function and figure out how to use more advanced functions available in the SDKs. We can step through our smart contract and examine variables, logic flow, called functions, the stack, and more.

Using the IDE method of development, we cannot test the smart contract via our web client because we have no security, and the full network is not operating. But from what we have learned, this is not necessary, because we can invoke all of the smart contract transactions from the command line by using the peer command, allowing us to focus on the development of smart contract transactions.

Smart contracts can start and stop, which allows quick iteration during development. This is important, because it eliminates the redeployment steps that slow down the development cycle. We can use our editor to write code, the command line to start and stop the smart contract, and the peer command to test it. If a test fails, we can set a breakpoint and execute code to hit the breakpoint and then debug it.

The debugger lets us see and analyze the runtime data, state, structures, stack, and more. Once we locate the problem, we make the edits and test again. This development cycle is repeated until we finish our initial implementation of the transactions. Once we complete this cycle of development, we can package and deploy our smart contract to the test network and test it in a systems environment, where security and multiple peers are involved in the execution of our new smart contract transactions. This is similar to the typical development process in practice today, where developers create and test code in a local controlled environment and promote it to systems or integration testing, then to a staging environment that mirrors production, and eventually to production. Using the setup we just went through is perfect for rapid local development of smart contracts.

Identifying and Reviewing Logs

Log files are a primary source of information for smart contract developers. Knowing how to access logs is an important task for developers to gather information on the performance and functioning of their code. In this section, we will identify available logs and show how to review them.

This first log is the developer's *console log*. In the previous section, where we set up a development environment for rapid testing and debugging, we started an orderer and peer. Both had console output that we can review and learn from as we invoke our smart contract transactions.

Here is an example of the log output from the orderer we started:

```
2021-02-28 00:52:42.488 CDT 000d INFO [orderer.common.server] Main -> Starting
orderer:
 Version: 2.4.0
 Commit SHA: 3acff50
 Go version: go1.14.2
 OS/Arch: darwin/amd64
2021-02-28 00:52:42.488 CDT 000e INFO [orderer.common.server] Main -> Beginning
to serve requests
2021-02-28 01:40:15.322 CDT 000f INFO [comm.grpc.server] 1 -> streaming call
completed
grpc.service=orderer.AtomicBroadcast grpc.method=Broadcast
grpc.peer_address=127.0.0.1:53484
grpc.code=OK grpc.call_duration=10.733427ms
2021-02-28 01:40:15.479 CDT 0010 INFO [blkstorage] newBlockfileMgr -> Getting
block information from
block storage
2021-02-28 01:40:15.980 CDT 0011 WARN [orderer.consensus.solo] HandleChain
-> Use of the Solo orderer is deprecated and remains only for use in test
environments but may be removed in the future.
2021-02-28 01:40:15.980 CDT 0012 INFO [orderer.commmon.multichannel] newChain
-> Created and started new channel ch1
2021-02-28 01:40:15.983 CDT 0013 INFO [comm.grpc.server] 1 -> streaming call
completed
grpc.service=orderer.AtomicBroadcast grpc.method=Deliver
grpc.peer_address=127.0.0.1:53483
grpc.code=OK grpc.call_duration=672.54711ms
2021-02-28 02:09:30.719 CDT 0014 INFO [comm.grpc.server] 1 -> streaming call
completed
grpc.service=orderer.AtomicBroadcast grpc.method=Broadcast
grpc.peer_address=127.0.0.1:53564
grpc.code=OK grpc.call_duration=119.986µs
```

And here is a sample of log output from the peer we started:

```
2021-02-28 17:13:58.348 CDT 05ca DEBU [chaincode] CheckInvocation -> [e0e0bca2]
getting chaincode data
for mycc on channel ch1
2021-02-28 17:13:58.348 CDT 05cb DEBU [chaincode] Execute -> Entry
2021-02-28 17:13:58.358 CDT 05cc DEBU [chaincode] handleMessage -> [e0e0bca2]
Fabric side handling
ChaincodeMessage of type: COMPLETED in state ready
2021-02-28 17:13:58.358 CDT 05cd DEBU [chaincode] Notify -> [e0e0bca2] notifying
Txid:e0e0bca28e413b66a92305c253ecc09d7c8cc250cddd444e1f47e8b9f27c8871,
channelID:ch1
2021-02-28 17:13:58.358 CDT 05ce DEBU [chaincode] Execute -> Exit
2021-02-28 17:13:58.358 CDT 05cf INFO [endorser] callChaincode -> finished
chaincode: mycc duration:
10ms channel=ch1 txID=e0e0bca2
2021-02-28 17:13:58.359 CDT 05d0 INFO [comm.grpc.server] 1 -> unary call
completed
grpc.service=protos.Endorser grpc.method=ProcessProposal
grpc.peer_address=127.0.0.1:56768
grpc.code=OK grpc.call_duration=11.46977ms
2021-02-28 17:14:00.926 CDT 05d1 INFO [gossip.privdata] StoreBlock -> Received
block [47] from buffer
channel=ch1
2021-02-28 17:14:00.928 CDT 05d2 INFO [committer.txvalidator] Validate -> [ch1]
Validated block [47] in 1ms
2021-02-28 17:14:01.459 CDT 05d3 INFO [kvledger] commit -> [ch1] Committed
block [47] with 1
transaction(s) in 531ms (state_validation=0ms block_and_pvtdata_commit=319ms
state_commit=111ms)
commitHash=[4d4207e9827e0c14c240f2f8912bdfb382d214575fca45cfb4d247fcacddbf97]
```

When we launch a test network, the first log of interest is the log output from the script that launches the network and deploys the Fabcar smart contract.. Reviewing this log offers a lot of knowledge about the commands used and the parameters supplied to those commands. Of interest to smart contract developers are the log entries that detail the several commands required to deploy a smart contract. The log entries are near the end of the log.

When the test network finishes launching, we can run a Docker command to display the containers started:

```
docker ps
```

This command will display a listing of the 11 Docker containers started along with port information, status, date created, command, image, and container ID:

```
dev-peer0.org1.example.com-fabcar_1
dev-peer0.org2.example.com-fabcar_1
cli
peer0.org1.example.com
peer0.org2.example.com
couchdb1
couchdb0
orderer.example.com
ca_org1
ca_org2
ca_orderer
```

It is possible to use the container ID to review any container's log output. We can even tail the log output with this command:

```
docker logs -f 9acf2852a0d5
```

We can aggregate the log output of all these containers using Logspout. The *monitor-docker.sh* script, which will launch Logspout for us, is located at the following:

```
/fabric-samples/commercial-paper/organization/digibank/configuration/cli/
```

To aggregate all of the container logs after launching the test network, just open a terminal and execute the following:

```
monitordocker.sh fabric_test
```

Now when you invoke smart contract transactions, the terminal will display the aggregated logs' output. If you want to review specific log output from a particular container, we can use Docker.

Creating Unit Test Contracts

In the rapid smart contract testing session, we discussed how to test Fabcar. In large projects, many smart contracts will be frequently updated by team members. In today's complex software development environment, unit tests are essential in the development life cycle, as they ensure that your specific module works under all expected conditions. A *unit test* isolates a function, class, or method and tests only that piece of code. It helps to debug code and improve code quality, which eventually results in more reliable code.

As you learned in previous chapters, the Hyperledger Fabric smart contract supports code based on Go, Java, and Node.js. Each language has plenty of mock test frameworks we can use. For example, in this book, we use Node.js as our smart contract language, and instead of using Hyperledger Fabric directly to test in the sample network, we can use the Mocha and Chai mock test frameworks to mock those Fabric

SDK interfaces and directly test the smart contract logic. You can include the following node dependency in the *package.json* node project for doing unit tests:

```
"chai": "^4.3.0",
"mocha": "^9.0.2",
"nyc": "^12.0.2",
"sinon": "^11.1.1",
"sinon-chai": "^3.7.0",
```

Chai is a behavior-driven development/test-driven development (BDD/TDD) assertion library, and Mocha and Sinon.JS are popular standalone test frameworks. Sinon–Chai provides a set of custom assertions for using the Sinon.JS and Chai assertion libraries.

Further, the following is an example to show how we can use the JS test framework to test smart contracts:

```
const { ChaincodeStub, ClientIdentity } = require('fabric-shim');
const { SomeContract } = require('..');
const chai = require('chai');
const sinon = require('sinon');
const sinonChai = require('sinon-chai');
chai.should();
chai.use(sinonChai);

class Context {
    constructor() {
        this.stub = sinon.createStubInstance(ChaincodeStub);
        this.clientIdentity = sinon.createStubInstance(ClientIdentity);
    }

}

describe('SomeContract', () => {

    describe('#instantiate', () => {
        it('should instantiate', async () => {
            const ctx = new Context();
            const contract = new SomeContract();
            const result = await contract.instantiate(ctx);
            assert(revertedAddAdmin)

        });

    });

    describe('#invoke transaction', () => {

        it('should invoke transaction', async () => {
            const ctx = new Context();
            const contract = new SomeContract();
            const result = await contract.txn(ctx, 'success');
```

```
                    assert(revertedAddAdmin)

            });

        });

    });
```

We first import the node library in the test class. Then, create a `Context` class to mock `ChaincodeStub` and `ClientIdentity`. With the mock `Context` defined, we can then start to instantiate a smart contract by creating a `SomeContract` instance, and then get the instantiated result. Similarly, we can invoke smart contract transactions by calling `contract.txn(ctx, 'success')` to verify the result.

Summary

In this chapter, you gained four vital skills for developing Hyperledger Fabric smart contracts: creating a smart contract web app, performing rapid smart contract testing, monitoring logs, and creating unit test contracts. The first vital skill was creating a UI client for Fabric smart contracts. We did this as a maintenance task that added a web UI client to the Fabcar smart contract. A great benefit from this is we can now use the Fabcar UI web client as a template and quick start for our next smart contract.

The second vital skill is all about testing smart contracts. We set up a testing environment that allows us to rapidly test smart contracts. Using this setup, you learned we can debug our smart contracts as they execute. The benefit of rapidly testing smart contracts is that it facilitates quick iteration for smart contract development and exploring the operation of other smart contracts. Without the setup, you learned we could use *test-network*. But that is slow, and debugging difficult. This setup skill alone is probably the most important skill you can possess for fast smart contract development, testing, and debugging.

In addition, you learned how to monitor logs and execute unit tests—two important skills for monitoring code execution and maintaining code quality.

You are now ready to take the knowledge and skills you have gained to Chapter 7, which covers the most popular use case for Hyperledger Fabric: supply chains.

Blockchain Supply Chain with Hyperledger

Part IV of the book shows you how to build an end-to-end pharma supply chain with Fabric. It is a complete project for putting knowledge obtained from previous chapters into practice. Along the way, you learn how to design an architecture for a blockchain supply chain, write a smart contract for tracking inventories, compile and deploy the smart contract, and more. Likewise, you learn how to develop an application with Fabric through the SDK.

## CHAPTER 7

Building Supply Chain DApps with Hyperledger Fabric

In Part III, you learned how to develop, deploy, and test chaincode in Hyperledger Fabric. In this chapter, we will put all this information together to design and build a simple supply chain blockchain application called Pharma Ledger Network (PLN). This project will give you a taste of how blockchain enables global business transactions with greater transparency, streamlined supplier onboarding, better response to disruptions, and a secure environment. Specifically, the PLN project illustrates how blockchain can help manufacturers, wholesalers, and other supply chain members like pharmacies deliver medical supplies.

This chapter will help you achieve the following practical goals:

- Designing a blockchain supply chain
- Writing chaincode as a smart contract
- Compiling and deploying Fabric chaincode
- Running and testing the smart contract
- Developing an application with Hyperledger Fabric through the SDK

Designing a Blockchain Supply Chain

The traditional supply chain usually lacks transparency and reliable reporting. Large organizations have built their own systems to enable global control of their daily operations while recording transactions between suppliers and distributors in real time. However, many small companies lack that information and have limited visibility to trace their products at any given moment. That means, in their entire supply chain product process flow (from production to consumption), the transparency from upstream to downstream is very limited. This could lead to inaccurate reports and a lack of interoperability.

By design, the blockchain is a shared-ledger, transparent, immutable, and secure decentralized system. It is considered a good solution for traditional supply chain industries at registering, controlling, and transferring assets. Indeed, the popularity of blockchain and its adoption, in part, stems from its use in supply chain systems around the world.

A smart contract, which defines a business function, can be deployed in blockchain and then accessed by multiple parties in the blockchain network. Each member in the blockchain will be assigned unique identifiers to sign and verify the blocks they add to the blockchain. During the life cycle of the supply chain, when authorized members in a consortium network invoke a smart contract function, the state data will be updated, after which current assets' status and the transaction data will become a permanent record in the ledger. Likewise, the processes related to assets can be easily and quickly moved from one step to another. The digital transactions in the ledger can be tracked, shared, and queried by all supply chain participants in real time. It provides organizations with new opportunities to correct problems within their supply chain system as it revolves around a single source of truth.

In this section, we discuss a simple supply chain system and build our PLN use case. It will provide a good foundation for analyzing and implementing an application based on Hyperledger Fabric. We will analyze the business process workflow, identify the organizations in the network, and then design the consortium network. We'll also define a smart contract function that each organization will perform.

Understanding the Supply Chain Workflow

Let's take a look at organizations in the PLN business scenario, as shown in Figure 7-1. For demonstration purposes, we simplified the pharma ledger process, as it can be much more complex in the real world

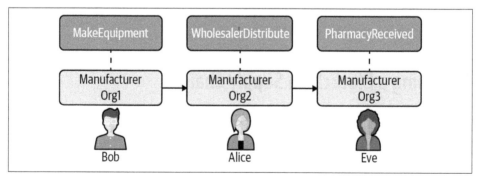

Figure 7-1. Organizations in the PLN

Our PLN process is divided into the following three steps:

1. A manufacturer makes equipment and ships it to the wholesaler.

2. A wholesaler distributes the equipment to the pharmacy.

3. The pharmacy, as a consumer, receives the equipment, and the supply chain workflow is completed.

Defining a Consortium

As we can see from the process workflow, our PLN involves three organizations: manufacturer, wholesaler, and pharmacy. These three entities will join together to build a consortium network to carry out the supply chain business. The consortium members can create users, invoke smart contracts, and query blockchain data. Table 7-1 depicts the organizations and users in the PLN consortium.

Table 7-1. The PLN consortium

Organization name	User	MSP	Peer
Manufacturer	Bob	Org1MSP	*peer0.org1.example.com*
Wholesaler	Alice	Org2MSP	*peer0.org2.example.com*
Pharmacy	Eve	Org3MSP	*peer0.org3.example.com*

In our PLN consortium, each of the three organizations has a user, an MSP, and a peer. For the manufacturer organization, we have a user called Bob as an application user. Org1MSP is an MSP ID to load the MSP definition. We define AnchorPeers with the hostname peer0.org1.example.com to gossip communication across. Similarly, the wholesaler is the second organization, Alice is its application user, and its MSP ID is Org2MSP. Finally, Eve is the pharmacy organization user with Org3MSP.

With the organizations identified, we can define our Hyperledger Fabric network topology, as shown in Figure 7-2.

Since installing and deploying PLN in multiple physical nodes may not be within the scope of this chapter, we define one peer with four organizations, representing the manufacturer, wholesaler, pharmacy, and orderer nodes.

The channel *plnchannel* provides a private communications mechanism used by the orderer and the other three organizations to execute and validate the transactions.

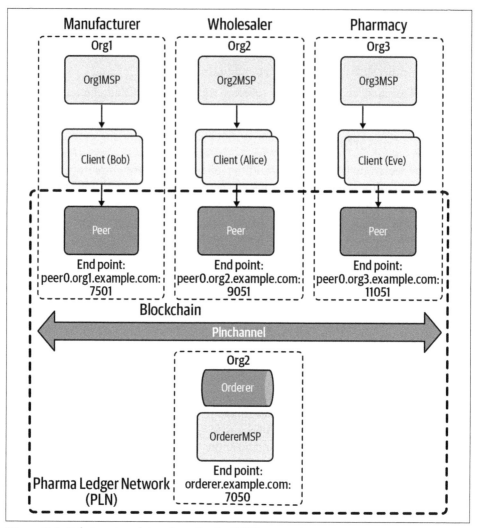

Figure 7-2. Fabric network topology for the PLN consortium

Reviewing the PLN Life Cycle

As we mentioned in the previous section, the PLN life cycle has three steps: the manufacturer makes equipment and ships to the wholesaler; the wholesaler distributes the equipment to the pharmacy; and finally, the pharmacy receives the equipment. The entire process can be traced by equipment ID. Let's look at this in more detail.

A piece of equipment with equipment ID 2000.001 was made by a manufacturer on January 1, with equipment and other attributes and values, as shown in Figure 7-3.

```
equipmentNumber: 2000.001
manufacturer: GlobalEquipmentCorp
equipmentName: e360-Ventilator
ownerName: GlobalEquipmentCorp
previousOwnerType: MANUFACTURER,
currentOwnerType: MANUFACTURER,
createDateTime: Jan 1, 2021,
lastUpdated: Jan 1, 2021, 10:01:02
```

Figure 7-3. Equipment attributes and their values for the manufacturer

Equipment attributes and values

Here we define a unique identification equipment number to represent equipment. Each equipment item is owned by an equipment owner at a certain period of time. In our case, we define three owner types: manufacturer, wholesaler, and pharmacy.

When a manufacturer makes a piece of equipment and records it in the PLN, the transaction result shows the equipment with a unique identification number of 2000.001 in the ledger. The current owner is GlobalEquipmentCorp. The current owner type and previous one are the same—manufacturer. The equipment was made on January 1, 2021. The `lastUpdated` entry is the date when the transaction was recorded in the PLN.

After a few weeks, the manufacturer ships the equipment to the wholesaler, and the equipment state will change, including ownership, previous and current owner type, and last update. Let's take a look at which equipment states change, as shown in Figure 7-4.

```
equipmentNumber: 2000.001
manufacturer: GlobalEquipmentCorp
equipmentName: e360-Ventilator
ownerName: GlobalEquipmentCorp
previousOwnerType: MANUFACTURER,
currentOwnerType: WHOLESALER,
createDateTime: Jan 1, 2021,
lastUpdated: Jan 20, 2021, 07:12:12
```

Figure 7-4. Equipment state changes for the wholesaler

Equipment state changes

One of the most significant changes is that the equipment is now owned by Global-WholesalerCorp. The previous owner type is the manufacturer. The last updated date has also changed.

After one month, the pharmacy finally receives this equipment order. The ownership is now transferred from the wholesaler to the pharmacy, as shown in Figure 7-5. The supply chain flow can be considered closed.

```
equipmentNumber: 2000.001
manufacturer: GlobalEquipmentCorp
equipmentName: e360-Ventilator
ownerName: PharmacyCorp
previousOwnerType: WHOLESALER,
currentOwnerType: PHARMACY,
createDateTime: Jan 1, 2021,
lastUpdated: Feb 25, 2021, 11:01:08
```

Figure 7-5. Updated equipment values for the pharmacy

Equipment in the hand of the pharmacy

With the same equipment identity, the peer organization can trace the equipment's entire history of transaction records by looking up the equipment number.

Understanding Transactions

As you've seen, the entire life cycle has three steps. Originating from the manufacturer, the equipment moves from wholesaler to pharmacy. As such, as a result of making a piece of equipment, the wholesaler distributes and the pharmacy receives the transaction. With all of this design and analysis, we can now start to write our PLN smart contract.

Writing Chaincode as a Smart Contract

We have discussed how equipment state and attributes change during the life cycle of a transaction, as the equipment moves among parties in our Pharma Ledger Network. As discussed in Part III, in Hyperledger Fabric, a smart contract is a program that implements the business logic and manages the world state of a business object during its life cycle. During deployment, this contract will be packaged into the chaincode and installed on each endorsing peer that runs in a secured Docker container.

The Hyperledger Fabric smart contract can be programmed in Go, JavaScript, Java, and Python.

In this section, we will write a smart contract implementation for our PLN by using JavaScript. All of the PLN code for this chapter is available in the book's GitHub repository. Also, we use Fabric v2.1.0 and Fabric CA v1.4.7 throughout the entire project.

Project Structure

To start our PLN smart contract development, first we need to create our smart contract project. Since we have three organizations, all peers must agree and approve of the new version of the smart contract that will be installed and deployed to the network. For our PLN, we will assume they are all the same:

```
We define a smart contract called pharmaledgercontract.js.  The project struc-
ture is shown here:
  +---manufacturer
  |   +---application
  |   |   |   app.js
  |   |   |   package.json
  |   |   +---public
  |   |   +---services
  |   |   \---views
  |   |           index.ejs
  |   \---contract
  |       |   index.js
  |       |   package.json
  |       \---lib
  |               pharmaledgercontract.js
```

The *package.json* file defines the two most important fabric libraries:

```
"dependencies": {
    "fabric-contract-api": "^2.1.2",
    "fabric-shim": "^2.1.2"
},
```

fabric-contract-api provides the contract interface. It has two critical classes that every smart contract needs to use, `Contract` and `Context`:

```
const { Contract, Context } = require('fabric-contract-api');
```

`Contract` has `beforeTransaction`, `afterTransaction`, `unknownTransaction`, and `createContext` methods that are optional and overridable in the subclass. You can specify the JavaScript explicit contract class name by using its superclass to initialize itself.

The Context class provides the transactional context for every transactional invocation. It can be overridden for additional application behavior to support smart contract execution.

Contract Class

Our pharma ledger contract implementation will extend from the default built-in contract class from the *fabric-contract-api* library. Let's first define PharmaLedgerContract with a constructor: org.pln.PharmaLedgerContract gives a very descriptive name with a unique namespace for our contract. The unique contract namespace is important to avoid conflict when a shared system has many contracts from different users and operations:

```
const { Contract, Context } = require('fabric-contract-api');
class PharmaLedgerContract extends Contract {

    constructor() {
        super('org.pln.PharmaLedgerContract');
    }
}
```

Transaction Logic

As we discussed, PharmaLedgerContract will need three business functions to move the equipment owner from the manufacturer to the wholesaler, and finally pharmacy:

```
async makeEquipment(ctx, manufacturer, equipmentNumber, equipmentName,
ownerName) {
// makeEquipment logic
}
async wholesalerDistribute(ctx, equipmentNumber, ownerName) {
// wholesalerDistribute logic
}
async pharmacyReceived(ctx, equipmentNumber, ownerName) {
// pharmacyReceived logic
}
```

The manufacturer will be initialized, and an equipment entry is created. As you will notice, these functions accept a context as the default first parameter with equipment-related arguments (manufacturer, equipmentNumber, equipmentName, ownerName) from client input. When makeEquipment is called, the function expects four equipment attributes from the client and assigns it to new equipment:

```
async makeEquipment(ctx, manufacturer, equipmentNumber, equipmentName, owner-
Name){
        let dt = new Date().toString();
        const equipment = {
            equipmentNumber,
            manufacturer,
```

```
                equipmentName,
                ownerName,
                previousOwnerType: 'MANUFACTURER',
                currentOwnerType: 'MANUFACTURER',
                createDateTime: dt,
                lastUpdated: dt
            };
    await ctx.stub.putState(equipmentNumber, Buffer.from(JSON.stringify(equip-
    ment))));
    }
```

At the end of `makeEquipment`, `ctx.stub.putState` will store the equipment's initial
state value with the equipment number key on the ledger. The equipment JSON data
will be stringified using `JSON.stringify`, then converted to a buffer. The buffer con-
version is required by the shim API to communicate with the peer.

The function uses the JavaScript `new Date` to get the current date time and assign it to
the `lastUpdated` date time. When transaction data is submitted, each peer will validate and commit a transaction.

After the equipment record is created by the manufacturer, the wholesaler and pharmacy will just need to update ownership to track the current owner. Both functions
are similar:

```
    async wholesalerDistribute(ctx, equipmentNumber, ownerName) {
            const equipmentAsBytes = await ctx.stub.getState(equipmentNumber);
            if (!equipmentAsBytes || equipmentAsBytes.length === 0) {
                throw new Error(`${equipmentNumber} does not exist`);
            }
            let dt = new Date().toString();
            const strValue = Buffer.from(equipmentAsBytes).toString('utf8');
            let record;
            try {
                record = JSON.parse(strValue);
                if(record.currentOwnerType!=='MANUFACTURER') {
        throw new Error(` equipment - ${equipmentNumber} owner must be MANUFACTURER`);
                }
                record.previousOwnerType= record.currentOwnerType;
                record.currentOwnerType = 'WHOLESALER';
                record.ownerName = ownerName;
                record.lastUpdated = dt;
            } catch (err) {
                throw new Error(`equipment ${equipmentNumber} data can't be
    processed`);
            }
        await ctx.stub.putState(equipmentNumber,
    Buffer.from(JSON.stringify(record)));
        }
```

In the `wholesalerDistribute` function, we query current equipment ledger data by
calling `ctx.stub.getState(equipmentNumber)`. Once data returns, we need to make

sure `equipmentAsBytes` is not empty and `equipmentNumber` is a valid number. Since ledger data is in JSON string byte format, that data needs to convert encoded data to a readable JSON format by using `Buffer.from().toString('utf8')`. We then verify that the current equipment owner type is the manufacturer by using the returned data.

Once all these conditions are met, `ctx.stub.putState` is called again. The equipment owner state would be updated to the wholesaler with the current timestamp. But as an immutable transaction log, all historical changes of the world state will permanently store in the ledger. We will define the `queryHistoryByKey` function to query all this data in the next step.

The `pharmacyReceived` function is similar to `wholesalerDistribute`, so it needs to validate that the current owner is the wholesaler and then transfer ownership to the pharmacy before updating the equipment record:

```
if(record.currentOwnerType!=='WHOLESALER') {
throw new Error(` equipment - ${equipmentNumber} owner must be WHOLESALER`);
}
record.previousOwnerType= record.currentOwnerType;
record.currentOwnerType = 'PHARMACY';Query Functions
```

After we implement all three equipment business functions, the ledger still needs a query function to search current equipment data, and a query history function to get all of the historical records.

`ChaincodeStub` is implemented by the *fabric-shim* library and provides `GetState` and `GetHistoryForKey` functions. In our case, the query definition is straightforward: we just need to call `ctx.stub.getState` to get the corresponding result.

`GetHistoryForKey` returns all historical transaction key values across time. We can iterate through these records and convert them to a JSON byte array and send the data back as a response. The timestamp tells us when the equipment state was updated. Each record contains a related transaction ID and a timestamp:

```
async queryHistoryByKey(ctx, key) {
  let iterator = await ctx.stub.getHistoryForKey(key);
  let result = [];
  let res = await iterator.next();
  while (!res.done) {
    if (res.value) {
      const obj = JSON.parse(res.value.value.toString('utf8'));
      result.push(obj);
    }
    res = await iterator.next();
  }
  await iterator.close();
  console.info(result);
```

```
        return JSON.stringify(result);
    }
```

That is all for the smart contract function we will implement for our PLN. Next, we will compile and deploy the Fabric chaincode.

Compiling and Deploying Fabric Chaincode

We have now successfully written our PLN chaincode using JavaScript. Before deploying our contract, we need to set up the Fabric network.

To get started with Hyperledger Fabric, we first need to meet some prerequisites. We assume you have already installed the software covered in Part II. If you haven't already done so, please install that first.

Install Prerequisites

Before advancing any further, we need to install the following third-party tools:

- Linux (Ubuntu)
- Python
- Git (*https://git-scm.com*)
- cURL (*https://curl.haxx.se*)
- Docker and Docker Compose: Docker version 17.06.2-ce or greater is required.
- Go version 1.14.*x*
- Node.js runtime and npm: Node.js version 8 is supported (from 8.9.4 and higher). Node.js version 10 is supported (from 10.15.3 and higher).

To set up a network, we generate crypto material for an organization by using Cryptogen, create a consortium, and then bring up PLN with Docker Compose. Let's first set up our project.

Review the Project Structure

We have defined all setup scripts and configuration files for our PLN project; the source code can be found on the book's GitHub page. The project structure is organized as follows:

```
|   loadFabric.sh
|---pharma-ledger-network
|   net-pln.sh
    +---channel-artifacts
    +---configtx
    |       configtx.yaml
    +---docker
```

```
+---organizations
|   +---cryptogen
|   +---manufacturer
|   +---pharmacy
|   +---wholesaler
+---scripts
```

Let's take a look at important configurations.

Cryptogen

Four crypto configurations are in the *cryptogen* folder for the orderer and the other three peer organizations. OrdererOrgs defines ordering nodes and creates an organization definition. PeerOrgs defines peers, organization, and managing peer nodes.

As we know, running components in the network requires a CA. The Fabric Cryptogen tool will use those four crypto configuration files to generate the required X.509 certificates for all organizations.

For OrdererOrgs, we define the following crypto configuration:

```
OrdererOrgs:
  - Name: Orderer
    Domain: example.com
    EnableNodeOUs: true
    Specs:
      - Hostname: orderer
        SANS:
          - localhost
```

For PeerOrgs, we define the following crypto configuration for Org1 (manufacturer). The other two orgs are similar:

```
PeerOrgs:
  - Name: Org1
    Domain: org1.example.com
    EnableNodeOUs: true
    Template:
      Count: 1
      SANS:
        - localhost
    Users:
      Count: 1
```

We set EnableNodeOUs to true, which enables the identity classification.

Configtx

The *configtx.yaml* file will generate OrdererSystemChannelGenesis and related artifacts by *configtx.yaml* configuration. In the *configtx.yaml* Organizations section, we define OrdererOrg and the other three peer organizations—Org1, Org2, and Org3, representing manufacturer, wholesaler, and pharmacy, respectively. Each organization will define its `Name`, `ID`, `MSPDir`, and `AnchorPeers`. `MSPDir` describes Cryptogen-generated output MSP directories. `AnchorPeers` specifies the peer node's host and port. It updates transactions based on peer policy for communication between network organizations and finds all active participants of the channel:

```
Organizations:
    - &OrdererOrg
        Name: OrdererOrg
        ID: OrdererMSP
        MSPDir: ../organizations/ordererOrganizations/example.com/msp
        Policies:
            ....
        OrdererEndpoints:
            - orderer.example.com:7050
    - &Org1
        Name: Org1MSP
        ID: Org1MSP
        MSPDir: ../organizations/peerOrganizations/org1.example.com/msp
        Policies:
...
        AnchorPeers:
            - Host: peer0.org1.example.com
              Port: 7051
    - &Org2
        AnchorPeers:
            - Host: peer0.org2.example.com
              Port: 9051
    - &Org3
        AnchorPeers:
            - Host: peer0.org3.example.com
              Port: 11051
```

The `Organization Policies` section defines who needs to approve the organization resource. In PLN, we use signature policies. For example, we define the `Org2 Readers` policy next, which allows the `Org2` admin, peer, and client to access the resource in this node and allows peers to do only transaction endorsement. You can define your own policy per your application's needs.

```
Policies:
            Readers:
                Type: Signature
                Rule: "OR('Org2MSP.admin', 'Org2MSP.peer', 'Org2MSP.client')"
            Endorsement:
                Type: Signature
                Rule: "OR('Org2MSP.peer')"
```

The `Profiles` section defines how to generate `PharmaLedgerOrdererGenesis`, including order configuration and organizations in the PLN consortiums:

```
Profiles:
    PharmaLedgerOrdererGenesis:
        <<: *ChannelDefaults
        Orderer:
            <<: *OrdererDefaults
            Organizations:
                - *OrdererOrg
            Capabilities:
                <<: *OrdererCapabilities
        Consortiums:
            PharmaLedgerConsortium:
                Organizations:
                    - *Org1
                    - *Org2
                    - *Org3
    PharmaLedgerChannel:
        Consortium: PharmaLedgerConsortium
        <<: *ChannelDefaults
        Application:
            <<: *ApplicationDefaults
            Organizations:
                - *Org1
                - *Org2
                - *Org3
            Capabilities:
                <<: *ApplicationCapabilities
```

Docker

The *docker* folder contains the Docker Compose configuration file, *docker-compose-pln-net.yaml*. The Docker Compose tool uses this configuration file to initialize the Fabric runtime environment. It defines volumes, networks, and services.

In our PLN project, we define our network name as pln. We first need to specify the Docker runtime environment variable for each organization service. For example, we define our blockchain network name as ${COMPOSE_PROJECT_NAME}_pln. When we assign the environment variable COMPOSE_PROJECT_NAME a net value, the network name will be net_pln. The container pulls the orderer images as well from *hyperledger/fabric-peer*. The volume configuration maps the directories where MSP, TLS, and other organization Fabric parts are used in the environment settings. Finally, working_dir sets the working directory for the peer:

```
services:
  orderer.example.com:
    container_name: orderer.example.com
    image: hyperledger/fabric-orderer:$IMAGE_TAG
    environment:..
    working_dir: /opt/gopath/src/github.com/hyperledger/fabric
    command: orderer
    volumes:..
```

```
    ports:
      - 7050:7050
    networks:
      - pln

  peer0.org1.example.com:
    container_name: peer0.org1.example.com
    image: hyperledger/fabric-peer:$IMAGE_TAG
    environment:
      - CORE_VM_DOCKER_HOSTCONFIG_NETWORKMODE=${COMPOSE_PROJECT_NAME}_pln
..
      - CORE_PEER_ADDRESS=peer0.org1.example.com:7051
      - CORE_PEER_LISTENADDRESS=0.0.0.0:7051
      - CORE_PEER_CHAINCODEADDRESS=peer0.org1.example.com:7052
      - CORE_PEER_CHAINCODELISTENADDRESS=0.0.0.0:7052
      - CORE_PEER_GOSSIP_BOOTSTRAP=peer0.org1.example.com:7051
      - CORE_PEER_GOSSIP_EXTERNALENDPOINT=peer0.org1.example.com:7051
      - CORE_PEER_LOCALMSPID=Org1MSP
    volumes:
...
    working_dir: /opt/gopath/src/github.com/hyperledger/fabric/peer
    command: peer node start
    ports:
      - 7051:7051
    networks:
      - pln
```

Install Binaries and Docker Images

We have reviewed important configurations in order to run the PLN network. The *net-pln.sh* script will bring up the PLN network, but we first need to download and install Fabric binaries to your system. Under the root project folder is a file called *loadFabric.sh*; run the following command to load Fabric binaries and configs:

```
./loadFabric.sh
```

This will install the Hyperledger Fabric platform-specific binaries and config files into the */bin* and */config* directories under the project. For this project, we use the current latest production releases: Fabric v2.1.0 and Fabric CA v1.4.7. Run docker images -a to check installed Fabric images.

 Make sure all of the scripts in the project are executable. For example, you can run chmod +x loadFabric.sh to make it executable.

It is now time to start our PLN network.

Start the PLN Network

As we mentioned before, to start the PLN network, we need to complete the following steps:

1. Generate peer organization certificates using the Cryptogen tool. Here is the command for Org1:

   ```
   cryptogen generate --config=./organizations/cryptogen/
   crypto-config-org1.yaml --output="organizations"
   ```

   The generated output is stored in the *organizations* folder.

2. Create orderer organization identities using Cryptogen:

   ```
   cryptogen generate --config=./organizations/cryptogen/
   crypto-config-orderer.yaml --output="organizations"
   ```

3. Generate a common connection profile (CCP) for Org1, Org2, and Org3:

   ```
   ./organizations/ccp-generate.sh
   ```

   ccp-generate.sh is under the *organizations* folder. It uses *ccp-template.json* and *ccp-template.yaml* files as templates; it defines placeholder variables for the org name, peer port, CA port, and CA PEM certificates. By passing these defined variables, we can generate org connection files when running *ccp-generate.sh*. And *ccp-generate.sh* will also copy generated connection files to the *peer orgs* folder:

   ```
   echo "$(json_ccp $ORG $P0PORT $CAPORT $PEERPEM $CAPEM)" >
   organizations/peerOrganizations/org1.example.com/connection-org1.json
   echo "$(yaml_ccp $ORG $P0PORT $CAPORT $PEERPEM $CAPEM)" >
   organizations/peerOrganizations/org1.example.com/connection-org1.yaml
   ```

   Each peer web client will use these connection files to connect to the Fabric network.

4. Create the consortium and generate an orderer system channel genesis block:

   ```
   configtxgen -profile PharmaLedgerOrdererGenesis -channelID
   system-channel -outputBlock ./system-genesis-block/genesis.block
   ```

   configtxgen reads the *configtx.yaml* profile and generates the *genesis.block* file under the *system-genesis-block* folder.

5. Bring up the peer and orderer nodes.

   The *docker-compose* file is defined under *docker/docker-compose-pln-net.yaml*. The command will pull the latest Fabric orderer and peer images, build the orderer and peer images, and start the services we defined in the *.yaml* file. Run the following docker-compose command to bring up the peer and orderer nodes:

   ```
   IMAGE_TAG=$IMAGETAG docker-compose ${COMPOSE_FILES} up -d 2>&1
   ```

6. Now, let's bring up the PLN network. Open a terminal window and run *net-pln.sh* under the *pharma-ledger-network* folder:

```
cd pharma-ledger-network
./net-pln.sh up
```

You should see the following success log:

```
Creating network "net_pln" with the default driver
Creating volume "net_orderer.example.com" with default driver
Creating volume "net_peer0.org1.example.com" with default driver
Creating volume "net_peer0.org2.example.com" with default driver
Creating volume "net_peer0.org3.example.com" with default driver
Creating orderer.example.com     ... done
Creating peer0.org2.example.com ... done
Creating peer0.org1.example.com ... done
Creating peer0.org3.example.com ... done
CONTAINER ID   IMAGE                         COMMAND    ..
NAMES
5a1fb5778a94   hyperledger/fabric-peer:latest   "peer node start" ...
peer0.org3.example.com
969a5a9f5a85   hyperledger/fabric-peer:latest   "peer node start" ...
peer0.org1.example.com
2f2cf2b0463d hyperledger/fabric-peer:latest   "peer node start" ...
peer0.org2.example.com
f327510667ff hyperledger/fabric-orderer:latest "orderer"         ...
orderer.example.com
```

We have four organizations, including three peers and one orderer, that are running in the *net_pln* network. In the next step, we will use the script to create a PLN channel for all orgs.

Monitor the PLN Network

The Fabric images in the PLN network are Docker based. During project development or the production life cycle, you may encounter many errors. Log monitoring is one of the most important things to do from a DevOps standpoint for troubleshooting the code. It will help troubleshoot and find the root cause much easier and faster.

Logspout is an open source container log tool for monitoring Docker logs. It collects Docker's logs from all nodes in your cluster to be aggregated into one place. In our PLN project, we will use Logspout to monitor channel creation, smart contract installation, and other actions. Navigate to the *pharma-ledger-network* folder and open a new terminal window:

```
cd pharma-ledger-network
```

Run the following command from the *net-pln.sh* script and start the Logspout tool for the containers running on the PLN network *net_pln*:

```
./net-pln.sh monitor-up

...
Starting docker log monitoring on network 'net_pln'
Starting monitoring on all containers on the network net_pln
Unable to find image 'gliderlabs/logspout:latest' locally
latest: Pulling from gliderlabs/logspout
cbdbe7a5bc2a: Pull complete
956fa3cf18b6: Pull complete
94f24e0675e0: Pull complete
Digest: sha256:872555b51b73d7f50726baeae8d8c138b6b48b550fc71d733df7ffcadc9072e1
Status: Downloaded newer image for gliderlabs/logspout:latest
e8a8ad1787b69cfb7387264ee6ff63fd5a805aabe50ca6af6356d4cd8b27e052
```

Here is the script logic to bring up the Logspout tool; it pulls *gliderlabs/logspout* images by passing the PLN network name:

```
docker run -d --name="logspout" \
  --volume=/var/run/docker.sock:/var/run/docker.sock \
  --publish=127.0.0.1:${PORT}:80 \
  --network  ${DOCKER_NETWORK} gliderlabs/logspout
```

This terminal window will now show the PLN network container output for the remainder of the project development.

> If you run into trouble during this process, check the Logspout terminal window to see errors.

Create a PLN Channel

To create the channel, we will use the `configtxgen` CLI tool to generate a genesis block, and then we'll use peer channel commands to join a channel with other peers. Creating a PLN channel requires several steps. All this script logic can be found in *scripts/createChannel.sh*:

1. Generate a channel configuration transaction file. In the *createChannel.sh* script, we define the `createChannelTxn` function. The critical command in this function is as follows:

   ```
   configtxgen -profile PharmaLedgerChannel -outputCreateChannelTx ./
   channel-artifacts/${CHANNEL_NAME}.tx
   -channelID $CHANNEL_NAME
   ```

   The `configtxgen` tool reads the profile `PharmaLedgerChannel` section from *configtx.yaml*, which defines channel-related configuration to generate the transaction and genesis block. It then generates the *plnchannel.tx* file.

2. Create an `AnchorPeer` configuration transaction file.

   Next, we define the `createAncorPeerTxn` function. Similar to the previous step, we have defined the different organizational identities in *configtx.yaml*. The con figtxgen tool reads the `PharmaLedgerChannel` organizational configuration and generates peer configuration transaction files:

   ```
   configtxgen -profile PharmaLedgerChannel -outputAnchorPeersUpdate ./
   channel-artifacts/${orgmsp}anchors.tx
   -channelID $CHANNEL_NAME -asOrg ${orgmsp}
   ```

   After `createAncorPeerTxn` runs, we should see the *Org1MSPanchors.tx*, *Org2MSPanchors.tx*, and *Org3MSPanchors.tx* transaction files generated.

3. Create a channel by using the `peer channel` command. The `createChannel` function uses the `peer channel create` command to create our PLN channel. When the command is issued, it will submit the channel creation transaction to the ordering service. The ordering service will check channel creation policy permissions defined in *configtx.yaml*. Only admin users can create a channel. The `setGlobalVars` function *scripts/utils.sh* will allow us to set the peer organization as the admin user. We use `Org1` as an admin to create our channel.

   The commands are as follows:

   ```
   setGlobalVars 1
   peer channel create -o localhost:7050 -c $CHANNEL_NAME --
   ordererTLSHostnameOverrideorderer.example.com
   -f ./channel-artifacts/${CHANNEL_NAME}.tx --outputBlock ./channel-
   ```

   `setGlobalVars` in *scripts/utils.sh* has the following logic for setting `Org1` as an admin user. We can also use this function to set other peer organizations as admin users:

   ```
   setGlobalVars() {
   ..
     if [ $USING_ORG -eq 1 ]; then
       export CORE_PEER_LOCALMSPID="Org1MSP"
       export CORE_PEER_TLS_ROOTCERT_FILE=$PEER0_ORG1_CA
       export CORE_PEER_MSPCONFIGPATH=${PWD}/organizations/
   peerOrganizations/org1.example.com/users/Admin@org1.example.com/msp
   export CORE_PEER_ADDRESS=localhost:7051
   ..
   }
   ```

4. After our PLN channel has been created, we can join all peers into this channel. `joinMultiPeersToChannel` in the *createChannel.sh* script will join all three peer orgs into our PLN channel by running the `peer channel join` command:

   ```
   for org in $(seq 1 $TOTAL_ORGS); do
     setGlobalVars $ORG
   ```

```
peer channel join -b ./channel-artifacts/$CHANNEL_NAME.block >&log.txt
done
```

When peer organizations join a channel, they need to be assigned as admin users by calling the `setGlobalVars` function and passing the `$ORG` parameter to it. The `peer channel join` command will use *genesis.block* to join peer orgs to the channel. Once the peer is joined to the channel, it can attend channel ledger block creation when receiving an ordering service transaction submission.

5. As the last step in the channel creation process, we need to select at least one peer as an anchor peer. An anchor peer's main role is private data and service discovery. The endpoints of the anchor peer are fixed. Other peer nodes belonging to different members can communicate with the anchor peers to discover all existing peers on a channel. To update an anchor peer, we set a selected peer as an admin user and issue a `peer channel update` command:

```
setGlobalVars $ORG
peer channel update -o localhost:7050 --ordererTLSHostnameOverride
orderer.example.com -c $CHANNEL_NAME -
f ./channel-artifacts/${CORE_PEER_LOCALMSPID}anchors.tx --tls
$CORE_PEER_TLS_ENABLED --cafile $ORDERER_CA
>&log.txt
```

You can use *net-pln.sh* to create the PLN channel by running the following command:

```
./net-pln.sh createChannel
```

Once channel creation is completed, you should see the following log:

```
...

***** [Step: 5]: start call updateAnchorPeers 3 on peer: peer0.org3,
channelID: plnchannel,
smartcontract: , version , sequence *****
Using organization 3
2020-06-06 03:24:36.333 UTC [channelCmd] InitCmdFactory -> INFO 001
Endorser and orderer connections
initialized
2020-06-06 03:24:36.392 UTC [channelCmd] update -> INFO 002
Successfully submitted channel update
***** completed call updateAnchorPeers, updated peer0.org3 on
anchorPeers on channelID: plnchannel,
smartcontract: , version , sequence *****

***** completed call updateOrgsOnAnchorPeers, anchorPeers updated on
channelID: plnchannel,
smartcontract: , version , sequence *****
```

```
========= Pharma Ledger Network (PLN) Channel plnchannel successfully
joined ===========
```

To see the related container information, you can check the Logspout terminal window that we opened earlier.

Running and Testing the Smart Contract

We need to package a smart contract before we can install it to the channel. Navigate to the manufacturer contract folder directory and run the npm install command:

```
cd pharma-ledger-network/organizations/manufacturer/contract
npm install
```

This will install the *pharmaledgercontract* node dependency under *node_modules*.

Install the Smart Contract

Now we can start installing our smart contract by running the following *deploySmartContract.sh* script:

1. The peer lifecycle chaincode package command will package our smart contract. We assign the manufacturer as an administrator user to run the package command:

   ```
   setGlobalVars 1
   peer lifecycle chaincode package ${CHINCODE_NAME}.tar.gz --path $
   {CC_SRC_PATH} --lang
   ${CC_RUNTIME_LANGUAGE} --label ${CHINCODE_NAME}_${VERSION}
   ```

2. Install the chaincode on all peer orgs as an admin with the peer lifecycle chaincode install command:

   ```
   for org in $(seq 1 $CHAINCODE_ORGS); do
   setGlobalVars $ORG
   peer lifecycle chaincode install ${CHINCODE_NAME}.tar.gz >&log.txt
   done
   ```

   When the chaincode package is installed, you will see messages similar to the following printed in your terminal:

   ```
   2020-06-06 03:30:50.025 UTC [cli.lifecycle.chaincode]
   submitInstallProposal -> INFO 001 Installed
   remotely: response:<status:200
   payload:"\nWpharmaLedgerCon-
   tract_1:1940852a477d7697bb3a12d032268ff48c741c585db166403dd35f5e0b5c4e74
   \022
   \026pharmaLedgerContract_1" >
   2020-06-06 03:30:50.025 UTC [cli.lifecycle.chaincode]
   submitInstallProposal -> INFO 002 Chaincode code
   ```

```
package identifier:
pharmaLedgerCon-
tract_1:1940852a477d7697bb3a12d032268ff48c741c585db166403dd35f5e0b5c4e74
***** completed call installChaincode, Chaincode is installed on
peer0.org1 on channelID: plnchannel,
smartcontract: pharmaLedgerContract, version 1, sequence 1 *****
```

3. After we install the smart contract, we need to query whether the chaincode is installed. We can query the `packageID` by using the `peer lifecycle chaincode queryinstalled` command:

```
peer lifecycle chaincode queryinstalled >&log.txt
```

If the command completes successfully, you will see logs similar to the following:

```
Installed chaincodes on peer:
Package ID: pharmaLedgerContract_1:
1940852a477d7697bb3a12d032268ff48c741c585db166403dd35f5e0b5c4e74,
Label: pharmaLedgerContract_1
***** completed call queryInstalled, Query installed successful with
PackageID is
pharmaLedgerCon-
tract_1:1940852a477d7697bb3a12d032268ff48c741c585db166403dd35f5e0b5c4e74
on channelID: plnchannel, smartcontract: pharmaLedgerContract, version
1, sequence 1 *****
```

4. With the returned package ID, we can now approve the chaincode definition for the manufacturer by using `approveForMyOrg`, which calls the `peer lifecycle chaincode approveformyorg` command:

```
peer lifecycle chaincode approveformyorg -o localhost:7050
--ordererTLSHostnameOverride
orderer.example.com --tls $CORE_PEER_TLS_ENABLED --cafile $ORDERER_CA
--channelID
$CHANNEL_NAME --name ${CHINCODE_NAME} -- version ${VERSION}
--package-id ${PACKAGE_ID} --sequence ${VERSION} >&log.txt
```

5. We can check whether channel members have approved the same chaincode definition by using `checkOrgsCommitReadiness`, which runs the `peer lifecycle chaincode checkcommitreadiness` command:

```
peer lifecycle chaincode checkcommitreadiness --channelID $CHANNEL_NAME
--name ${CHINCODE_NAME} --
version ${VERSION} --sequence ${VERSION} --output json >&log.txt
```

As expected, we should see approvals for `Org1MSP` as `true`; the other two orgs are `false`:

```
***** [Step: 5]: start call checkCommitReadiness org1 on peer:
peer0.org1, channelID: plnchannel,
smartcontract: pharmaLedgerContract, version 1, sequence 1 *****
Attempting to check the commit readiness of the chaincode definition on
peer0.org1, Retry after 3
```

```
seconds.
+ peer lifecycle chaincode checkcommitreadiness --channelID plnchannel
--name pharmaLedgerContract --
version 1 --sequence 1 --output json
{
        "approvals": {
                "Org1MSP": true, "Org2MSP": false, "Org3MSP": false
        }
}
```

6. The endorsement policy requires a set of majority organizations to endorse a transaction before it can commit the chaincode. We continue to run the `peer lifecycle chaincode approveformyorg` command for Org2 and Org3:

```
## approve org2
approveForMyOrg 2
## check whether the chaincode definition is ready to be committed, two
orgs should be approved
checkOrgsCommitReadiness 3 1 1 0
## approve org3
approveForMyOrg 3
## check whether the chaincode definition is ready to be committed, all
3 orgs should be approved
checkOrgsCommitReadiness 3 1 1 1
```

If all commands execute successfully, all three orgs will approve the chaincode installation:

```
{
        "approvals": {
                "Org1MSP": true, "Org2MSP": true, "Org3MSP": true
        }
}
***** completed call checkCommitReadiness, Checking the commit
readiness of the chaincode definition successful on peer0.org3
on channel 'plnchannel' on channelID: plnchannel,
```

7. Now that we know for sure that the manufacturer, wholesaler, and pharmacy have all approved the *pharmaledgercontract* chaincode, we commit the definition. We have the required majority of organizations (three out of three) to commit the chaincode definition to the channel. Any of the three organizations can commit the chaincode to the channel by using the `peer lifecycle chaincode commit` command:

```
peer lifecycle chaincode commit -o localhost:7050
--ordererTLSHostnameOverride orderer.example.com
--tls $CORE_PEER_TLS_ENABLED --cafile $ORDERER_CA
--channelID $CHANNEL_NAME --name ${CHINCODE_NAME}
$PEER_CONN_PARMS -- version ${VERSION} --sequence ${VERSION} >&log.txt
```

8. We will use `peer lifecycle chaincode querycommitted` to check the chaincode commit status:

```
peer lifecycle chaincode querycommitted --channelID $ CHANNEL_NAME
--name ${CHINCODE_NAME} >&log.txt
```

9. Now that we've completed the chaincode deployment steps, let's deploy the *pharmaledgercontract* chaincode in our PLN network by running the following command:

```
./net-pln.sh deploySmartContract
```

If the command is successful, you should see the following response in the last few lines:

```
Committed chaincode definition for chaincode 'pharmaLedgerContract' on
channel 'plnchannel':
Version: 1, Sequence: 1, Endorsement Plugin: escc, Validation Plugin:
vscc, Approvals:
[Org1MSP: true, Org2MSP: true, Org3MSP: true]
***** completed call queryCommitted, Query committed on channel
'plnchannel' on channelID: plnchannel,
smartcontract: pharmaLedgerContract, version 1, sequence 1 *****
***** completed call queryAllCommitted, Chaincode installed on
channelID: plnchannel, smartcontract: pharmaLedgerContract, version 1,
sequence 1 *****
=== Pharma Ledger Network (PLN) contract successfully deployed on
channel plnchannel  ====
```

After the chaincode is installed, we can start to invoke and test the chaincode methods for *pharmaledgercontract*.

Test the Smart Contract

We have created *invokeContract.sh* for this project. It defines an invocation method for `makeEquipment`, `wholesalerDistribute`, `pharmacyReceived`, and a query function. Now we can start testing our smart contract for these functions:

1. Call the `makeEquipment` chaincode method:

```
./net-pln.sh invoke equipment GlobalEquipmentCorp 2000.001 e360-
Ventilator GlobalEquipmentCorp
```

2. We pass `manufacturer`, `equipmentNumber`, `equipmentName`, and `ownerName` as arguments. The script basically calls `peer chaincode invoke` commands by passing related function arguments:

```
peer chaincode invoke -o localhost:7050  --ordererTLSHostnameOverride
orderer.example.com --tls
$CORE_PEER_TLS_ENABLED --cafile $ORDERER_CA -C $CHANNEL_NAME -n ${CHIN-
CODE_NAME} $PEER_CONN_PARMS  -c
```

```
'{"function":"makeEquipment","Args":["' $manufacturer'",
"'$equipmentNumber'", "' $equipmentName'","'$ownerName'"]}' >&log.txt
```

You will see logs similar to the following:

```
invokeMakeEquipment--> manufacturer:GlobalEquipmentCorp, equipmentNum-
ber:2000.001, equipmentName: e360-
Ventilator,ownerName:GlobalEquipmentCorp
+ peer chaincode invoke -o localhost:7050 --ordererTLSHostnameOverride
orderer.example.com --tls true
--cafile /home/ubuntu/Hyperledger-Fabric-V2/chapter7-supplychain/
pharma-ledger-
network/organizations/ordererOrganizations/example.com/orderers/
orderer.example.com/msp/tlscacerts/tlsc
a.example.com-cert.pem -C plnchannel -n pharmaLedgerContract
--peerAddresses localhost:7051
--tlsRootCertFiles /home/ubuntu/Hyperledger-Fabric-V2/chapter7-
supplychain/pharma-ledger-
network/organizations/peerOrganizations/org1.example.com/peers/
peer0.org1.example.com/tls/ca.crt --
peerAddresses localhost:9051 --tlsRootCertFiles /home/ubuntu/
Hyperledger-Fabric-V2/chapter7-
supplychain/pharma-ledger-
network/organizations/peerOrganizations/org2.example.com/peers/
peer0.org2.example.com/tls/ca.crt --
peerAddresses localhost:11051 --tlsRootCertFiles /home/ubuntu/
Hyperledger-Fabric-V2/chapter7-
supplychain/pharma-ledger-
network/organizations/peerOrganizations/org3.example.com/peers/
peer0.org3.example.com/tls/ca.crt -c
'{"function":"makeEquipment","Args":["GlobalEquipmentCorp","2000.001",
"e360-Ventilator",
"GlobalEquipmentCorp"]}'
2020-06-06 03:43:09.186 UTC [chaincodeCmd] chaincodeInvokeOrQuery ->
INFO 001 Chaincode invoke
successful. result: status:200
```

3. After invoking makeEquipment, we can run a query function to verify the ledger result. The query function uses the peer chaincode query command:

```
peer chaincode  query -C $CHANNEL_NAME - n ${CHINCODE_NAME} -c
'{"function":"queryByKey","Args":["'$QUERY_KEY'"]}' >&log.txt
```

4. Issue the following script command to query equipment:

```
./net-pln.sh invoke query 2000.001
```

The query should return current equipment state data:

```
{"Key":"2000.001","Record":{"equipmentNumber":"2000.001",
"manufacturer":"GlobalEquipmentCorp","equipmentName":
"e360-Ventilator","ownerName":"GlobalEquipmentCorp",
"previousOwnerType":"MANUFACTURER","currentOwnerType":"MANUFACTURER",
```

```
"createDateTime":"Sat Jun 06 2020 03:43:09 GMT+0000 (Coordinated
Universal Time)","lastUpdated":"Sat Jun 06 2020 03:43:09 GMT+0000
(Coordinated Universal Time)"}}
```

5. Continue to invoke the remaining equipment functions for the wholesaler and pharmacy:

```
./net-pln.sh invoke wholesaler 2000.001 GlobalWholesalerCorp
./net-pln.sh invoke pharmacy 2000.001 PharmacyCorp
```

6. Once equipment ownership is moved to the pharmacy, the supply chain reaches its final state. We can issue queryHistoryByKey from the peer chaincode query command. Let's check equipment historical data:

```
./net-pln.sh invoke queryHistory 2000.001
```

We can see the following output in the terminal:

```
***** start call chaincodeQueryHistory on peer: peer0.org1, channelID:
plnchannel, smartcontract:
pharmaLedgerContract, version 1, sequence 1 *****
+ peer chaincode query -C plnchannel -n pharmaLedgerContract -c
'{"function":"queryHistoryByKey","Args":["2000.001"]}'
[{"equipmentNumber":"2000.001","manufacturer":"GlobalEquipmentCorp",
"equipmentName":"e360-Ventilator","ownerName":"PharmacyCorp",
"previousOwnerType":"WHOLESALER","currentOwnerType":"PHARMACY",
"createDateTime":"Sat Jun 06 2020 03:43:09 GMT+0000
(Coordinated Universal Time)","lastUpdated":"Sat Jun 06 2020 03:48:48
GMT+0000 (Coordinated Universal Time)"},{"equipmentNumber":"2000.001",
"manufacturer":"GlobalEquipmentCorp","equipmentName":"e360-Ventilator",
"ownerName":"GlobalWholesalerCorp","previousOwnerType":"MANUAFACTURER",
"currentOwnerType":"WHOLESALER","createDateTime":"Sat Jun 06 2020
03:43:09 GMT+0000 (Coordinated Universal Time)","lastUpdated":"Sat
Jun 06 2020 03:46:41 GMT+0000 (Coordinated Universal Time)"},
{"equipmentNumber":"2000.001","manufacturer":"GlobalEquipmentCorp",
"equipmentName":"e360-Ventilator","ownerName":"GlobalEquipmentCorp",
"previousOwnerType":"MANUAFACTURER","currentOwnerType":"MANUAFACTURER",
"createDateTime":"Sat Jun 06 2020 03:43:09 GMT+0000 (Coordinated
Universal Time)","lastUpdated":"Sat Jun 06 2020 03:43:09 GMT+0000 (Coor-
dinated Universal Time)"}]
***** completed call chaincodeQuery, Query History successful on
channelID: plnchannel,
smartcontract: pharmaLedgerContract, version 1, sequence 1 *****
```

All of the transaction history records are displayed as output. We have tested our smart contract, and it works as expected.

Developing an Application with Hyperledger Fabric Through the SDK

We just deployed our Pharma Ledger Network in the Fabric network. The next step is to build a Pharma Ledger client application to interact with the smart contract function in the network. Let's take a moment to examine the application architecture.

At the beginning of our PLN network section, we generated a CCP for Org1, Org2, and Org3. We will use these connection files to connect to our PLN network for each peer org. When the manufacturer application's user Bob submits a makeEquipment transaction to the ledger, the pharma-ledger process flow starts. Let's quickly examine how our application works (Figure 7-6).

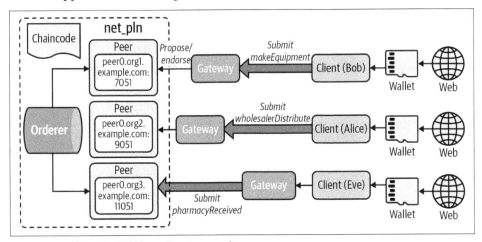

Figure 7-6. How the PLN application works

The manufacturer web user Bob connects to the Fabric network through a wallet. A wallet provides users an authorized identity that will be verified by the blockchain network to ensure access security. The Fabric SDK then submits a makeEquipment transaction proposal to *peer0.org1.example.com*. Endorsing peers verify the signature, simulate the proposal, and invoke the makeEquipment chaincode function with required arguments.

The transaction is initiated after the proposal response is sent back to the SDK. The application collects and verifies the endorsements until the endorsement policy of the chaincode is satisfied with producing the same result. The client then broadcasts the transaction proposal and proposal response to the ordering service.

The ordering service orders them chronologically by channel, creates blocks, and delivers the blocks of transactions to all peers on the channel. The peers validate transactions to ensure that the endorsement policy is satisfied and to ensure that no changes have occurred to the ledger state since the proposal response was generated by the transaction execution. After successful validation, the block is committed to the ledger, and world states are updated for each valid transaction.

You now understand the transaction end-to-end workflow. It is time to start building our pharma-ledger client application. Figure 7-7 shows the application client project structure. The same folder structure is available for the wholesaler and pharmacy.

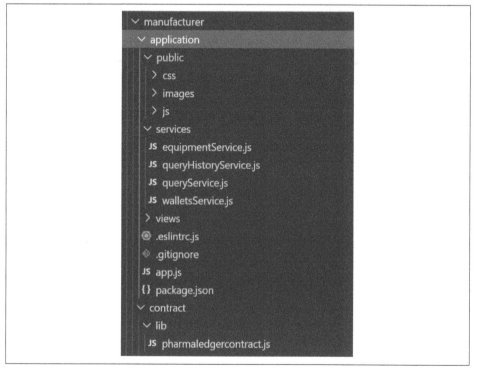

Figure 7-7. The application client project structure

We use *express.js* to build our node application. Let's review some important files.

The *package.json* file defines two Fabric-related dependencies:

```
"dependencies" : {
    "fabric-contract-api" : "^2.1.2",
    "fabric-shim" : "^2.1.2"
}
```

app.js defines all entry points for the manufacturer, and addUser will add a client user for the manufacturer, which in our case is Bob. makeEquipment will create equipment records when the manufacturer is an owner. queryByKey and queryHistoryByKey are common functions for all three orgs. The wholesaler and pharmacy will have similar functions:

```
app.post('/addUser', async (req, res, next) => {
});
app.post('/makeEquipment', async (req, res, next) => {
})
app. get('/queryHistoryByKey', async (req, res, next) => {
})
app. get('/queryByKey', async (req, res, next) => {
})
```

addUser will call walletsService to add a user. Let's take a look at addToWal let(user) in walletsService:

```
const wallet = await Wallets.newFileSystemWallet('../identity/user/'+user+'/
wallet');
```

newFileSystemWallet will create a wallet for an input user (Bob) under the provided filesystem directory. Next, we find the user certificate and privateKey and generate an X.509 certificate to be stored in the wallet:

```
const credPath = path. join(fixtures,
'/peerOrganizations/org1.example.com/users/User1@org1.example.com');
const certificate = fs.readFileSync(path. join(credPath, '/msp/signcerts/
User1@org1.example.com-
cert.pem')).toString();
const privateKey = fs.readFileSync(path.join(credPath, '/msp/keystore/
priv_sk')).toString();
```

The wallet calls key class methods to manage X509WalletMixin.createIdentity, which is used to create an Org1MSP identity using X.509 credentials. The function needs three inputs: mspid, the certificate, and the private key:

```
const identityLabel = user;
const identity = {
        credentials: {
            certificate,
            privateKey
        },
        mspId: 'Org1MSP',
        type: 'X.509'
}
const response = await wallet.put(identityLabel, identity);
```

Users from the manufacturer will call the equipmentService makeEquipment function. Before any user can call any of the smart contract functions, it needs to be authorized. To authorize user access to the blockchain, we need to follow these steps:

1. Find the user wallet created by adding a user function:

```
const wallet = await Wallets.newFileSystemWallet('../identity/
user/'+userName+'/wallet');
```

2. Load the connection profile associated with the user. Then the wallet will be used to locate and connect to a gateway:

```
const gateway =  new Gateway();
    let connectionProfile =
yaml.safeLoad(fs.readFileSync('../../../organizations/peerOrganizations/
org1.example.com/connection-org1.json', 'utf8'));
        // Set connection options; identity and wallet
         let connectionOptions = {
          identity: userName,
          wallet: wallet,
          discovery: { enabled: true, asLocalhost: true }
        };
        await gateway.connect(connectionProfile, connectionOptions);
```

3. Once a gateway is connected to a channel, we can find our `pharmaLedgerContract` with a unique namespace when creating a contract:

```
const network = await gateway.getNetwork('plnchannel');
const contract = await network.getContract('pharmaLedgerContract',
'org.pln.PharmaLedgerContract');
```

4. Submit the `makeEquipment` chain code invocation:

```
const response = await contract.submitTransaction('makeEquipment',
manufacturer, equipmentNumber, equipmentName, ownerName);
```

5. To verify that equipment records are stored in the blockchain, we can use Fabric query functions to retrieve the result. The following code shows how we can submit a `query` or `queryHistory` function to get equipment results:

```
const response = await contract.submitTransaction('queryByKey', key);
const response = await contract.submitTransaction('queryHistoryByKey',
key);
```

6. Let's bring up a manufacturer, create the user Bob, and then submit a transaction to our PLN blockchain. Navigate to the *pharma-ledger-network/organizations/manufacturer/application* folder and run `npm install`. When we start the application, we also make sure to update the client IP address in *plnClient.js* under *public/js*:

```
var urlBase = "http://your-machine-public-ip:30000";

npm install
pharma-ledger-network/organizations/manufacturer/application$ node
app.js
App listening at http://:::30000
```

7. In the manufacturer, we define the application port as 30000:

Make sure this port is open, or you can change it to another available port number under the `app.js` line.

```
var port = process.env.PORT || 30000;
```

8. Open a browser and enter `http://your-machine-public-ip:30000`:

   We will see the screen shown in Figure 7-8.

Figure 7-8. Adding a user to the wallet for the manufacturer

9. The default page is *addToWallet*. Since we have not added any user to the wallet so far, you can't submit `makeEquipment` and query history transactions at this moment. You have to add a user to the wallet. Let's add Bob as a manufacturer user, as shown in Figure 7-9.

Figure 7-9. New user (Bob) is added

10. With the user wallet set up, the application can now connect to our PLN and interact with the chaincode. Click MakeEquipment on the left menu, enter all required equipment information, and submit the request (Figure 7-10). The success response will be returned from the blockchain.

Figure 7-10. Adding equipment to the PLN network

11. We can now query equipment data in the PLN network by equipment number. Figure 7-11 shows the result.

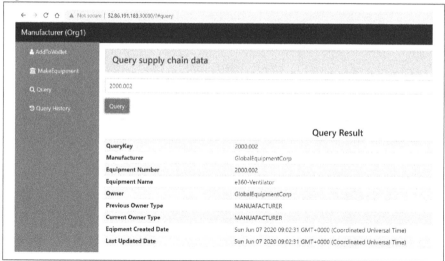

Figure 7-11. Query equipment on PLN network

12. Now open two other terminal windows, which will bring up node servers for the wholesaler and pharmacy, respectively. Navigate to */pharma-ledger-network/ organizations/wholesaler/contract*. Run npm install to install the smart contract dependency first.

13. Make sure to update the base URL to *http://your-machine-public-ip:30001* in *plnClient.js*. Then navigate back to the *pharma-ledger-network/organizations/ wholesaler/application* folder and run the following:

```
npm install
node app.js
This starts the wholesaler web App. Open a browser and enter: http://
your-machine-public-ip:30001
```

14. Add Alice as a wholesaler user (Figure 7-12) and submit a `wholesalerDistri`
    bute request:

Figure 7-12. Adding a user (Alice) to the wholesaler

15. Follow the same steps by bringing up the pharmacy node server and add Eve as a
    pharmacy user (Figure 7-13). Submit a `pharmacyReceived` request:

Figure 7-13. Adding a user (Eve) to the pharmacy

Now the pharma ledger supply chain flow ends. Bob, Alice, and Eve can query equipment data and trace the entire supply chain process by querying historical data. Simply go to any user, and on the Query History page, search equipment **2000.002**, and
you should see all query history results, as shown in Figure 7-14.

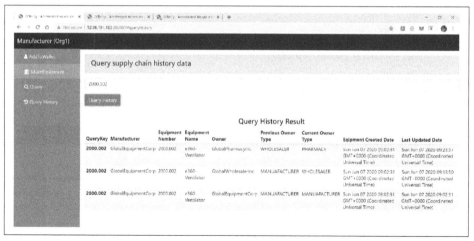

Figure 7-14. Querying equipment historical data

Summary

In this chapter, you learned how to build supply chain DApps with Hyperledger Fabric. We have introduced, among other things, how to define a consortium, analyze the Pharma Ledger Network life cycle, and trace the equipment's entire transaction history. We spent a lot of time writing chaincode as a smart contract, including the logic for the manufacturer, wholesaler, and pharmacy. After setting up a pharma ledger Fabric network environment, we installed and deployed our smart contract to blockchain step by step.

We tested a smart contract function through a command-line script to make sure that all functions we defined work as expected. With this work completed, we started to work on a UI page, where you learned how to add users into a wallet and connect to the Fabric blockchain through SDK. We also built UI pages for the manufacturer, wholesaler, and pharmacy, allowing users in these organizations to submit related requests to invoke the smart contract in the PLN blockchain.

You can see that it is quite a lot of work to build the end-to-end Hyperledger Fabric application. So we hope you are not tired because in the next chapter we will explore another exciting topic: deploying Hyperledger Fabric on the cloud.

Hyperledger Fabric—Other Topics

Part V, which includes Chapters 8, 9, and 10, covers Fabric application production on popular cloud platforms, Fabric migration from an older version of Fabric, and more. In Chapter 8, we discuss how to deploy Fabric on three popular cloud platforms. In Chapter 9, we review considerations for migration to Fabric v2. In Chapter 10, we cover four more members of the Hyperledger family: Aries, Avalon, Besu, and Grid.

## CHAPTER 8

Deploying Hyperledger Fabric on the Cloud

In Chapter 7, you built an end-to-end blockchain supply chain with Hyperledger Fabric by applying all the concepts from Part III, where you learned how to build, deploy, test, invoke, and maintain Fabric smart contracts. This chapter builds on top of what you learned in Parts III and IV; you'll put all of your Fabric skills into practice by creating and deploying Fabric applications on the Amazon, IBM, and Oracle cloud platforms. As such, this chapter covers highly practical steps for those interested in moving their Fabric application from the pilot step to production.

This chapter will help you achieve the following practical goals:

- Setting up Amazon Managed Blockchain for Fabric applications
- Creating and deploying a Fabric application on AWS
- Reviewing the IBM cloud platform for building blockchain applications
- Creating and joining a Fabric network on the IBM cloud platform
- Reviewing Oracle Blockchain Platform and its offerings
- Building and running a Fabric application on Oracle Blockchain Platform

We start by reviewing essential features of AWS for building and deploying Hyperledger Fabric and then do the same for the IBM and Oracle cloud platforms. Each platform has its own requirements, considerations, and features necessary for successfully deploying and managing Fabric applications. We follow a concise yet holistic approach, covering practical steps from the ground up—from setting up a network through installing and instantiating the chaincode.

Deploying Hyperledger Fabric on Amazon Blockchain Services

Amazon offers a variety of cloud services for deploying and managing both centralized and decentralized applications. For the sake of brevity, this section focuses on only the Amazon Managed Blockchain service and how to deploy and manage Hyperledger Fabric on it. Amazon Web Services (AWS) has an active community with practitioners ranging from system architects to developers and engineers.

AWS provides the following three ways to create blockchain services:

Amazon Quantum Ledger Database (QLDB)
> This fully managed NoSQL (Semi-SQL and Semi-NoSQL) immutable and transparent ledger database is powered by blockchain. The append-only ledger data provides a cryptographically verifiable transaction history with an audit log owned by a central trusted authority. AWS QLDB automatically scales when applications need more capacity for read and write limits.

AWS Blockchain Templates
> These templates provide you with a fast and easy way to create and deploy blockchain projects on the network, and test applications on the AWS platform. Building users' preset blockchain frameworks through AWS CloudFormation stacks helps developers focus on building blockchain applications and spend less time setting up a blockchain network. AWS currently provides two types of blockchain templates: Ethereum and Hyperledger Fabric.
>
> AWS CloudFormation loads AWS Blockchain Templates and deploys the blockchain framework as containers on an Amazon Elastic Container Service (ECS) cluster or directly on an Amazon Elastic Compute Cloud (EC2) instance running Docker. The network runs inside your own Amazon virtual private cloud (VPC). A VPC is a virtual datacenter in the cloud that provides a completely separate environment to host your machine in a custom way. A subnet is a logical subdivision of an IP network; a network inside a VPC subnet makes networks more efficient. With VPC subnets and network access control lists (ACLs) in Amazon, you can control how clients can access the AWS blockchain network. You can define a permission policy using AWS Identity and Access Management (IAM) to restrict which resources an Amazon ECS cluster or Amazon EC2 instance can access.

Amazon Managed Blockchain
> This fully managed service provides a production-level blockchain network. It can easily be scaled to support thousands of applications running millions of transactions. You can use AWS Management Console, the AWS Command Line Interface (CLI), or the Managed Blockchain software development kit (SDK) to set up a managed blockchain application quickly.

Managed Blockchain manages your certificates; the participants can transact with peer nodes without having to know or trust each other.

This section covers how to use Amazon Managed Blockchain to create and work with a Hyperledger Fabric blockchain network.

Set Up Amazon Managed Blockchain with Prerequisites

We can set up Amazon Managed Blockchain in multiple ways, as we discussed earlier. While setting up a Managed Blockchain application, we will use AWS Management Console to create a blockchain network and a member. Then, we'll create a VPC and security policy, and assign the policy to IAM roles. We will also create and configure an EC2 instance to run AWS CLI to interact with Amazon Managed Blockchain. The EC2 instance will be the primary node that runs the blockchain network. With AWS Management Console, we will create a peer node to join the network. Finally, we will create a channel in the network and then install and run chaincode.

To deploy Fabric on AWS Managed Blockchain, you need to have already created the following:

- An AWS account.
- VPC and subnet—name it **HF-VPC**.
- The AWS EC2 security group—name it **HF-SG**. The Hyperledger Fabric client Amazon EC2 instance must have an inbound rule that allows SSH traffic (port 22) from trusted SSH clients.
- An EC2 instance (as a bastion host); we use Amazon Linux 2 AMI (HVM) as an Amazon Machine Image (AMI) with a `t2.micro` AWS free usage instance type for this setup. Name the EC2 instance **HF-Node** by entering the tag. Associate HF-SG with the HF-Node EC2 instance.
- Elastic IP addresses allocated to the HF-Node EC2 instance.
- AWS IAM policy with the following policy statement—name it **HyperledgerFabricClientAccess**, replace *youraccountId* with your actual AWS account ID, and replace *us-east-1* with the appropriate Region. Then attach to an IAM role for an HF-Node EC2 instance:

```
{
    "Version": "2012-10-17",
    "Statement": [
      {
        "Sid": "ListNetworkMembers",
        "Effect": "Allow",
        "Action": [
            "managedblockchain:GetNetwork",
            "managedblockchain:ListMembers"
```

```
      ],
      "Resource": [
          "arn:aws:managedblockchain:*:youraccountId:networks/*"
      ]
  },
  {
    "Sid": "AccessManagedBlockchainBucket",
    "Effect": "Allow",
    "Action": [
      "s3:GetObject"
    ],
    "Resource": "arn:aws:s3:::us-east-1.managedblockchain/*"
  },
  {
    "Sid": "ManageNetworkResources",
    "Effect": "Allow",
    "Action": [
      "managedblockchain:CreateProposal",
      "managedblockchain:GetProposal",
      "managedblockchain:DeleteMember",
      "managedblockchain:VoteOnProposal",
      "managedblockchain:ListProposals",
      "managedblockchain:GetNetwork",
      "managedblockchain:ListMembers",
      "managedblockchain:ListProposalVotes",
      "managedblockchain:RejectInvitation",
      "managedblockchain:GetNode",
      "managedblockchain:GetMember",
      "managedblockchain:DeleteNode",
      "managedblockchain:CreateNode",
      "managedblockchain:CreateMember",
      "managedblockchain:ListNodes"
    ],
    "Resource": [
      "arn:aws:managedblockchain:*::networks/*",
      "arn:aws:managedblockchain:*::proposals/*",
      "arn:aws:managedblockchain:*:youraccountId:members/*",
      "arn:aws:managedblockchain:*:youraccountId:invitations/*",
      "arn:aws:managedblockchain:*:youraccountId:nodes/*"
    ]
  },
  {
    "Sid": "WorkWithNetworksForAcct",
    "Effect": "Allow",
    "Action": [
      "managedblockchain:ListNetworks",
      "managedblockchain:ListInvitations",
      "managedblockchain:CreateNetwork"
    ],
    "Resource": "*"
```

```
      }
    ]
  }
```

- An AWS IAM role called **ServiceRoleForHyperledgerFabricClient**. Select the previously created policy, *ServiceRoleForHyperledgerFabricClient*, and attach this role with the HF-Node EC2 instance.

We now have completed all of the prerequisites for setting up the Hyperledger Fabric network using the AWS Managed Blockchain console. We will start to set up a blockchain network in the next section.

Set Up the Hyperledger Fabric Network

In this section, we will start to set up our HF network and run a Fabric application on it. Currently, AWS Managed Blockchain supports only version 1.4 of Hyperledger Fabric. Follow these steps:

1. Open the Managed Blockchain console and click "Create a network" and then enter a network name. You can keep most of the default settings.

2. On the Create Member page, create a member by entering **member1** as a member name.

3. Under Hyperledger Fabric Certificate Authority (CA) configuration, specify an Admin username and password to be used by the administrator on the Hyperledger Fabric CA.

4. Create the network and members.

   Creating your first network will take several minutes. Once the network is created, you will see its summary. AWS Managed Blockchain creates a network and assigns a network ID and a member ID to our member1. Write down these two important pieces of information, as we will use them in a later setup step.

5. We need to associate HF-VPC, which we created earlier, with the first network by creating a VPC endpoint. On the first network summary screen, click "Create VPC endpoint" and then select HF-VPC as the VPC. Select the HF-SG EC2 security group to create the VPC endpoint.

Set Up the Hyperledger Fabric Client

Now we will install our Fabric client and join a peer node. But first, we need to set up all necessary packages and samples in the HF-Node EC2 client node so you can run a Managed Blockchain command to build our Fabric network and chaincode.

You'll start by using ssh to access the HF-Node EC2 instance. You can use this command to connect to your instance, or you can use another SSH client tool to log in:

```
ssh -i /path/.../your-aws-private-ket.pem ec2-user@your-ec2-public-ip
```

Once you access your EC2 instance, check the AWS version by entering **AWS -version**.

This EC2 instance must have version 1.16.149 or later of the AWS CLI installed. Earlier versions of the AWS CLI do not have the Managed Blockchain command. We assume you have installed Go, Docker, Docker Compose, and the other utilities that are prerequisites for installing and using Hyperledger tools (refer to Chapter 4).

Let's set up the Hyperledger Fabric CA client next. In this step, you will verify that you can connect to the Hyperledger Fabric CA by using the VPC endpoint you configured previously. You'll then install the Hyperledger Fabric CA client, which issues certificates to administrators and network peers.

To verify connectivity to the Hyperledger Fabric CA, you need the CAEndpoint. Run the following AWS managedblockchain get-member command by passing the network-id and member-id. You can get these two IDs from the AWS Managed Blockchain console:

```
aws managedblockchain get-member \
--network-id n-UYEFPPMBENFFFEITGTS6IJ6TDY \
--member-id m-G4Q5XLRCCJFBTII7PYINITSZH4
{
    "Member": {
        "NetworkId": "n-UYEFPPMBENFFFEITGTS6IJ6TDY",
        "Status": "AVAILABLE",
        "Name": "member1",
        "FrameworkAttributes": {
            "Fabric": {
                "AdminUsername": "admin",
                "CaEndpoint": "ca.m-g4q5xlrccjfbtii7pyinitszh4.n-
uyefppmbenfffeitgts6ij6tdy.managedblockchain.us-east-1.amazonaws.com:30002"
            }
        },
        ..
        "Id": "m-G4Q5XLRCCJFBTII7PYINITSZH4"
    }
}
```

Use cURL or Telnet to verify that the CAEndpoint resolves. Replace the CAEndpoint with the CAEndpoint returned by the get-member command:

```
curl https://ca.m-g4q5xlrccjfbtii7pyinitszh4.n-
uyefppmbenfffeitgts6ij6tdy.managedblockchain.us-east-
1.amazonaws.com:30002/cainfo -k
```

The command should return output similar to the following:

```
{"result":{"CAName":" m-G4Q5XLRCCJFBTII7PYINITSZH4",
"CAChain":"LongStringOfCharacters","Version":"1.4.7",
"errors":[],"messages":[],"success":true}
```

Alternatively, you can connect to the Fabric CA by using Telnet:

```
telnet CaEndpoint-Without-Port CaPort
```

The command should return output similar to the following:

```
Trying 10.0.0.24...
Connected to ca.m-g4q5xlrccjfbtii7pyinitszh4.n-
uyefppmbenfffeitgts6ij6tdy.managedblockchain.us-east-
1.amazonaws.com.
Escape character is '^]'..
```

Now that you have verified that you can connect to the Hyperledger Fabric CA, run the following commands to configure the CA client:

```
mkdir -p /home/ec2-user/go/src/github.com/hyperledger/fabric-ca
cd /home/ec2-user/go/src/github.com/hyperledger/fabric-ca
wget https://github.com/hyperledger/fabric-ca/releases/download/v1.4.7/
hyperledger-fabric-ca-linux-
amd64-1.4.7.tar.gz
tar -xzf hyperledger-fabric-ca-linux-amd64-1.4.7.tar.gz
```

Clone the Samples Repository

We will use *fabric-samples* as an example HF application in AWS Managed Blockchain. Let's clone the Git code in the EC2 instance by running the following command:

```
cd /home/ec2-user
 git clone --branch v1.4.7 https://github.com/hyperledger/fabric-samples.git
```

Enroll an administrative user

Because only admin identities can install, instantiate, and query chaincode in Fabric, we need to register and issue certificate files for an administrative user. We first need to create the certificate file by running the following command to copy the *managedblockchain-tls-chain.pem* file to the */home/ec2-user* directory. Replace *us-east-1* with the AWS Region you are using:

```
aws s3 cp s3://us-east-1.managedblockchain/etc/managedblockchain-tls-chain.pem
/home/ec2-user/managedblockchain-tls-chain.pem
```

Run the following command to test that you correctly copied the contents to the file:

```
openssl x509 -noout -text -in /home/ec2-user/managedblockchain-tls-chain.pem
```

The command should return the contents of the certificate in a human-readable format. Once the certificate file is created, we need to enroll the member administrator. Run the `fabric-ca-client enroll` command to enroll the member administrator by providing the CA endpoint, administrator profile, and certificate file:

```
[ec2-user@ip-10-0-0-235 ~]$ fabric-ca-client enroll \
 > -u https://admin:Password_1234@ca.m-g4q5xlrccjfbtii7pyinitszh4.n-
uyefppmbenfffeitgts6ij6tdy.managedblockchain.us-east-1.amazonaws.com:30002 \
 > --tls.certfiles /home/ec2-user/managedblockchain-tls-chain.pem -M
```

In Fabric, the MSP identifies which root CAs and intermediate CAs are permitted to define the members of a trust domain. In our setup, we will store certificates for the administrator's MSP in */home/ec2-user/admin-msp*. Let's copy certificates for the MSP by running this command:

```
cp -r /home/ec2-user/admin-msp/signcerts admin-msp/admincerts
```

Create a peer node in your membership

Fabric peer nodes perform the validation and updates to the ledger data. They keep a local copy of the shared ledger. A typical Fabric network will have more than one peer node in the network. In our setup, we will create a peer node in the HF network.

To create a peer node using AWS Management Console, open the Managed Blockchain console at *https://console.aws.amazon.com/managedblockchain*.

Choose Networks, select the network from the list, and then choose View Details. Next, select a Member from the list and click "Create peer node." Choose configuration parameters for your peer node. We can leave all default settings in this setup. Then choose "Create peer node." Once a peer node is created, you can get all peer node information from the member page by clicking the peer node ID. We will use a peer endpoint in our later setup.

Run the Hyperledger Fabric Application

After bringing up peer nodes in the previous step, in this section we will finally start to configure and run the Hyperledger Fabric application. Let's first start the Hyperledger Fabric CLI.

Configure and run Docker Compose to start the Hyperledger Fabric CLI

Create a Docker Compose configuration file *docker-compose-cli.yaml* in the */home/ec2-user* directory:

```
touch docker-compose-cli.yaml
```

You will configure this file to run the Hyperledger Fabric CLI. Let's open *docker-compose-cli.yaml*. Copy the following contents into the file and replace the `MyMem berID` and `MyPeerNodeEndpoint` values. You can find the member ID and peer node ID from the AWS Managed Blockchain console's Member page:

```
version: '2'
services:
  cli:
    container_name: cli
    image: hyperledger/fabric-tools:1.4
    tty: true
    environment:
      - GOPATH=/opt/gopath
      - CORE_VM_ENDPOINT=unix:///host/var/run/docker.sock
      - FABRIC_LOGGING_SPEC=info # Set logging level to debug for more verbose
logging
      - CORE_PEER_ID=cli
      - CORE_CHAINCODE_KEEPALIVE=10
      - CORE_PEER_TLS_ENABLED=true
      - CORE_PEER_TLS_ROOTCERT_FILE=/opt/home/managedblockchain-tls-chain.pem
      - CORE_PEER_LOCALMSPID=m-G4Q5XLRCCJFBTII7PYINITSZH4
      - CORE_PEER_MSPCONFIGPATH=/opt/home/admin-msp
      - CORE_PEER_ADDRESS=nd-fmwonqhh6vgexehznnpv4ydzyq.m-
g4q5xlrccjfbtii7pyinitszh4.n-
uyefppmbenfffeitgts6ij6tdy.managedblockchain.us-east-1.amazonaws.com:30003
    working_dir: /opt/gopath/src/github.com/hyperledger/fabric/peer
    command: /bin/bash
    volumes:
      - /var/run/:/host/var/run/
      - /home/ec2-user/fabric-samples/chaincode:/opt/gopath/src/github.com/
      - /home/ec2-user:/opt/home
```

Run `docker-compose` to start the Hyperledger Fabric CLI:

```
docker-compose -f docker-compose-cli.yaml up -d
```

Once Hyperledger Fabric CLI Docker Compose is up, you can start creating the Hyperledger Fabric channel as usual.

Create configtx for Hyperledger Fabric channel creation

The *configtx.yaml* file contains details of the channel configuration. For more information, see Chapter 4.

Create a *configtx.yaml* file under the */home/ec2-user* directory by using vi.

Replace `MemberID` with your own member ID.

`MSPDir` is set to the same directory location, */opt/home/admin-msp*, that you established using the `CORE_PEER_MSPCONFIGPATH` environment variable in the Docker container for the Hyperledger Fabric CLI in *docker-compose-cli.yaml*:

```
Organizations:
  - &Org1
      Name: m-G4Q5XLRCCJFBTII7PYINITSZH4
      ID: m-G4Q5XLRCCJFBTII7PYINITSZH4
      MSPDir: /opt/home/admin-msp
  ..
Profiles:
  OneOrgChannel:
      Consortium: AWSSystemConsortium
      Application:
          <<: *ApplicationDefaults
          Organizations:
              - *Org1
```

After the configuration is completed, run this Docker command to generate the channel *configtx*:

```
docker exec cli configtxgen -outputCreateChannelTx /opt/home/mychannel.pb \
-profile OneOrgchannel -channelID mychannel \
--configPath /opt/home
```

Set environment variables for the orderer

Set the $ORDERER environment variable for convenience by editing *.bash_profile*. Replace the ORDERER value with your own ordering service endpoint. You can find the endpoint on the Managed Blockchain console.

After updating *.bash_profile*, apply the changes by running the source command:

```
source ~/.bash_profile
```

In the next step, we will start creating the channel. Run the following command to read a genesis block from *channel.tx* that will create the channel:

```
docker exec cli peer channel create -c mychannel \
-f /opt/home/mychannel.pb -o $ORDERER \
--cafile /opt/home/managedblockchain-tls-chain.pem --tls
```

After the channel is created, join the peer node to the channel by running this Docker command:

```
docker exec cli peer channel join -b mychannel.block \
-o $ORDERER --cafile /opt/home/managedblockchain-tls-chain.pem -tls
```

With the successful creation of *mychannel*, we can install the sample chaincode in our network. Run the following command to install the example chaincode on the peer node:

```
docker exec cli peer chaincode install \
-n mycc -v v0 -p github.com/chaincode_example02/go
```

Now we need to instantiate the chaincode:

```
docker exec cli peer chaincode instantiate \
-o $ORDERER -C mychannel -n mycc -v v0 \
-c '{"Args":["init","a","100","b","200"]}' \
--cafile /opt/home/managedblockchain-tls-chain.pem --tls
```

It may take a minute to get a result; you can use the following command to verify the instantiation result:

```
docker exec cli peer chaincode list --instantiated \
-o $ORDERER -C mychannel \
--cafile /opt/home/managedblockchain-tls-chain.pem --tls
```

At this stage, we can interact with chaincode in the HF network. Let's start querying the chaincode. Run this command to query a value:

```
docker exec cli peer chaincode query -C mychannel \
-n mycc -c '{"Args":["query","a"]}'
```

Since we initialized variable a and have set its value to 100, the command should return a value of 100. You should see a result similar to this:

```
> -n mycc -c '{"Args":["query","a"]}'
100
```

In the previous command, we instantiated and queried a value of 100. Use the invoke command to subtract 10 from that initial value:

```
docker exec cli peer chaincode invoke -C mychannel \
-n mycc -c  '{"Args":["invoke","a","b","10"]}' \
-o $ORDERER --cafile /opt/home/managedblockchain-tls-chain.pem --tls
```

Query again using the following command:

```
docker exec cli peer chaincode query -C mychannel \
-n mycc -c '{"Args":["query","a"]}'
```

It should return the new value 90, as shown in the following output:

```
docker exec cli peer chaincode query -C mychannel \
> -n mycc -c '{"Args":["query","a"]}'
90
```

The video "Build a Blockchain Track-and-Trace Application" (*https://oreil.ly/cIlPR*) by Carl Youngblood provides a demo of setting up a Fabric network in AWS by using the Blockchain service offering.

Using IBM Cloud for Blockchain Applications

As one of the major contributors to the Hyperledger Fabric project, IBM offers a complete and intuitive platform, IBM Blockchain Platform, for building a Fabric network and deploying Fabric applications. IBM Cloud allows users to fully manage their deployments, certificates, and private keys. It provides a simplified UI that allows developers to easily deploy Fabric components into a Kubernetes/Red Hat OpenShift cluster.

Understand the Platform Features

In a nutshell, IBM Blockchain Platform features can be divided into three areas: development, operation, and scalability.

Development

While developing Fabric applications, IBM offers a set of developer tools that simplifies the job of development and deployment. In particular, you can do the following:

- Use Ansible Playbooks or Red Hat Marketplace to deploy networks faster
- Go from proof of concept to production in a single environment by increasing Kubernetes resources
- Leverage IBM Blockchain Platform developer tools to easily code

Operation

While running a Fabric application on IBM Cloud, you can take advantage of these great features:

- Ability to deploy peers to multiple channels on multiple clouds, or to permit other members to join your consortium.
- The Unified Codebase feature allows you to run your components on any environment backed by IBM Cloud and third-party, public clouds.
- The Dynamic Signature Collection feature facilitates collaborative governance over channel configurations.
- Removal of Docker-in-Docker for chaincodes makes chaincode pods run more securely, without peers requesting privileged access.
- Ability to easily upgrade nodes running on older Fabric versions to the latest version of Fabric. Upon upgrade, the capabilities of your channels and network will also be increased accordingly.
- Integration of Logging and Monitoring tools leveraging IBM Cloud services like IBM Log Analysis; IBM Cloud Monitoring is helpful for managing the blockchain network.

Scalability

As a prominent performance factor, scalability plays a vital role in the growth of Fabric applications. IBM Cloud gives you the following capabilities for scalability:

- Flexibility on the amount of compute power being utilized in your network by setting the amount of CPU, memory, and storage you wish to provision in your Kubernetes cluster

- Ability to adjust the amount of resources being utilized in your network by easily scaling up and down the resources in your Kubernetes cluster

- Ability to replicate your Kubernetes deployment among multiple regions or zones to ensure high availability of your components as well as disaster recovery

Further, using the IBM Blockchain Platform console, you can easily create and manage blockchain applications. Specifically, once a blockchain service instance is provisioned on IBM Cloud, you can link it to your Kubernetes cluster, after which you can create and manage your blockchain components like CA, peer, and ordering service images through the console. However, before using the console, you should know that you will be responsible for the following:

- Monitoring the health, security, and logging of Kubernetes clusters.

- Managing and securing your certificates and private keys. IBM does not save your certificates in the Kubernetes cluster.

For an additional list of considerations or requirements for using the IBM Blockchain Platform, see the IBM Cloud documentation (*https://oreil.ly/uy3VF*).

Create an IBM Cloud Account

Before proceeding with our discussion on creating and managing a Fabric network on IBM Cloud, you need to create or have an IBM Cloud account. For new user registration, visit the IBM Cloud site and follow the instructions.

Once you have an IBM Cloud account, you can add IBM Blockchain Platform from either the IBM Cloud Catalog or the Red Hat Marketplace. See the IBM documentation for more details. Note that if you want to use a hardware security module (HSM) to generate and save the private key for your peer and orderer nodes, you should configure the HSM prior to deploying your platform. For more details on HSM implementation on IBM Cloud and other considerations, visit the IBM documentation page.

 Storage Manage permissions are required for all users who link the service to the Kubernetes cluster. Just go to the dashboard, choose Manage → Access (IAM), select Users, and click the user who will connect the service to the Kubernetes cluster. Click the Classic infrastructure tab, expand the Services part, and choose Storage Manage. Click Apply to give the permission to the user.

Decide the Structure of the Blockchain Network

As you know, the various parties of a business have to agree to be part of a blockchain network. The type of participants and transactions of the blockchain network plays a crucial role in deciding its structure. As a first step, you need to decide the number of blockchain participants, number of organizations, number of peers in each organization, certificate authorities, and so on as per the business requirements. Once the blockchain network components are finalized, you can proceed further to set up the network.

As an example, let's say our Fabric network includes the following:

- Two CAs
- Two MSPs
- One peer
- One orderer
- One channel that includes one peer organization and one orderer organization

This sample network structure is good for learning purposes, but we would need to add more peers and organizations for it to look like an actual blockchain network. The following sections will walk you through step-by-step instructions for creating the sample Fabric network on IBM Cloud, and then you'll add Fabric components like peer, orderer, and channel to it.

Create and Join the Fabric Network

The blockchain service on IBM Cloud that allows you to set up a Fabric network is called IBM Blockchain Platform and is considered a blockchain-as-a-service system.

Start by logging in to IBM Cloud. This will take you to the IBM Cloud dashboard, which lists resources (applications, storage services, clusters, etc.) created (if any) for your account. The list of all available services on IBM Cloud can be found on the Catalog tab.

To create a new service instance, click the Catalog tab and search for `Blockchain`. Then, click the service tile IBM Blockchain Platform. This will redirect you to the blockchain service instance creation.

First, select a location. The location specifies the region in the various geographical areas like Asia-Pacific, North America, Europe, and so on. Then, select the pricing plan. Next, provide a service name. This can be any name you choose. After this, select the resource group. A resource group is a way to organize resources in your cloud account. The `default` resource group will be created by default in your cloud account. If you want to create a new resource group, choose Manage → Account → Account resources → Resource groups → Create.

After providing all the required values, click Create to create an instance of the block-chain service. This service instance acts as a placeholder for your Fabric network; the network has not been created yet. The service creation will take you to the welcome page to set up your network step by step. The welcome page shows you the required steps to manage your blockchain service. As you know, Hyperledger Fabric uses containers to build the network, so you can use either an IBM Cloud Kubernetes cluster or Red Hat OpenShift on IBM Cloud to deploy blockchain network components. The next step is to create a new cluster and link the existing cluster to the setup network.

Make a note that if a cluster exists in your Cloud account (i.e., you have created a cluster already), skip this step. You do not need to create a new cluster again.

If you create a new cluster on IBM Cloud through the Manage Service page, it lists the cluster requirements, so first refer to those and decide the appropriate size (number of worker nodes, vCPUs, RAM size, single zone or multizone).

While creating a Kubernetes/Red Hat OpenShift cluster, you will be asked to provide the cluster name, location, size, etc. Each has its own pricing plan. Once you create the cluster, setting it up will take some time. Wait until the cluster is completely deployed.

Next is to link your cluster with this blockchain service. Click that option, and it provides you a list of all available clusters in your account. Choose the cluster that you want to use for your blockchain network. It will associate the cluster to your blockchain service. Now you are ready to launch the service console.

You can launch the IBM Blockchain Platform console by successfully linking your blockchain service with the cluster. It will take you to the IBM Blockchain Platform page, where you will start creating your actual network components.

Build the Blockchain Network

The concepts of CA, MSP, peer, orderer, organization, channel, and more have been explained in Chapter 3; refer to that chapter for more details. This section focuses on setting up the Fabric network on IBM Cloud, using the IBM Blockchain Platform.

We will detail the steps to set up the sample network—an ordering service, a single peer organization, and a peer on a single channel—as explained in "Decide the Structure of the Blockchain Network" on page 190.

The IBM Blockchain Platform console provides an interface to work with nodes (peers, CAs, ordering service), channels, smart contracts, wallets, organizations, and users. Let's get started.

Add a certificate authority

To deploy peers, you first need to create their organizations. This requires an MSP definition of your organization, which in turn requires an organization admin user identity. A CA creates identities for all network participants. Therefore, as a first step to setting up the blockchain network, you need to create the CA for the organization.

From the IBM Blockchain Platform console, choose Nodes → Add Certificate Authority. To create a new CA, provide the following values:

- CA Display Name (for example, Org1CA).
- CA Administrator Enroll ID.
- CA Administrator Enroll Secret.
- The advanced deployment options, like creating a high-availability CA, multi-zone CA, and HSM are also available. Refer to the IBM documentation for more details.

You can use your own CA as well. If you have your own CA, you need to import it by using a JSON file. The CA has to fulfill certain specifications, such as the format of the issued certificates. You can refer to the IBM docs for specifications.

Associate the admin identity

After deploying the CA, you need to associate an admin identity. This identity will allow you to work with the CA and will be used to create the organization's MSP, register users, and add peers in the network.

From the IBM Blockchain Platform console, choose Nodes → [CA node] → Associate Identity.

Provide the CA Administrator Enroll ID and the Enroll Secret that you provided in the previous step. On clicking "Associate identity," the CA admin identity becomes associated with the CA node and is added into the wallet. You can check the wallet by going to the IBM Blockchain Platform console and selecting Wallet. This admin identity will be used to register new users and generate certificates.

Register users

As previously noted, every node requires a certificate and a private key to participate in the blockchain network. So using the CA admin identity of the organization, you need to register the two following identities:

- An identity that will work as an admin of the organization
- The identity of the peer itself, which will be used for signing the peer's action

Make a note that if an organization has more than one peer, one admin identity is sufficient, but you need to create a peer identity for each peer.

To proceed with identity registration, go to IBM Blockchain Platform console and choose Nodes → [*CA node*] → Register User. If this is the first time you are registering the admin for your organization, use the following steps:

 Except for step 1, these steps are for more advanced users. Refer to the IBM documentation for further details.

1. Provide the Enroll ID and Enroll Secret for the organization administrator and select Admin for the Type.
2. For the affiliation needed for role-based access control, keep the default selection.
3. For the optional Maximum Enrollments field, keep the default value, which is blank.
4. Create key-value pairs if you wish to set up attribute-based access control.

Now that the admin user is registered, we can proceed with registering the peer identity. To do that, repeat step 1 by selecting Peer for Type instead of Admin.

Check the wallet to view these identities. You might think that these identities are not available in the wallet yet. That's correct!

You have registered the identities but not yet enrolled them. Once an identity gets enrolled, its certificates will be generated, and the identity can be viewed in the wallet. In the upcoming sections, you will learn about enrolling these identities.

Create the peer organization's MSP definition

Now we will create the MSP, a formal definition of the peer's organization. To do that, go to IBM Blockchain Platform console and choose Organizations → Create MSP definition. Provide the required values as listed here:

- MSP name (for example, Org1MSP) and its ID
- The Root CA details, like the root CA that was used to create nodes and identities for the organization
- Admin Certificate, like the ID and secret of the user that you registered with the admin identity in the previous section

The certificates of the admin identity are generated in this step, while this identity gets exported to the wallet. Likewise, you can manage the certificates by exporting the admin certificates and saving them into your filesystem.

For the next step, we create an MSP definition, with which you can add peers in the organization.

Create the peer node

Peers are the nodes that host smart contracts and maintain the ledger. To create a peer node, go to IBM Blockchain Platform console and choose Nodes → Add Peer. Creating a peer node requires the following details:

- A name for the peer node (for example, peer1).
- CA details—use the CA that you used to create the organization's MSP.
- The user ID and secret, which was registered as a Peer type.
- Select the Organization MSP.
- Associate the peer admin identity. This will act as the administrator of your peer. You can make the organization admin the same as the peer admin; however, you can register and enroll a different identity with the organization CA to make that the admin of your peer.

With all this information, you've created the peer node. Advanced deployment options are also available—for example, if you want to use your own CA, state database, or HSM, refer to the IBM documentation for more information.

 To add more peers to the same organization, you need to register a new user with the Peer identity and repeat the steps as mentioned.

Create the ordering service

The ordering service is a node or a cluster of nodes. You can create one node ordering service (sufficient for testing purposes) or a crash fault-tolerant ordering service using multiple nodes. Refer to the IBM documentation for more information.

To create an ordering service node, we need to follow the same steps as for the peer node. As before, you must create a CA, create new identities using that CA, and create an organization definition; similarly, you need to perform the same steps given next before creating an ordering service:

1. Create a CA for the ordering service organization (say, OrdererCA). Follow the same steps as in "Add a certificate authority" on page 192.

2. Associate the CA admin identity by following the same steps as in "Associate the admin identity" on page 192.

3. Register new identities. You need to register two identities, one admin identity as type Admin and another node identity as type Orderer. Repeat the same steps as given in "Register users" on page 192.

4. Create an MSP for the ordering service organization (for example, OrdererMSP) in the same way as in "Create the peer organization's MSP definition" on page 193. Make sure in this step that you use the identities related to the ordering service appropriately.

5. Create the ordering service node from the IBM Blockchain Platform console by choosing Nodes → Add Ordering Service.

While creating an ordering service node, you need to enter the ordering service name, number of ordering nodes, and details of the ordering service CA, the user with the orderer identity, and MSP. At the end, associate the identity from your wallet, which will act as an admin of your ordering service. You can choose the Ordering Service MSP admin for this or create a new identity.

Add the organization as a consortium member

Now that you have created peer(s), its organizations, and the ordering service, the ordering service should know about the organizations before creating a channel in the blockchain network. Hence you need to add organizations to the ordering service. This process is called *joining the consortium*.

From the IBM Blockchain Platform console, in the Consortium Members section, choose Nodes → [*Ordering Service Node*] → Add Organization. Choose the organization from all the available organizations and click Add Organization. Repeat the same step for all of the organizations that will be part of the consortium.

After completing this step, the organizations can create or join a channel hosted on the ordering service in the blockchain network.

Create a channel

The channels act as a messaging medium among peers through the ordering service. Before creating the channel, make sure you have deployed an ordering service and peer organization, and that the organization has joined the consortium. To create a channel, go to the IBM Blockchain Platform console and choose Channels → Create Channel. Then complete the following steps:

1. Provide the channel name and choose the ordering service.

2. Add the organization's MSP as a channel member along with its permissions as operator, reader, or writer. Each channel must have at least one organization with operator permission.

3. The channel update policy specifies the number of organizations that need to approve the updates to the channel configuration whenever required. If you have one organization in your network, the policy will be "1 out of 1."

4. Next, select the channel creator organization and its admin identity. This specifies which organization is creating the channel.

After creating the channel, the next step is to join a channel.

Join the channel

After the peer joins the channel, the setup of the sample blockchain network is completed. To join the channel, go to the IBM Blockchain Platform console and choose Channels.

The channel created in the previous step has no peer that has joined yet and shows a status of "Pending – add peer." Clicking this will give you the available peers list, from which you can choose the peer.

Alternatively, you can go to the IBM Blockchain Platform console and choose Channels → Join Channel. You then need to choose the ordering service associated with your channel and provide the channel name. Then you'll see the available peers list, from which you can choose the peer.

After the selection of peers, you'll see an option to make your peer an anchor peer. For more information on anchor peers, refer to Chapter 3. You can have one anchor peer or many/all peers as anchors. Make your peer an anchor peer and proceed with joining the channel.

Now the setup of your blockchain network is completed, and with this, you have a fully functional blockchain network. As a next step, you can start deploying your smart contract on the channel and start transacting in the network.

Deploy the Smart Contract

Through the IBM Blockchain Platform console, you can manage the deployment of the smart contract, but not its development. The smart contract should be packaged as *.cds* (for older Fabric versions) or *.tgz* or *.tar.gz* before installing it on the Fabric network.

For older versions of Fabric (< 2.x) go to the IBM Blockchain Platform console and choose Smart Contracts → Install Smart Contract.

Provide the packaged (*.cds*) smart contract, and it will be installed on all peers. Once it's installed, you have the option to instantiate the smart contract. During this process, you set the endorsement policy, function name, and its required arguments to initialize the contract. On successful instantiation, the contract can be viewed under Instantiated Smart Contracts.

For current Fabric versions (> 2.*x*), smart contracts are managed differently. You need to take the following three steps:

1. Propose the smart contract.

    From the IBM Blockchain Platform console, choose Channels → [*Your Channel Node*] → Propose smart contract definition. Then provide the peer admin identity, smart contract name and its version, and endorsement policy. Then click Propose. This will install the packaged smart contract on the selected peer's node and propose the smart contract to the channel. Proposing the smart contract to the channel means it will notify the channel members for their approval.

2. Assign members to the smart contract.

    The channel members can view this proposed smart contract under Channels on the console. Select your organization and associated peer admin identity to proceed with your approval/rejection for the proposal.

3. Commit the smart contract to the channel.

    Once all the required approvals are in place, you commit the smart contract. This process is similar to smart contract instantiation. Any channel member can commit the smart contract on the channel. Select your organization, provide the peer admin identity, and commit the smart contract.

Once the smart contract is instantiated, or committed to the channel, your network is ready to accept the transactions.

Create the Application

Once the blockchain network is successfully created, and the smart contract has been committed in a channel of your network, you can start writing your client application to transact in the network. An application can interact with the Fabric network by using Fabric SDKs. Fabric provides several SDKs for various programming languages. The SDK uses the connection profile to connect to your network. The connection profile contains the endpoint information of the peers, CA, and organization MSP.

To download the connection profile, go to IBM Blockchain Platform console and choose Organizations → [*Organization Name*] → Create connection profile. Then select the peer and download the connection profile.

The next step is to connect to your blockchain network from your application by using the SDK and connection profile and then perform transactions to create, update, or transfer the assets in your network.

Oracle Blockchain Platform Overview

In this section, we dive into Oracle's platform for blockchain and its offerings. This is followed by complete coverage of a blockchain use case designed and deployed on Oracle.

Oracle Blockchain Platform (OBP) is a preassembled platform that offers the ease of building and running chaincodes and maintaining an immutable distributed ledger. Before we delve into OBP, it's important to understand that the blockchain platform uses the Oracle Cloud Infrastructure (OCI) VM to deploy and run the blockchain network and other supporting services including object storage (product and related binaries and logs), identity services (user, role, authentication, security), and load balancers.

A typical blockchain network on OBP will consist of nodes that validate transactions and respond to queries by executing the chaincode. External applications can use the SDK or REST APIs to invoke transactions on the blockchain network. One or more endorsing peers digitally sign (endorse) the chaincode execution results, which are further verified by the ordering service. Upon reaching a consensus, transactions are ordered, grouped, and sent to peer nodes for validation before being appended to the ledger.

The console allows administrators to configure a blockchain network and monitor its operations, check logs, and more. While configuring a blockchain network, you complete a few simple instance creation steps, and then Oracle takes care of service management, patching, backup and restoration, and other service life-cycle tasks. You start by creating a blockchain instance that includes all that you need to build, deploy, run, and monitor a production-grade permissioned blockchain ledger powered by Fabric.

In this section, you'll use Oracle Blockchain Platform Cloud Service to build a sample use case that demonstrates OBP. Oracle offers the following blockchain products:

Oracle Blockchain Platform Cloud Service
> This cloud service includes a preassembled platform as a service (PaaS) with template-based provisioning. It leverages OCI, which takes care of dependencies like containers, virtual machines, identity management, and block and object storage.

Oracle Blockchain Platform Enterprise Edition

This is designed for customers who need greater data privacy or prefer to manage their data on premises. This edition offers a preassembled, on-premises blockchain, which can be deployed on your datacenter. It has feature parity with the cloud-based Oracle Blockchain Platform and offers the same APIs and portability of applications.

Prebuilt solution

This prebuilt option offers pre-integrated, quickly deployable blockchain solutions. These solutions can seamlessly connect with SaaS applications like supply chain management. For example, Intelligent Track and Trace is a pre-integrated blockchain solution to achieve end-to-end supply chain visibility.

Tamper-resistant blockchain tables in Oracle Database

This solution is designed for an enterprise that needs immutable storage for use cases such as tamper-resistant transaction logs, audit trails, compliance data, financial ledgers, or legal hold data. It is a tamper-resistant option in Oracle Database that allows only insert operations. Each row contains the previous row's hash, thus chaining the rows. Nonrepudiation is guaranteed as users sign the content of the rows with a PKI-based signature.

Figure 8-1 shows the high-level architecture of OBP. This permissioned blockchain offers a closed ecosystem in which the founder organization invites other participating organizations. It follows a three-step consensus process: endorsement, ordering, and validation. The platform itself is a managed service with zero-downtime managed patching, upgrades, and backups of ledger and configurations.

Based on the OCI infrastructure tenancy model, this architecture helps isolate the organization's data and offers enhanced security and in-transit and at-rest data encryptions. It offers a Web Application Firewall (WAF) to protect against attacks. The identity management cloud service offers user and role management. It also provides a simplified ecosystem to form consortiums, ease participant onboarding to the blockchain network, and provide authentication of the CA, REST proxy, and platform console.

Each organization's instance uses managed VMs and containers per node. To avoid outages, the *orderers*, *console*, REST proxy, and *fabric-ca* nodes are replicated. A separate VM is provisioned for the chaincode execution container. And to withstand datacenter outages, object stores are automatically replicated across OCI availability domains (ADs).

Now that we have covered various offerings and OBP architecture, let's focus on Oracle Blockchain Platform by starting with a sample use case.

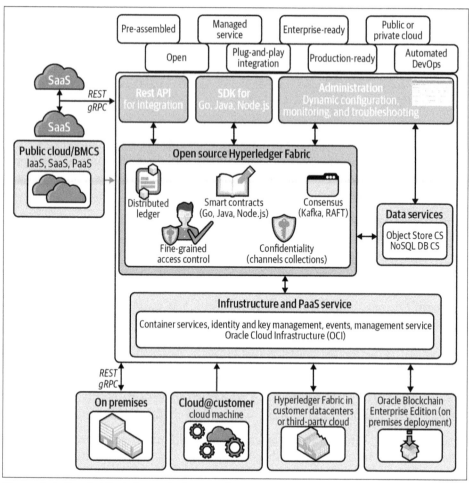

Figure 8-1. Oracle Blockchain Platform architecture

Oracle Blockchain Platform Use Case

In this section, we set up and deploy a Fabric application on OBP by going through four steps sequentially: Explore, Engage, Experiment, and Experience. Specifically, we start the Explore step by defining the use case. Then we follow the Engage step by reviewing transactions, channels, digital assets, and other relevant artifacts for our use case. At the Experiment step, we configure the Fabric network and the transaction infrastructure on OBP. Finally, at the Experience step, we add the "smartness" to our Fabric network by deploying and instantiating our chaincode.

Explore the Use Case

Before we begin any work, we need to assess the use case to determine whether it is a fit for a blockchain-based solution and identify the type of network that will help set up the business case.

This section briefly describes our use case. In this example, a university uses Fabric to manage the authenticity of its students' credentials. Along the way, you'll learn how to solve a business problem with Fabric as well as how to deploy solutions on OBP.

Like other industries, universities and other higher education institutions are investing in and adopting digital solutions to enhance students' efficiency and experiences. Higher-education institutions are preparing the future workforce, and that workforce is already tech-savvy. They need a thriving ecosystem, efficient anytime-anywhere learning capabilities, and tamper-proof credential storage to showcase their skills to future employers. In general, the education industry faces key challenges in building this ecosystem, such as legacy technology, data silos, low collaboration with peer universities, credential verification, paper-based degrees and certificates, tracking and protecting IPs, and seamless and fair allocation of grants to the bright and needy.

Our use case targets credential verification. Many will agree that credential verification is slow and mostly a manual process. Fake certificates and degrees can tarnish universities and harm employers in many ways.

This use case deals with issuing certificates by a CA and allowing a certificate owner (student/learner), employers, and other institutions to verify a tamper-proof credential of the certificate owner. This example includes the following stakeholders:

Certificate viewer/verifiers (CVs)
  Student, employer, other universities

Oracle Business School (OBS)
  Certificate creator (school of studies)

Oracle Global University (OGU)
  Certificate approver and issuer (university)

Engage with the Solution

To begin, we need to define the holistic design of the solution, shown in Figure 8-2, to ensure synchronicity among the process flows, use cases, and technology. This stage focuses on defining a blockchain-based business network and its components, such as business topology, access control, digital assets, transactions, events, and channels. Finally, it ends with defining the solution architecture.

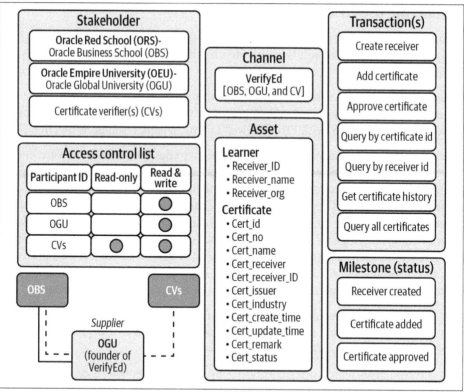

Figure 8-2. Solution components

Business topology

Our use case has three stakeholders. Oracle Global University (OGU) is the governing body with several affiliated business schools such as Oracle Business School (OBS). Learners are enrolled in OBS, and OBS submits their credentials to OGU, which issues a digital certificate to the learner. The following are the stakeholders:

Oracle Global University (OGU)
   This is the certificate authority (digital asset), acting as approver and issuer of the certificates. It is also the founder of the network.

Oracle Business School (OBS)
   The certificate (digital asset) creator and requestor.

Digital certificate verifier (CVs)
   Potential employers, other certificate providers (for example, Pearson VUE), universities, and other authorities. It also includes the certificate owner, which is the learner.

Access control

Different stakeholders have different permissions for accessing and managing the network. Such permissions are set via access rights, like read or write privileges assigned to each stakeholder, as listed in Table 8-1.

Table 8-1. Network participant access-control list

Organization	Entity type	Access type
OGU	Founder	Read/write
OBS	Endorsing participant	Read/write
CVs	Participant	Read

Channel

In our founder-initiated business network, participating stakeholders (like OBS and CVs) will communicate over a blockchain channel. In addition, all the stakeholders are dealing with the same digital asset; participants need to be on the same channel with appropriate access rights. Hence, we will have one channel, defined by the founder, and other participants will join the channel.

Digital asset

Once the stakeholders and network topology are defined, you need to focus on defining the digital asset(s) that will be stored in the ledger. For this use case, we will have two digital assets: the learner (certificate owner) information and the digital certificate data.

Transactions

While designing the solution for a use case, we recommend charting the transactions and events. During the life cycle of the digital asset, stakeholders will perform the transactions listed in Table 8-2.

Table 8-2. Transactions and events

Transaction	Stakeholders	Milestone	Description
CreateReceiver	OBS	Receiver created	Creates a new receiver or student
AddCertificate	OBS	Certificate added	Inserts a certificate for a receiver
ApproveCertificate	OGU	Certificate approved	Approves a certificate
Search operation			
QueryByCert_id	All	N/A	Queries a certificate
QueryByRecev_id	All	N/A	Queries a receiver by ID
GetCertificateHistory	OGU/OBS/receiver	N/A	Queries history of one key for the record
QueryAllCerts	OGU/OBS	N/A	Queries all certificates of all students

Solution architecture

Let's examine the high-level solution architecture for the use case. Several components interact and integrate at various levels by working in tandem to realize the solution:

OBP dashboard
> This is the console that allows authorized participants to perform various tasks. For example, OGU users can create compartments (Oracle infrastructure logical partitions), define blockchain networks, create channels, and allow other participants to collaborate on the channel.

Client UI
> Various participants and certificate viewers can use the client application UI to perform tasks, such as these:
>
> - Users with OBS access control can search for certificate data for a given learner. They can also create a learner entry, request certificate approval, and insert certificate data for the student on the ledger.
>
> - Users with OGU access control can search for certificate data for a given learner and can also approve or reject a learner's certificate data.
>
> - Certificate verifiers (CVs) include learners and viewers. Learners (the certificate owner) can use client applications to view their certificate data and its approval state, and to generate a token to share with other certificate verifiers to validate their credentials. Viewers are users who can verify a learner's credentials by using the token.

Experiment with Oracle Blockchain Platform

Now that we've defined the key components, we can start using OBP to create network stakeholders with OBP instances, configure the OBP network infrastructure, and configure the OBP transaction infrastructure. Figure 8-3 shows the major tasks and subtasks in this section. Adding smartness will be covered in "Experience the Solution" on page 210.

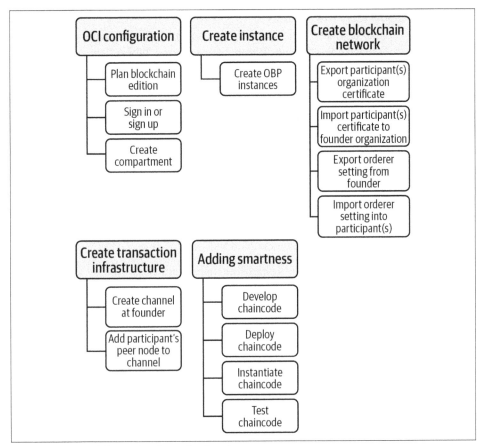

Figure 8-3. Workflow of tasks and subtasks

Configure Oracle Cloud Infrastructure

Before you dive into creating a blockchain network and run transactions, you will start with OCI configurations. The tasks that need to be performed are signing in or signing up, planning for different blockchain editions, and creating a compartment.

Signing in or signing up

    To start, you need an Oracle Cloud account. You can sign up for a free Oracle cloud promotion or place an order for OBP. Your Oracle Cloud account will include Oracle Identity and Access Management (IAM) and Identity Cloud Service (IDCS). With IAM, you can control who can access which cloud resources. As a cloud admin, you use IDCS to add users, assign roles, and manage access to the blockchain platform. Roles are mapped against IAM.

Planning for different blockchain editions

OBP is available in many regions, including Europe, North America, and APAC —and its popularity is growing. Before you set up a blockchain network, you need to plan for using any specific blockchain platform edition. OBP Cloud Service offers two editions: the Standard Edition with two CPUs, 50 GB storage, and two peers; and the Enterprise Edition, which can range from 4 to 32 CPUs, 150 GB storage, and two to six peers, depending on the size (small, medium, large, or XL). You can scale (up or down) the enterprise shape as per your load. For the sake of simplicity, we will create an instance with the Standard Edition.

Creating a compartment

We recommend that you create a separate compartment for a blockchain network. When you first log in to OCI, Oracle autocreates a root compartment in your tenancy. As an OCI admin, you can create additional compartments under the root compartment for the blockchain network.

Log in as an admin user, navigate to the blockchain platform, and choose the appropriate compartment. We have created a separate compartment, OracleBlockchainCompartment, for this use case.

Create OBP instances

As per the business topology, you will create three blockchain instances: one for the founder (OGU) and one for each participant (OBS and CV). Following are the subtasks for this section:

1. Create the founder blockchain instance for OGU.

2. Create the participant blockchain instance for OBS.

3. Create the participant blockchain instance for the CVs.

The steps are as follows:

1. Sign in to your Oracle Cloud Infrastructure account as a federated Oracle Identity Cloud Service admin user.

2. At the console, click the Navigation menu in the top-left corner and select Blockchain Platform.

3. From the list of compartments, select the compartment (OracleBlockchainCompartment) in which you want to create the service.

4. Enter the founder's blockchain instance display name, **OGUInstance**, and a description.

5. Choose "Create a new network" as a platform role, because this is a founder instance.

6. Choose the Standard Edition, which will offer two CPUs, 50 GB storage, and two peers.

7. Click Create Instance.

8. The instance goes to Creating status. Provisioning the blockchain instance takes a few minutes. Once the instance is created, the state changes to Active.

9. Click the service console to navigate to the founder's blockchain instance.

10. At the blockchain instance dashboard, navigate to the Nodes tab. This tab lists all the nodes, as follows:

   a. With the Standard Edition, you will receive two peer nodes (peer0 and peer1), three orderer nodes, one CA, and one proxy node. Also there will be a console node.

   b. You will also get a default channel.

Similarly, create other participant instances. However, while creating a participant instance, choose "Join a network" as the participant role.

Create a blockchain network

Once the stakeholder instances are established, we will create a blockchain transaction network for blockchain instances, which will establish connectivity among blockchain instances and enable an underlying shared ledger infrastructure between them. To proceed, the initial task is to export the participant(s) organization certificate, and then import the participant(s) certificate to the founder organization. In the next step, export the Orderer setting from the founder, followed by importing the Orderer setting into the participant(s).

Export participant(s) organization certificate

A participant certificate contains keys for admin, CA, and TLS, along with its signature. It's a JSON file. Follow these steps:

1. Navigate to a participant(s) blockchain instance and go to their dashboard.

2. Navigate to the Network tab.

3. Select the export certificate option for one of the participants.

4. Repeat steps 1 to 3 for all other participants.

Import participant(s) certificate to founder organization

In this section, we will import participant certificates into the founder organization. Here are the steps:

1. Go to the founder blockchain dashboard.
2. Navigate to the Network tab.
3. Click Add Organization.
4. At the Add Organization dialog, browse the exported certificate's JSON file and click Add.
5. Once the file is added successfully, click Finish.

Export orderer settings from founder

Next we will export the orderer configuration from the founder to the participant. Orderers are associated with founders, and to ensure that the same orderers validate the transaction submitted by participants, we recommend exporting the orderer setting from the founder and importing them into the participants.

Orderer settings contain the founder's certificate, signatures, and orderer endpoints, so follow these steps:

1. Go to the founder blockchain instance's dashboard.
2. Navigate to the Network tab.
3. Click Export Ordering Settings.
4. Download the JSON file, which will be imported at the participants.

Import orderer settings to participants

Now we will import the orderer configuration to participants by following these steps:

1. Go to the participant blockchain instance's dashboard.
2. Navigate to the Network tab.
3. Click the Orderer setting.
4. Choose the Import option.
5. Browse to the founder's orderer settings JSON file.
6. Click Submit to import the orderer settings.

Create the transaction infrastructure

Once a blockchain network and instances are created and the orderer information is exchanged between the founder and participants, you can create the blockchain transaction infrastructure. Essentially, this step will define a shared ledger and the associated transacting blockchain instances to read or read/write to the shared ledger.

Create a channel at the founder

In this section, we will create channels. Channels include peers, the shared ledger, instantiated chaincode, and one or more orderers. Channels allow stakeholders (blockchain instances) to share data via a shared ledger. Follow these steps to create the channel:

1. Go to the founder's dashboard.
2. Navigate to the Channels tab.
3. Click Create a New Channel.
4. Enter the name of the channel: **verifyed** (lowercase).
5. Select one or more participant organizations.
6. Choose the participant's access control as per the access control defined in the preceding section.
7. For each participant, select one or more peers to join the channel. We have selected peer0 for both participants.
8. Click Submit to create the channel.

Add the participant's peer node to the channel

Once a channel is created at the founder instance, we will add a participant's peer to the same channel. This ensures that transactions performed by client applications on the blockchain network are handled by the defined peer nodes. These peer node(s) will validate and execute chaincode and will perform RWSet (ReadWriteSet) creation. These RWSets are later submitted to orderer nodes for sequencing and adding to the ledger. Follow these steps to add a participant to the channel:

1. Go to the participants dashboard.
2. Click Nodes.
3. Find the peer (peer0).
4. Select "Join new channel."
5. Choose the channel verifyed.
6. Click Submit.

These steps will add the OBS and CV participant's `peer0` to the channel.

 You can check the blockchain platform and Hyperledger Fabric version by going to the Oracle Blockchain Platform console. Then locate your login username and click About. This displays the version number of the blockchain platform and the Hyperledger version number as well.

Experience the Solution

Now that we've defined the OBP instance, configured the OBP network infrastructure, and configured the OBP transaction infrastructure, we can focus on developing chaincode and verifying it. Let's proceed with the final step of *adding smartness* to our Fabric network by deploying and instantiating our Fabric chaincode.

Develop chaincode

Chaincode can be developed in various languages like Go, Node.js, and Java. All chaincode needs to be packaged into a ZIP file for deployment. But if your chaincode is a single *.go* file, you can directly deploy and instantiate the chaincode on OBP without packaging it. For our use case, you can find the source code file *verifyed.go* at *https://myhsts.org/hyperledger-fabric-book*.

Use OBP's app builder

OBP offers blockchain app builders to simplify and ease the process of chaincode development; this injects speed and agility to chaincode development. The platform autogenerates CRUD methods that can be used directly via REST APIs or can be invoked from custom functions. It supports various types of assets, including embedded assets (modular and nested asset structure) and user-controlled chaincode versioning.

OBP allows you to generate chaincode from a specification file, where you can specify assets in TypeScript (for Node.js chaincode) or Go (for Go chaincode). The specification file allows you to define multiple assets, their data mode, behaviors, and validation rules. It facilitates quick chaincode generation that can be tested on a local machine on a preconfigured blockchain instance inside the blockchain app builder or by deploying on an OBP network (cloud or on-premises edition). The platform includes two interfaces: CLI (command line) for CI/CD automation, and a Visual Studio Code extension for IDE-based interactive development.

Deploy and instantiate the chaincode

OBP offers two deployment options: quick and advanced. The quick deployment option can be used for testing and developing a proof of concept (PoC). The advanced option is used for selected peers and the endorsement policy; thus, the steps for the advanced option are as follows:

1. Go to the founder dashboard.
2. Navigate to the Chaincodes tab.
3. Click Deploy a New Chaincode and then choose the Advanced option.
4. In the Advanced Option dialog, enter the chain code name (**verifyed**) and chaincode version (v1). Choose the peer node (peer0) and select the chaincode source, which will be a single (dot) Go file.
5. Click Next to install (deploy) the chaincode.
6. After successful chaincode installation, the Advance Deployment dialog will jump to instantiate the chaincode option. Enter the channel name (**verifyed**).
7. Select the peer (peer0) that will participate in the transactions and opt for the other default values.
8. Click Next.

REST proxies are enabled by default. The REST proxy for the founder and other participants is listed on the dashboard's Node tab.

Deploy chaincode to participants

Once the chaincode is deployed and instantiated at the founder node, you can navigate to the participant's dashboard and go to the Chaincodes tab to deploy the same version of the chaincode to all the participants since you don't need to instantiate the chaincode. Once instantiated at the founder, the chaincode stays instantiated for all the participants because instantiation is specific to the channel, not to the organization or peer.

Test the chaincode

Once chaincode is deployed and instantiated, you can invoke it via the REST proxy or by using a mock shim. OBP offers a REST proxy to connect to chaincode via REST endpoints. Post instantiation, the ledger is empty, so let's proceed with running a test.

First, navigate to the founder or participant's dashboard and go to the Nodes tab. The RESTPROXY node is enabled. Copy this URL for the REST proxy:

https://<blockchain instance name>-<tenancy>-region.blockchain.ocp.oraclecloud.com:port/restproxy

Next, send a request for the `restproxy` endpoints, which are in JSON format and contain channel and chaincode information. Because you can configure multiple chaincodes in a single REST proxy, channel and chaincode information helps in dispatching the request to the correct chaincode. Every call should contain authorization and content type. Also, the REST proxy offers two target endpoints: *transaction/invocation* and *transaction/query*. You can use any REST testing tool like Postman or ReadyAPI to test the rest endpoint. The header has the following three parts:

Authorization
> Use your Oracle cloud username and password.

Content-Type
> Use *application/json*.

Target Endpoint
> Use this format:
>
> *https://<blockchaininstancename>-<tenancy>-region.blockchain.ocp.oraclecloud.com:port/ restproxy/bcsgw/rest/v1/transaction/invocation*

Once the testing step is completed, you can perform an invocation to insert the certificate receiver information. Set the target endpoint to `/invocation` and the target method to `insertReceiver`. Also, set `Input JSON` as shown here:

```
Input JSON - {
    "channel": "verified",
    "chaincode": "verifyed",
    "method": "insertReceiver",
    "args": [
       "008",
       "Noah",
       "App Dev"
    ],
    "chaincodeVer": "v1"
}
```

For the final step, we query the endpoint. Similar to querying a certificate owner (receiver), you can query it by its ID, using the query endpoint with three parameters: the target endpoint (`/query`), the target method (`queryReceiverById`), and `Input JSON`:

```
Input JSON - {
   "channel": "verifyed",
   "chaincode": "verifyed",
   "method": "queryReceiverById",
   "args": [
      "008"
   ],
   "chaincodeVer": "v1"
}
```

Verify transactions at the ledger

Each channel has only one ledger, which is shared by the founder and participating organizations. OBP offers the option to view transaction blocks on the shared ledger for a given channel. Follow these steps to access the ledger and view transactions:

1. Go to the founder dashboard.

2. Navigate to the channel.

3. Choose the channel `verifyed`.

4. Click the ledger.

This lists all the blocks on the ledger. You can find blocks from the genesis to the latest blocks. It also segregates user transactions from system and genesis blocks. It is evident that each block stores various information such as transaction ID, status, chaincode name, method name, arguments, results, initiator, and endorser.

Summary

In this chapter, you learned how to deploy Fabric on the AWS, IBM, and Oracle cloud platforms. We started out with a discussion on the Amazon cloud platform. You learned to set up Amazon Managed Blockchain services, a Fabric network, and a Fabric client to run and manage chaincodes. We completed our AWS journey by configuring and running the Fabric application.

Next we explained the features, considerations, and capabilities of the IBM cloud platform for building Fabric applications. Specifically, we showed you how to create and join a Fabric network on IBM Cloud, including how to build a Fabric network and create an orderer or a channel. We concluded our IBM section by going over smart contract deployment on IBM Cloud.

Finally, we explored the Oracle Blockchain Platform including its offerings and architecture. We delved into defining business topology, access control, partitions, assets, and transactions. In addition, you experimented with Oracle Blockchain Platform to experience the ease of setting up a Fabric network and deploying and testing chaincodes.

The next chapter covers the new features of Hyperledger Fabric v2, such as new chaincode application patterns and an external chaincode launcher. We also discuss how to update Fabric components as well as the capability level of a channel.

## CHAPTER 9

Hyperledger Fabric V2 Integration

Since Hyperledger Fabric v1.0.0 released in 2017, many minor versions have been rolled out for Fabric v1.*x* (1.1, 1.2, 1.3, 1.4). As an open source, permissioned distributed ledger, Hyperledger Fabric has quickly become one of the most popular enterprise blockchain frameworks, adopted by many organizations from small businesses to enterprises worldwide. The major cloud vendors—including AWS, IBM, and Oracle —have included Fabric in their blockchain cloud services, as you saw in Chapter 8. Fabric's benefits and popularity stem from its powerful architecture for building enterprise blockchain applications.

In 2020, the Hyperledger Community released Hyperledger Fabric v2, bringing many improvements over v1. This significant milestone has boosted the adoption of enterprise blockchains and enhanced the efficiency and security of production deployments.

This chapter will help you understand the following:

- New features of Hyperledger Fabric v2
- Updating the capability level of a channel
- Upgrading components
- Considerations for getting to v2

New Features of Hyperledger Fabric V2

Hyperledger Fabric version 2, or v2, builds on what the community has learned in the past four years, delivering several new features and improvements that have made v2 shine as a production-ready enterprise blockchain. The new features of Hyperledger Fabric v2 include support for enhanced governance around smart contracts, improvements in chaincode life cycle management, introduction of a new raft consensus mechanism, new patterns for working with and sharing private data, and stronger token support. Let's explore these features.

Decentralized Governance for Smart Contracts

Prior to v2, the chaincode life cycle process was composed of these steps: package, install, and instantiate. If multiple organization participants own the same chaincode, the packaging step is needed. Only one organization is required to install chaincode, with an optional instantiation policy. The chaincode is installed on endorsing peer nodes of chaincode owners. With signed packaged chaincode, chaincode can be instantiated and sent to other owners for inspection and signing. When other peers refuse to install the chaincode, the original owner will not be able to execute the chaincode, but still can validate and commit the transactions. Once chaincode gets installed, chaincode is not yet in the channel since it is not instantiated to the channel. When the selected peer performs chaincode instantiation, the instantiated transaction invokes the life cycle system chaincode (LCSC). The chaincode enters the active state and can be executed on the channel.

Figure 9-1 shows the Hyperledger Fabric 1.4 chaincode life-cycle operation.

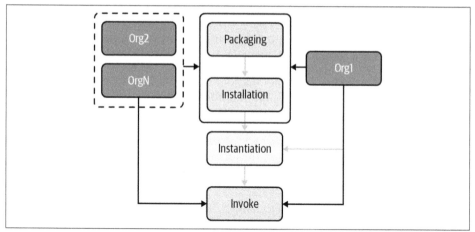

Figure 9-1. Hyperledger Fabric 1.4 chaincode life-cycle operation

One major drawback in this chaincode life-cycle operation was chaincode governance: only one organization had to instantiate, write, deploy, and update chaincode for all the peers in the network. This centralized process limits other organizations from participating in chaincode governance.

Hyperledger Fabric v2 introduces decentralized governance for the chaincode life cycle. Instead of instantiating by one organization, the new process requires multiple organizations to agree to the parameters of a chaincode and approve how it will be operated on the channel. This more democratic process has significantly improved security across the network. For example, approval of the chaincode definition in a two-organization network is required for both channel members before chaincode can be committed to the channel.

Figure 9-2 shows the Hyperledger Fabric v2 chaincode life-cycle operation.

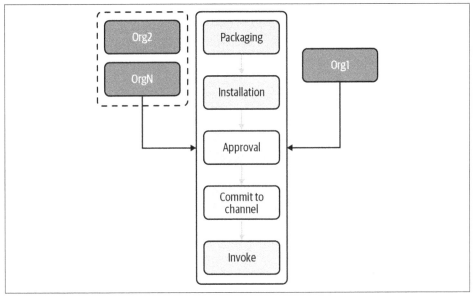

Figure 9-2. Hyperledger Fabric v2 chaincode life-cycle operation

In comparison with 1.4, the new life cycle eliminates the instantiate step and replaces it with two new steps: approving the chaincode (which is done by all organization members) and committing the chaincode definition.

Here is a list of peer commands for chaincode initialization:

```
peer lifecycle chaincode package ${CHAINCODE_NAME}.tar.gz
peer lifecycle chaincode install ${CHAINCODE_NAME}.tar.gz
peer lifecycle chaincode approveformyorg
peer lifecycle chaincode commit
```

In Chapter 7, we walked through the entire chaincode operation process; let's quickly review how the chaincode life-cycle endorsement policy is defined in the configuration.

Open *configtx.yaml* under the project *configtx* folder. The Application section defines the values to encode into a config transaction or block for application-related parameters:

```
Application: & ApplicationDefaults

    # Organizations is the list of orgs which are defined as participants on
    # the application side of the network
    Organizations:

    # Policies defines the set of policies at this level of the config tree
    # For Application policies, their canonical path is
    #     /Channel/Application/<PolicyName>
    Policies:
        Readers:
            Type: ImplicitMeta
            Rule: "ANY Readers"
        Writers:
            Type: ImplicitMeta
            Rule: "ANY Writers"
        Admins:
            Type: ImplicitMeta
            Rule: "MAJORITY Admins"
        LifecycleEndorsement:
            Type: ImplicitMeta
            Rule: "MAJORITY Endorsement"
        Endorsement:
            Type: ImplicitMeta
            Rule: "MAJORITY Endorsement"

    Capabilities:
        <<: *ApplicationCapabilities
```

Here you can define the types of life-cycle endorsement policies. In our case, we define governance as MAJORITY Endorsement. This MAJORITY Endorsement policy will be used as the default if an endorsement policy is not explicitly specified. It requires a majority of peers to participate in the chaincode transaction validation and execution in the channel and to commit the transaction to the ledger.

We use the channel configuration to define our supply chain endorsement policy. You can also explicitly specify a signature policy for the endorsement; for example, the following command will require that a member of both Org1 and Org2 sign the transaction:

```
peer lifecycle chaincode approveformyorg --signature-policy "AND('Org1.member',
'Org2.member')" --tls
$CORE_PEER_TLS_ENABLED --cafile $ORDERER_CA --channelID $CHANNEL_NAME --name $
{CHINCODE_NAME} --version
${VERSION}  --package-id ${PACKAGE_ID} --sequence ${VERSION}
```

Channel configuration policies in *configtx.yaml* can be customized or overridden by editing the file *configtx.yaml* for a specific channel.

New Chaincode Application Patterns

As discussed in the previous section, the new chaincode decentralized life-cycle management will apply in chaincode operation. This will ensure that multiple organizations must agree to the parameters of a chaincode and approve how it will be operated on the channel. The new chaincode application patterns will allow the following:

Automated checks
> Organizations can automate checks and validate additional chaincode information before submitting a transaction proposal request to the orderer service.

Decentralized agreement
> Personal decisions can be modeled on a chaincode process that requires several transactions. Based on the defined ledger transaction policy, the chaincode may need different organizations to agree to process the transaction. Once all the individual transactors are met and verified by a final chaincode proposal, the business transaction is finalized across all channel members.

Private Data Enhancements

In a centralized application, the superuser can view all the database data and grant selected members permission to access it. In the blockchain network, the transaction data is stored in the ledger, which is shared with all participants. Prior to v2, in order to keep data private from other organizations on the channel, we had to create a new channel that consisted of the organizations requiring data access.

Today, Hyperledger Fabric MSP will ensure the privacy of all members of the network. MSP provides an abstraction of membership operations and defines the rules of how memberships are governed and authenticated. Fabric has three types of MSPs:

Network MSP
> Defines members in the network

Channel MSP
> Defines who can participate in certain actions on a given channel according to channel policies

Peer/orderer MSP
> The local MSP for a single peer or orderer, for identifying members of the same organization

In building our supply chain DApps example, we have manufacturer, wholesaler, and pharmacy organizations in the blockchain. They share all device ownership transition data in the ledger by creating a channel from the manufacturer to the pharmacy.

In Figure 9-3, we can see that all three organizations can view that channel 1 ledger data.

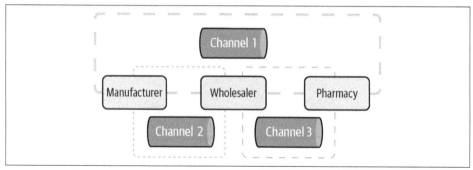

Figure 9-3. Channel 1 ledger data for three organizations

After completing a trade with the manufacturer, the wholesaler may also want to keep the trade's confidential data from the pharmacy. They can create channel 2, in which the pharmacy can't see transactions. The wholesaler may also want to have a private data relationship with the pharmacy, so they create channel 3. Similarly, the manufacturer can't see transactions in channel 3.

The channel design is elegant, providing a subnetwork to keep all transactions confidential within a set of organizations. However, this design has some downsides. First, it requires additional administrative overhead (to create a channel, deploy chaincode, update policies and MSPs, etc.). Second, it doesn't allow all channel participants to see the transaction data, but keeps partial data privacy for selected members. Third, when many members (hundreds) participate in the consortium network, those members could create a large number of channels in the network. This will make the network very complex and hard to maintain, and tracking communications will be difficult.

Instead of creating many multiple channels, Hyperledger Fabric v2 offers enhanced private data collection or policy configuration by introducing a new endorsement policy. Fabric can create private data collections on a peer node, sometimes called a *SideDB*, which can be shared with selected peers. Private data collections have two elements: the actual private data and a hash of private data.

The *actual private data* is sent between authorized peers through the gossip data dissemination protocol. Each gossiped message is signed, and other unauthorized peers will be prevented from seeing the message. The data is stored in a SideDB. This process does not involve an ordering service, which may be controlled by an unauthorized organization.

Figure 9-4 shows how public data and a private data collection are stored in a peer node.

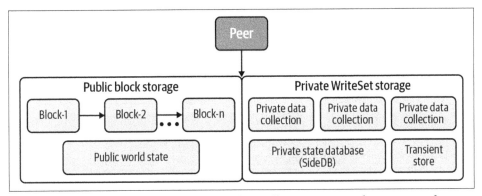

Figure 9-4. How public data and a private data collection are stored in a peer node

Public block storage contains transaction logs for each channel and public world-state data. The world state keeps the current state of data. Channel members can view this data. The endorsed transaction logs are stored in blocks linked in sequence with the hashing mechanism.

Private block storage consists of private `writeSet` storage, a private state database, and a transient store. Private `writeSet` stores a number of private data collections, and all private historical transactions for each private data collection. A private state database is world-state storage that keeps the current state of private data collections. The transient store is used to store temporally private data during a transaction invocation process. The transient data is used to determine whether a peer has already received the private data at chaincode endorsement time.

After the orderer validates the transactions, the *hash of private data* is packaged into blocks and written to the ledger. The cryptographic hash serves as evidence of the transaction and allows authorized organizations in the channel to endorse, commit, or query private data.

In our supply chain example, all three peers have the private state database instance for each related private collection. The private data between manufacturer and wholesaler is privately managed by Org1's peer and Org2's peer only. Similarly, Org2's peer and Org3's peer will maintain wholesaler and pharmacy private data collections. Figure 9-5 illustrates these three peers with two collections of private data on the same channel.

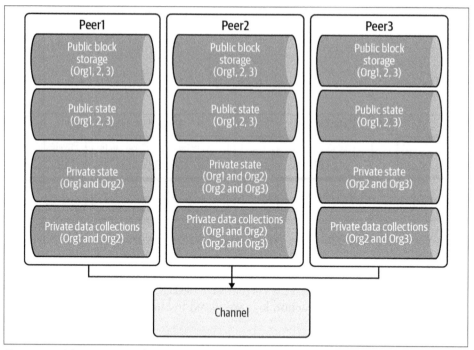

Figure 9-5. Three peers with two collections of private data on the same channel

To understand how Fabric private data works, let's look at how a transaction flow gets performed in the transaction life cycle. Figure 9-6 depicts the end-to-end system flow for processing a private data transaction in Hyperledger Fabric v2.

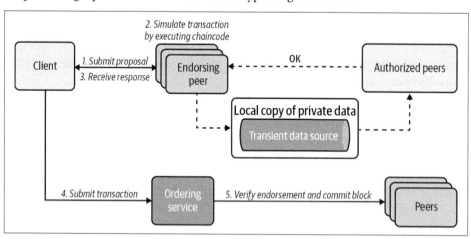

Figure 9-6. The end-to-end system flow for processing a private data transaction in Hyperledger Fabric v2

Here are the steps of the flow:

1. The client initiates a transaction by sending a transaction proposal request with private data to endorsing peers. Those endorsing peers are authorized organizations for private data collections.

2. The endorsing peers simulate the transaction by using a local copy of private data in a transient data store to execute the chaincode. This chaincode execution distributes the private data to authorized peers via gossip and sends back the results to the application.

3. At this point, the client application combines the transaction along with the endorsements (including the proposal response with the private data hashes) and broadcasts it to the ordering service. The private data hashes are distributed to all peers. Without knowing the actual private data, all peers on the channel can be involved in transaction validation in a consistent way.

4. Finally, authorized peers check the collection policy to make sure the client has permission to access the private data. If authorized peers don't have private data in the local transient data store, they will pull data from other authorized peers to get the private data.

5. Once the private data is validated against the hashes in the public block, the transaction will be committed in the block. The private state database and private `writeSet` storage in authorized peers will get updated. The private data in the transient data store then gets deleted.

You now understand how private data works. Before moving to the next new v2 features, let's quickly review how private data collection is defined. Here is a sample collection definition JSON file:

```
[
  {
    "name": "ORG12-PD",
    "policy": "OR('Org1MSP.member', 'Org2MSP.member')",
    "requiredPeerCount": 1,
    "maxPeerCount": 3,
    "blockToLive": 1000000,
"memberOnlyRead": true,
"memberOnlyWrite": true
  },
  {
    "name": " ORG23-PD ",
    "policy": "OR('Org2MSP.member', 'Org3MSP.member')",
    "requiredPeerCount": 1,
    "maxPeerCount": 3,
    "blockToLive": 0,
"memberOnlyRead": true
  ]
```

The file contains two private data collection definitions. In each one, we need to specify the collection name. Table 9-1 shows the keyword definitions of the JSON configuration.

Table 9-1. Keywords in a private data configuration

Keyword	Definition
name	The name of the collection.
policy	Defines which organizations' peers are authorized to operate on collection data.
requiredPeer Count	A minimum number of peers must successfully disseminate private data.
maxPeerCount	For data redundancy purposes, when maxPeerCount is larger than requiredPeerCount, and an endorsing peer becomes unavailable between endorsement time and commit time, any peers that haven't received private data yet can pull it from other peers that are participating in the process.
blockToLive	Defines how long the data should live on the private database in terms of blocks.
memberOnly Read	Defines how long the data should live on the private database in terms of blocks; memberOnlyRead defines the client

When using the peer CLI to approve and commit the chaincode definition, you can use the `--collections-config` flag with a collection definition file similar to the following:

```
peer lifecycle chaincode commit --collections-config path/
collections_config.json
```

To read or write private data, we can use a shim API. For example, we can use `PutPri vateData(collection,key,value)` to store private data in private `writeSet` storage and `GetPrivateData(collection,key)` to query private data.

External Chaincode Launcher

Prior to Hyperledger Fabric v2, the process of chaincode maintenance was quite complex and cumbersome. Being in a decentralized environment, maintenance is a real challenge. In most cases, the code is required to be installed by a number of peers in the multiorganization consortium network.

Here's a rundown of some of the Hyperledger v1 limitations:

- The process used to build and launch chaincode was part of the peer implementation. To customize the process, you had to change the source code and rebuild the chaincode.

- All chaincode installed on the peer was built by passing a hardcoded language-specific logic. For example:

```
peer chaincode install -n mychannel -l golang
```

- This build process required Docker as the part of the deployment environment. The process would generate a Docker container image for executing chaincode in a Docker container. The client could connect to the peer through the container.
- To build and launch chaincode, peers needed the privileges to access a Docker daemon, which could cause issues in production environments.

To enhance the development and deployment process, v2 comes with external builders and launchers whose functions are to empower operators to optimally customize the building process in such a way that chaincode can be deployed and executed independently (outside the Fabric system). This opens up further opportunities to deploy other popular container systems like Kubernetes pods.

Before this update, the chaincode in different languages like Java and Node.js needed to be compiled and built into a chaincode binary, then packaged with the Go shim libraries for creating a chaincode server. Now the Go shim API can be packaged to become independent of a chaincode server. The user chaincode can be packaged independently and run as an external service and connected to the chaincode server through the chaincode ID, server endpoint address, TLS information, and so forth.

This loose coupling module design provides a flexible way to run in a cloud service–based environment like Kubernetes. The Hyperledger Fabric external builders and launchers are loosely based on Heroku buildpacks. To leverage external builders and launchers, you will need to create your own buildpack and then modify the `external Builder` configuration in the peer *core.yaml*. If no configured external builder is specified, Fabric will use the standard Fabric packaging tools, such as the peer CLI or node SDK. Let's explore this in more detail.

Buildpacks are sets of open source scripts that are responsible for transforming deployed code into the target environment. Depending on the programming language chosen, the scripts will examine your apps, download related dependencies, and determine how to configure the application chaincode to communicate with the bound chaincode server.

An external builder and launcher repository contains the following four scripts in the *bin* directory:

The first script is the *detect* script. This script determines whether the buildpack should apply to build the chaincode package and launch it. The peer invokes *detect* with two arguments: `CHAINCODE_SOURCE_DIR` is the location for the chaincode source, and `CHAINCODE_METADATA_DIR` is the directory for the *metadata.json* file from the chaincode package installed to the peer.

Fabric runs the *detect* script to determine whether the chaincode source package should be applied based on return values. So if the script returns a value of 0, it should apply the chaincode source package; conversely, it takes no action when the script returns nonzero values.

Here is an example of a simple *detect* script for Go chaincode:

```bash
#!/bin/bash

if [ $# -ne 2 ]; then
    echo "Expected 2 input got $#"
    exit 1
fi


CHAINCODE_METADATA_DIR="$2"

if [ "$(jq -r .type "$CHAINCODE_METADATA_DIR/metadata.json" | tr '[:upper:]'
'[:lower:]')" = "golang" ]; then
    exit 0
fi


exit 1
```

This script uses jq, a lightweight command-line JSON processor, to check whether the chaincode language is Go and that at least two arguments are passed when running the script.

The second script is *build*. This script executes the buildpack logic and converts the chaincode package into executable chaincode.

The peer invokes *build* with three arguments:

```
bin/build SOURCE_DIR METADATA_DIR BUILD_OUTPUT_DIR
```

The following is an example of a simple *build* script for Go chaincode:

```bash
#!/bin/bash

if [ $# -ne 3 ]; then
    echo "Expected 3 input got $#"
    exit 1
fi

SOURCE_DIR="$1"
METADATA_DIR="$2"
OUTPUT_DIR="$3"

# extract package path from metadata.json
GO_PACKAGE="$(jq -r .path "$METADATA_DIR/metadata.json")"
if [ -f "$SOURCE_DIR/src/go.mod" ]; then
    cd "$SOURCE_DIR/src"
    go build -v -mod=readonly -o "$BUILD_OUTPUT_DIR/chaincode" "$GO_PACKAGE"
else
    GO111MODULE=off go build -v  -o "$BUILD_OUTPUT_DIR/chaincode" "$GO_PACKAGE"
fi
```

```
# save statedb index metadata to provide at release
if [ -d "$SOURCE_DIR/META-INF" ]; then
cp -a "$SOURCE_DIR/META-INF" "$OUTPUT_DIR/"
```

Fabric runs the *build* script. If the script returns the success code 0, the contents of BUILD_OUTPUT_DIR will copy to peer persistent storage; otherwise, the build step should be considered a failure.

The third script is *release*. This script provides metadata to the peer, indicating how the chaincode should be executed.

The fourth script is *run*. This script runs the chaincode.

To implement the external builder, you can create your own external builder directory within the *bin* subfolder. Then create all four scripts under that directory:

```
external-builder/bin
detect
build
run
release
```

To ensure that the peer picks up the external builder, you need to add external Builder information at the peer's *core.yaml*. We can check the *fabric-samples* folder (*/path/fabric-samples/config*) to see *core.yaml*. The default externalBuilders section is an empty array []. You can update the externalBuilders section with the required information. The following example defines one external builder:

```
externalBuilders:
    - path: /path-to-external-builder/external-builder
      name: externalBuilders-sample
      environmentWhitelist:
          - GOPROXY
          - GONOPROXY
          - GOSUMDB
          - GONOSUMDB
          - GOCACHE
          - GOPATH
          - GOROOT
          - HOME
          - XDG_CACHE_HOME
```

In this example, we define externalBuilders-sample, which has an *external-builder* script under */path-to-external-builder/external-builder*.

The environment allow list contains the values that will propagate only when the peer invokes the build scripts.

If the external builder scripts contain commands that are not included under the *hyperledger/fabric-peer* Docker image (for example, the *jq* library in our example), then you need to build your own peer image.

The Fabric Docker images are available at *https://github.com/hyperledger/fabric.git*, so you can clone and modify the Docker image in your own environment. Under the *fabric/images/peer* folder, you can update the peer Dockerfile. For example, you can add the jq command as follows:

```
RUN apk add --no-cache tzdata jq
```

Once you update the Dockerfile, you can build a new peer image with a new name— for example:

```
docker build -t fabric-peer:2.1.0-external-builder
```

Once an image is built successfully, it will include *jq*.

Since the peer Docker image has been updated, you need to update the related peer Docker Compose file. The following example shows the peer section in this file:

```
peer0.org2.example.com:
    container_name: peer0.org2.example.com
    image: fabric-peer:2.1.0-external-builder
    environment:
    volumes:
        - peer0.org2.example.com:/var/hyperledger/production
        - /path../external-builder:/etc/hyperledger/external-builder
```

After this step, you can start a Fabric network with new peer images. You can run external builders and launchers.

State Database Cache for CouchDB

Fabric supports two peer state databases: LevelDB and CouchDB. The default state database embedded in the peer node is LevelDB.

LevelDB is an open source, on-disk, fast key-value store. *CouchDB* is a document storage NoSQL database. It can store data in the flexible document-based struct (JSON format) and supports powerful data mapping that allows rich queries that combine and filter information. You can create indexes to support rich queries.

Prior to Fabric v2, when using the external CouchDB state database, the query would cross the network to get results during the endorsement and validation phases. This caused a performance bottleneck. With Fabric v2, the state data caches in peers. Instead of expensive lookups, Fabric queries and reads the state data from the local cache to fetch results. This can greatly improve the performance of your network.

To set up cache size, update the peer *core.yaml* `cacheSize` property. The following is an example of a *core.yaml* CouchDB configuration under the `ledger -> state` section:

```
ledger:
  state:
    stateDatabase: CouchDB
    totalQueryLimit: 100000
    couchDBConfig:
      couchDBAddress: 127.0.0.1:5984
      username:
      password:
      maxRetries: 3
      maxRetriesOnStartup: 10
      requestTimeout: 35s
      internalQueryLimit: 1000
      maxBatchUpdateSize: 1000
      warmIndexesAfterNBlocks: 1
      createGlobalChangesDB: false
      cacheSize: 128
```

We first define the database as CouchDB. The default `totalQueryLimit` is 100000, regardless of whether the pagination APIs are utilized. `couchDBConfig` specifies a CouchDB-related configuration. When setting the optional `createGlobalChangesDB` flag to `true`, Fabric will synchronize the network state data changes and maintain the database, which requires additional system resources. The default is `false`. The `cacheSize` setting defines how state data will be allocated for in-memory storage, expressed in megabytes (MB). The `cacheSize` value needs to be a multiple of 32 MB, or Fabric will round the size to the next multiple of 32 MB. We can define 0 MB to disable the cache.

Alpine-Based Docker Images

Starting from release 2.0, the Hyperledger Fabric Docker image now builds based on security-oriented, lightweight *Alpine Linux*. This community-developed operating system is built around the *musl* libc and BusyBox. It is widely adopted in cloud, microservices, and container environments because of its small image size.

BusyBox is a single executable file that provides many tiny versions of common Unix utilities. It runs in a variety of Portable Operating System Interface (POSIX) environments such as Linux, Android, and FreeBSD. With a modular, size-optimized, and limited resource design, BusyBox is fairly easy to customize for any small or embedded system.

musl is a C implementation for standard library functionality described in the ISO C and POSIX standards. By using static linking in *musl*, applications are able to fetch essential code or data to operate, which in turn leads to more efficient application deployment. *musl* integrates the entire standard library implementation, including threads, math, and the dynamic linker itself into a single shared object. This eliminates most of the startup time and memory overhead of dynamic linking.

With the *musl* libc and BusyBox, Alpine's size is typically around 8 MB; it is quite small compared to a minimal disk installation, which might be around 130 MB. This results in a faster boot time for the operating system, which is heavily used in containers. All Userland (user space) binaries are compiled as Position Independent Executables (PIE) with stack smashing protection in Alpine Linux, making it very secure.

Let's take a look at the Docker images in Hyperledger Fabric 1.3 and 2.0—the Docker images with the latest tag and also different tagged versions of Docker images that will get downloaded as part of the Fabric binaries download. Table 9-2 shows the size of Docker images in Hyperledger Fabric 1.3.

Table 9-2. Docker images in Hyperledger Fabric 1.3

Package	Version	Size
hyperledger/fabric-ca	1.3.0-rel	244 MB
hyperledger/fabric-ca	Latest	244 MB
hyperledger/fabric-tools	1.3.0-rel	1.5 GB
hyperledger/fabric-tools	Latest	1.5 GB
hyperledger/fabric-ccenv	1.3.0-rel	1.38 GB
hyperledger/fabric-ccenv	Latest	1.38 GB
hyperledger/fabric-orderer	1.3.0-rel	145 GB
hyperledger/fabric-orderer	Latest	145 GB
hyperledger/fabric-peer	1.3.0-rel	151 MB
hyperledger/fabric-peer	Latest	151 MB
hyperledger/fabric-zookeeper	0.4.12	1.39 GB
hyperledger/fabric-zookeeper	Latest	1.39 GB
hyperledger/fabric-kafka	0.4.12	1.4 GB
hyperledger/fabric-kafka	Latest	1.4 GB
hyperledger/fabric-couchdb	0.4.12	1.45 GB
hyperledger/fabric-couchdb	Latest	1.45 GB

Next, let's take a look at Docker image sizes in Hyperledger Fabric v2, which are listed in Table 9-3.

Table 9-3. Docker images in Hyperledger Fabric v2

Package	Version	Size
hyperledger/fabric-javaenv	2.1.0-external-builder	56.9 MB
hyperledger/fabric-javaenv	None	895 MB
hyperledger/fabric-javaenv	None	1.12 GB
hyperledger/fabric-tools	3.10	5.58 MB
hyperledger/fabric-tools	2.0	505 MB
hyperledger/fabric-tools	2.0.1	505 MB
hyperledger/fabric-peer	Latest	505 MB
hyperledger/fabric-peer	2.0	512 MB
hyperledger/fabric-peer	2.0.1	512 MB
hyperledger/fabric-orderer	Latest	512 MB
hyperledger/fabric-orderer	2.0	57.2 MB
hyperledger/fabric-orderer	2.0.1	57.2 MB
hyperledger/fabric-ccenv	Latest	57.2 MB
hyperledger/fabric-ccenv	2.0	39.7 MB
hyperledger/fabric-ccenv	2.0.1	39.7 MB
hyperledger/fabric-baseos	Latest	39.7 MB
hyperledger/fabric-baseos	2.0	529 MB
hyperledger/fabric-baseos	2.0.1	529 MB
hyperledger/fabric-ca	Latest	529 MB
hyperledger/fabric-ca	2.0	6.9 MB
hyperledger/fabric-ca	2.0.1	6.9 MB

We can see that the image size is significantly reduced in v2—for example, *fabric-tools* in v1.3 is 1.5 GB, but only 512 MB in v2.

Sample Test Network

Prior to v2, *first-network* was the most common example used to demonstrate how Hyperledger Fabric works. In v2, a new Fabric test network is included in the *fabric-samples* repository, as the long-term replacement of the *first-network* sample.

Project structure

The v2 test network project structure is more organized. For instance, all Docker files are placed under the *docker* folder, and organization-related configuration is put under the *organizations* folder. The *scripts* folder contains smart contract installation- and deployment-related scripts. This makes the test network easy for testing applications and smart contracts. We have built a similar project structure in the Chapter 7 supply chain project. In the first network, most Docker files are under the root project folder, so there is no organization folder.

Peers and orgs

The test network defines one peer as two organizations, while the first network comes with two peers, and each peer has two organizations. Table 9-4 shows the peers and organizations in these two sample networks.

Table 9-4. Peers and organizations in the test and first networks

Test network	First network
peer0.org1.example.com	peer0.org1.example.com
peer0.org2.example.com	peer1.org1.example.com
	peer0.org2.example.com
	peer1.org2.example.com

Generating crypto material

In the first network, only Cryptogen is supported for generating crypto material. However, in the test network, crypto material can be generated either through Cryptogen or by the organization CA. Here is the script in the test network to handle these two types of crypto material:

```
function createOrgs() {
  # Create crypto material using cryptogen
  if [ "$CRYPTO" == "cryptogen" ]; then
echo "##### Generate certificates using cryptogen tool #########"
    ....
    cryptogen generate --config=./organizations/cryptogen/
crypto-config-org1.yaml --output="organizations"
    ...
    cryptogen generate --config=./organizations/cryptogen/
crypto-config-org2.yaml --output="organizations"
    ....
    cryptogen generate --config=./organizations/cryptogen/
crypto-config-orderer.yaml --output="organizations"
  fi
  # Create crypto material using Fabric CAs
  if [ "$CRYPTO" == "Certificate Authorities" ]; then
    echo "##### Generate certificates using Fabric CA's ###########"
    IMAGE_TAG=${CA_IMAGETAG} docker-compose -f $COMPOSE_FILE_CA up -d 2>&1
    . organizations/fabric-ca/registerEnroll.sh
    ....
    createOrg1
    createOrg2
    createOrderer
  fi

}
```

Since the test network supports using CAs for crypto material, this makes enrolling application users into the network easier.

Updating the Capability Level of a Channel

When upgrading to the latest 2.*x* release, we need to upgrade the Fabric channel and components in the channel—for example, orderer and peers. In this section, we discuss how to update the capability level of a channel.

Fabric enables capability levels in the configuration of each channel. These version capabilities need to be closely related to node binary versions. When a capability level is defined, it must be present in a Fabric binary. For example, when a new MSP type is added, newer binaries (v2) can validate those signatures of transactions, while older binaries (v1.*x*) may fail. This could lead to multiple versions of the Fabric binaries with different world states.

Three capabilities for an entire channel can be configured in the `capabilities` section of *configtx.yaml*.

The following is a sample configuration for capabilities for 2.*x* and 1.*x*:

2.*x*	1.*x*
Capabilities:	Capabilities:
• Channel: &ChannelCapabilities	• Channel: &ChannelCapabilities
— V2_0: true	— V1_4_3: true
• Orderer: &OrdererCapabilities	— V1_3: false
— V2_0: true	— V1_1: false
• Application: &ApplicationCapabilities	• Orderer: &OrdererCapabilities
— V2_0: true	— V1_4_2: true
	— V1_1: false
	• Application: &ApplicationCapabilities
	— V1_4_2: true
	— V1_3: false
	— V1_2: false
	— V1_1: false

Channel capabilities apply to both the peer organizations and the ordering service. The binary level of the ordering service and peers need to be at least the defined minimum level in order to process the capability. When `ChannelCapabilities V2_0` is set to `true`, it expects that all orderers and peers on a channel need to be at v2.0.0 or later.

Orderer capabilities apply only to the ordering service. Orderer capabilities don't involve peers or transaction processes, so when the ordererer fails, only the ordering service admins get impacted.

Application capabilities apply only to peers. In the case of private data, ordering service admins and channel administration are not involved in setting up private data between peer organizations, so we can enable these capabilities for only private data.

While defining the capability level in *configtx.yaml*, we also need to upgrade binaries to at least the level of the relevant capabilities; otherwise, binaries will crash, which may cause a ledger fork. Once a capability has been enabled, it is permanent and not reversible. Even after rolling back the configuration changes, the old binaries will not be able to participate in transactions of the channel.

> Prior to enabling capabilities in production, we recommend trying the new capabilities in a test environment to ensure the expected result.

Update to the Newest Capability Levels

When we start upgrading to v2, it becomes necessary to update to the newest capability depending on your own use case or requirement. Note that it may be necessary to update to the newest capability levels before using the features in the latest release, and it is considered a best practice to always be at the latest binary versions and capability levels. At a high level, this process has three steps (for each channel):

1. Retrieve the latest channel configuration.
2. Modify the necessary channel configuration.
3. Create a config update transaction.

Retrieve the latest channel config

Before you start to retrieve the channel config, you need to set up environment variables for your config update. The following variables need to be exported as environment variables:

CH_NAME
    The name of the system channel for updating

CORE_PEER_LOCALMSPID
    ID of orderer organization that proposes the channel update

`TLS_ROOT_CA`

The absolute path to the TLS certificate of your orderer node(s)

`CORE_PEER_MSPCONFIGPATH`

The absolute path to the MSP representing your organization

`ORDERER_CONTAINER`

The name of an orderer node container

Once we set up environment variables, we can pull the channel configuration in Protocol Buffers format, which is a method of serializing structured data, and create a file called *config_block.pb*.

In the peer container, you can issue the following command:

```
channel fetch config config_block.pb -o $ORDERER_CONTAINER -c $CH_NAME --tls
--cafile $TLS_ROOT_CA
```

Next, we'll convert the Protobuf file to a human-readable JSON file called *config_block.json*:

```
configtxlator proto_decode --input config_block.pb --type common.Block --output
config_block.json
```

Finally, use the jq command to remove all unnecessary metadata, and generate a new file (in this example, we'll call it *config.json*):

```
jq .data.data[0].payload.data.config config_block.json > config.json
```

Before starting to modify the JSON config file, we need to copy *config.json* as a new JSON file called *modified_config.json*. In a later step, we need to compare the differences between these two files and submit the changed configuration.

Run this command to copy *config.json*:

```
cp config.json modified_config.json
```

Modify the necessary channel config

In this step, you can open a text editor or other JSON tool like *jq* to modify the channel configuration to make all necessary changes. We define *capabilities.json* as a sample config and then add the capabilities to the `orderer` or `application` channel sections. Here is the *capabilities* config file:

```
{
    "channel": {
        "mod_policy": "Admins",
            "value": {
                "capabilities": {
                    "V2_0": {}
                }
            },
```

```
            "version": "0"
        },
        "orderer": {
            "mod_policy": "Admins",
                "value": {
                    "capabilities": {
                        "V2_0": {}
                    }
                },
            "version": "0"
        },
        "application": {
            "mod_policy": "Admins",
                "value": {
                    "capabilities": {
                        "V2_0": {}
                    }
                },
            "version": "0"
        }
    }
}
```

To add the orderer group capabilities to *modified_config.json*, issue this command:

```
jq -s '.[0] * {"channel_group":{"groups":{"Orderer": {"values":
{"Capabilities": .[1].orderer}}}}}'
config.json ./capabilities.json > modified_config.json
```

Similarly, to add the channel group capabilities to *modified_config.json*, issue this command:

```
jq -s '.[0] * {"channel_group":{"values": {"Capabilities": .[1].channel}}}'
config.json ./capabilities.json > modified_config.json
```

Three parts of the channel capability configurations can be updated:

- Orderer group
- Channel group
- Application group

The orderer group and channel group are similar to the orderer system channel. To add the application group capability, issue this command:

```
jq -s '.[0] * {"channel_group":{"groups":{"Application": {"values": {"Capabili-
ties": .[1].application}}}}}' config.json ./capabilities.json >
modified_config.json
```

> For incremental change, you need to repeat the three-step process per change.

Create a config update transaction

To update the JSON configuration file, we first need to run the `configtxlator` tool and submit a modified configuration. Then we convert the configuration from JSON format back to Protobuf format:

```
configtxlator proto_encode --input config.json --type common.Config
--output config.pb

configtxlator proto_encode --input modified_config.json --type common.Config
--output
modified_config.pb

configtxlator compute_update --channel_id $CH_NAME --original config.pb
--updated modified_config.pb
--output config_update.pb
```

With the `compute_update` command from the `configtxlator` tool, we get the calculated difference between the old config and the modified one. Next, we apply the changes to the config:

```
configtxlator proto_decode --input config_update.pb --type common.ConfigUpdate
--output
config_update.json

echo '{"payload":{"header":{"channel_header":{"channel_id":"'$CH_NAME'",
"type":2}},"data":{"config_update":'$(cat config_update.json)'}}}' | jq . >
config_update_in_envelope.json

configtxlator proto_encode --input config_update_in_envelope.json
--type common.Envelope --output
config_update_in_envelope.pb
```

Finally, we submit the config update transaction. The ordering service will convert it to a full channel configuration:

```
peer channel update -f config_update_in_envelope.pb -c $CH_NAME -o $ORDERER_CON-
TAINER --tls --cafile
$TLS_ROOT_CA
```

To enable channel and application capabilities, you can either bundle all changes at the same time or do it incrementally.

Upgrade Components

Upgrading a component to a newer version (including v2) in Hyperledger Fabric typically is a four-step process:

1. Back up the ledger and MSPs.
2. Upgrade the orderer binaries in a rolling fashion to the latest Fabric version.
3. Upgrade the peer binaries in a rolling fashion to the latest Fabric version.
4. Update the orderer system channel and any application channels to the latest capability levels.

For native deployments, you will also need to back up the *orderer.yaml* or the *core.yaml* file and update the content with release artifacts including new port changes if required.

Set Environment Variables for the Binaries

To run a peer or an orderer node operation, you typically need to set environment variables relevant to Fabric CLI commands on each upgraded node. Here's a list of some of the peer environment variables, based on actual need; some of the variables are optional:

```
CORE_PEER_TLS_ENABLED=true
CORE_PEER_GOSSIP_USELEADERELECTION=true
CORE_PEER_GOSSIP_ORGLEADER=false
CORE_PEER_PROFILE_ENABLED=true
CORE_PEER_TLS_CERT_FILE=/etc/hyperledger/fabric/tls/server.crt
CORE_PEER_TLS_KEY_FILE=/etc/hyperledger/fabric/tls/server.key
CORE_PEER_TLS_ROOTCERT_FILE=/etc/hyperledger/fabric/tls/ca.crt
CORE_PEER_ID=peer0.org1.example.com
CORE_PEER_ADDRESS=peer0.org1.example.com:7051
CORE_PEER_LISTENADDRESS=0.0.0.0:7051
CORE_PEER_CHAINCODEADDRESS=peer0.org1.example.com:7052
CORE_PEER_CHAINCODELISTENADDRESS=0.0.0.0:7052
CORE_PEER_GOSSIP_BOOTSTRAP=peer0.org1.example.com:7051
CORE_PEER_GOSSIP_EXTERNALENDPOINT=peer0.org1.example.com:7051
CORE_PEER_LOCALMSPID=Org1MSP
```

Here's a list of some of the orderer environment variables. Again, some of the variables are optional:

```
ORDERER_GENERAL_LISTENADDRESS=0.0.0.0
ORDERER_GENERAL_GENESISMETHOD=file
ORDERER_GENERAL_GENESISFILE=/var/hyperledger/orderer/orderer.genesis.block
ORDERER_GENERAL_LOCALMSPID=OrdererMSP
ORDERER_GENERAL_LOCALMSPDIR=/var/hyperledger/orderer/msp
ORDERER_GENERAL_TLS_ENABLED=true
```

```
ORDERER_GENERAL_TLS_PRIVATEKEY=/var/hyperledger/orderer/tls/server.key
ORDERER_GENERAL_TLS_CERTIFICATE=/var/hyperledger/orderer/tls/server.crt
ORDERER_GENERAL_TLS_ROOTCAS=[/var/hyperledger/orderer/tls/ca.crt]
ORDERER_GENERAL_CLUSTER_CLIENTCERTIFICATE=/var/hyperledger/orderer/tls/
server.crt
ORDERER_GENERAL_CLUSTER_CLIENTPRIVATEKEY=/var/hyperledger/orderer/tls/server.key
ORDERER_GENERAL_CLUSTER_ROOTCAS=[/var/hyperledger/orderer/tls/ca.crt]
```

Back Up and Restore the Ledger

A ledger backup can reduce time and computational costs when restarting nodes and bootstrapping from the genesis block and reprocessing all transactions. The process may take quite a long time if the size of the ledger is large.

We can back up ledger data in two ways:

- Create a new peer to join the same channel. The new node will synchronize with the network and rebuild its ledger by initiating the genesis block and state DB for all joined channels.
- Log in to the peer node as the peer admin, stop the peer, and then go to the peer data folder. By default, peer data is stored under */var/hyperledger/production/*. Back up folders such as *chaincodes*, *ledgersData*, and *transientStore*. Some subfolders under *ledgersData* (including *stateLeveldb*, *historyLeveldb*, and *chains/index*) can be ignored to reduce the storage demand for the backup, but reconstructing them will take more time when peer starts.

Upgrade the Orderer Nodes

You should upgrade orderer nodes in a rolling fashion (one at a time). Before upgrading orderer nodes, we need to set up the following environment variables:

- `ORDERER_CONTAINER`
- `LEDGERS_BACKUP`: the location of the local filesystem where the ledger data will be backed up
- `IMAGE_TAG`: the Fabric version you are upgrading to

The process to upgrade the orderer node typically follows these steps:

1. Stop the orderer node and run this docker CLI command:

   ```
   docker stop $ORDERER_CONTAINER
   ```

2. Back up the ledger and MSP in the orderer node. Remember that the default orderer nodes data is located under */var/hyperledger/production/orderer*:

   ```
   docker cp $ORDERER_CONTAINER:/var/hyperledger/production/orderer/ ./
   $LEDGERS_BACKUP/$ORDERER_CONTAINER
   ```

3. Delete the orderer node container:

```
docker rm -f $ORDERER_CONTAINER
```

4. Start a new orderer node container with the newer version image tag:

```
docker run -d -v /opt/backup/$ORDERER_CONTAINER/:/var/hyperledger/
production/orderer/ \
            -v /opt/msp/:/etc/hyperledger/fabric/msp/ \
            --env-file ./env<name of node>.list \
            --name $ORDERER_CONTAINER \
            hyperledger/fabric-orderer:$IMAGE_TAG orderer
```

5. Repeat this process for each node of the ordering service until the entire ordering service has been upgraded.

Upgrade the Peers

Similar to upgrading the orderer nodes, peer upgrading should be done in a rolling fashion. Before upgrading the peer nodes, we need to set up the following environment variables:

- PEER_CONTAINER
- LEDGERS_BACKUP
- IMAGE_TAG

The process to upgrade the peer node is as follows:

1. Stop the peer with the following command and then bring down the peer:

```
docker stop $PEER_CONTAINER
```

2. Back up the peer's ledger and MSP:

```
docker cp $PEER_CONTAINER:/var/hyperledger/production ./$LEDGERS_BACKUP/
$PEER_CONTAINER
```

3. Remove the chaincode containers and images:

```
//remove chaincode containers

CC_CONTAINERS=$(docker ps | grep dev-$PEER_CONTAINER | awk '{print
$1}') if [ -n "$CC_CONTAINERS" ] ;
then docker rm -f $CC_CONTAINERS ; fi

//remove chaincode images
CC_IMAGES=$(docker images | grep dev-$PEER | awk '{print $1}') if [ -n
"$CC_IMAGES" ] ; then docker rmi
-f $CC_IMAGES ; fi
```

4. Remove the peer container:

```
docker rm -f $PEER_CONTAINER
```

5. Start a new peer container by using the relevant image tag and issuing the following command:

```
docker run -d -v /opt/backup/$PEER_CONTAINER/:/var/hyperledger/
production/ -v
/opt/msp/:/etc/hyperledger/fabric/msp/ --env-file ./env<name of
node>.list --name $PEER_CONTAINER
hyperledger/fabric-peer:$IMAGE_TAG peer node start
```

Once the peer node starts, you can issue the chaincode invocation and query to verify that the peer functions upgraded normally.

Upgrade the Node SDK Clients

Upgrading the node SDK client follows a regular npm upgrade; you issue a Node.js `npm install` command under the project root directory containing the *package.json* file. Issue this command to upgrade to the latest Fabric client and Fabric CA client:

```
$ npm install fabric-client@latest
```

```
$ npm install fabric-ca-client@latest
```

Considerations for Moving to V2

We have reviewed new features in v2; Hyperledger Fabric supports rolling upgrades from v1.4.*x* to v2.0 without downtime. When upgrading from v1.4.*x* to v2.2, we need to consider many factors.

Chaincode Life Cycle

As you learned earlier, Hyperledger Fabric v2 decentralized governance for the chaincode life cycle requires that multiple organizations agree to the parameters of the chaincode and approve how it will be operated on the channel. When peers participate in the new chaincode process, the peers and orderer nodes must be at v2.*x*; otherwise, the peer will crash after the channel capability has been enabled. This requires that all peers first be upgraded on the channel before enabling channel capability. Once channel capability is enabled, we enable application capability to `V2_0` on a channel.

To package, install, approve, and commit new chaincodes on the channel, we must use the Hyperledger Fabric v2 chaincode life-cycle operation. Since the release of the new decentralized governance chaincode life cycle, the endorsement policy needs to be updated in the channel configuration (e.g., a `MAJORITY` of organizations).

Chaincode Shim Changes (Go Chaincode Only)

If your chaincode is written in Go, the *fabric-chaincode-go/shim* libraries need an upgrade to the 2.*x* version before making upgrades to the peers and channels. The best practice approach is to vendor (or manage) the shim in your v1.4 Go chaincode.

Many tools are available for vendoring shim dependencies. One of the popular tools is `govendor`, a Go package dependency management command-line tool. This tool will flatten out all the project dependencies and import dependencies from your `GOPATH`. The following demonstrates how to use `govendor`:

```
clone and cd to the Fabric repository to your $GOPATH/src/github.com/
hyperledger directory
govendor init
govendor add +external  // Add all external package, or
govendor add github.com/external/pkg // Add specific external package
```

This imports the external dependencies into a local vendor directory.

If you do not want to vendor the shim in your v1.4 chaincode, you have two options:

- Upgrade the chaincode on all peers and on the channel.
- Set up peer environment variables to specify the v1.4 chaincode, including new packages in chaincode. Use v1.4 *ccenv* to rebuild the chaincode images; the v1.4 *ccenv* should still work with a v2.*x* peer.

Chaincode Logger (Go Chaincode Only)

In v1.4, the shim provides logging objects for the chaincode to use via the `NewLogger` API, which allows the chaincode to control the severity level; this has been removed in v2. The chaincode logs in the peer and orderer use the log API library under *common/flogging*. This package supports the following:

- Various levels of control for logging, based on the severity of the message
- Logging control based on the application logger generating the message
- Various log message formatting options, including pretty-printing format message support

You can set up the `FABRIC_LOGGING_SPEC` environment variable to specify the logging levels.

The full logging-level specification is of the following form:

```
[<logger>[,<logger>...]=]<level>[:[<logger>[,<logger>...]=]<level>...]
```

Peer Databases Upgrade

When upgrading peer components to 2.*x*, you should also upgrade the peer database to the new version. The data format in v2.*x* is different from the earlier format. The databases of all peers including the state database, historical database, and other internal databases for the peer must be rebuilt.

For the peer database upgrading process, you can perform the `peer node upgrade-dbs` command to drop the local database volume directory. Before doing it, you should back up the peer data. Set up the peer container and ledger environment first; then run the following Docker command:

```
set the PEER_CONTAINER and LEDGERS_BACKUP environment variables
docker run --rm -v /opt/backup/$PEER_CONTAINER/:/var/hyperledger/production/ \
           -v /opt/msp/:/etc/hyperledger/fabric/msp/ \
           --env-file ./env<name of node>.list \
           --name $PEER_CONTAINER \
           hyperledger/fabric-peer:2.x peer node upgrade-dbs
```

The peer node will rebuild the databases by using the v2.*x* data format after it restarts. Rebuilding the database could take a while, depending on the data volumes of your databases.

Capabilities

In "Updating the Capability Level of a Channel" on page 233, we noted that three new capabilities are introduced in the v2 release:

- Channel capabilities
- Application capabilities
- Orderer capabilities

Before updating the application and channel capabilities, you need to upgrade your peer binaries to newer binaries (v2). Also, upgrade your orderer binaries before updating the orderer and channel capabilities; otherwise, the old binaries (v1.*x*) may fail. The failure could lead to multiple versions of the Fabric binaries with different world states.

Define orderer node endpoint per organization

It is a best practice to define the orderer endpoints in both the system channel and in all application channels by adding new `OrdererEndpoints`.

If you haven't included `OrdererEndpoints` per organization, you can create an endpoints config JSON file. The process to define and update orderer node endpoints per organization is as follows:

1. Create an orderer endpoint config JSON file (for example, *newOrdererEndpoint-Conf.json*):

```
{
  "OrdererEndpoint": {
    "Endpoints": {
      "mod_policy": "Admins",
      "value": {
        "addresses": [
          "127.0.0.1:30000"
        ]
      }
    }
  }
}
```

2. Export the environment variables. Once you create an OrdererEndpoint JSON file, you can start using the command line to update the orderer endpoint configuration. Before doing that, as usual, we need to set up environment variables as follows:

CH_NAME
> The updated name of the system channel

CORE_PEER_LOCALMSPID
> ID of one of the orderer organizations that proposes the channel update

TLS_ROOT_CA
> The absolute path to the TLS certificate of your orderer node(s)

CORE_PEER_MSPCONFIGPATH
> The absolute path to the MSP representing your organization

ORDERER_CONTAINER
> The name of an orderer node container

ORGNAME
> The name of the organization you are currently updating

3. Pull and translate the config and add the life-cycle organization policy (as listed in *orglevelEndpoints.json*) to *modified_config.json* by issuing the following command:

```
jq -s ".[0] * {\"channel_group\":{\"groups\":{\"Orderer\": {\"groups\":
{\"$ORGNAME\": {\"values\":.[1].${ORGNAME}Endpoint}}}}}" config.json
./ newOrdererEndpoinConf.json > modified_config.json
```

4. Finally, submit the config. This will define the orderer endpoints in your system channel and application channels.

Summary

In this chapter, we discussed the important new features of Hyperledger Fabric v2. We explored how to upgrade the components and the capability level of a channel. By showing the detailed upgrading steps, you have a better understanding of the upgrading process of the peer and orderer services.

It is a best practice to consider upgrading to a newer major release version and reap the benefits of important new features. We discussed the many significant factors you need to consider when changing to the v2 release from 1.*x*. Throughout this chapter, you gained lots of practical knowledge for smart contract development with Hyperledger Fabric v2. The next chapter provides an overview of other new Hyperledger projects.

## CHAPTER 10

Overview of Other Hyperledger Projects

In Chapter 2, we briefly reviewed 16 Hyperledger projects and tools and discussed the design philosophy, core components, and architecture of the Hyperledger ecosystem. In this chapter, we will continue our journey by delving into some of these projects in more detail.

This chapter will help you achieve the following practical goals:

- Building a decentralized identity management system with Hyperledger Aries
- Running off-chain transaction processing with Hyperledger Avalon
- Using Hyperledger Besu as an open source Ethereum client to bring public blockchain to the enterprise
- Building and managing supply chain solutions with Hyperledger Grid

Hyperledger Avalon addresses blockchain scalability and privacy challenges through trusted off-chain processing. By exploring Hyperledger Besu modular architecture, you will learn how this open source Ethereum client brings public blockchain to the enterprise. As a platform to build supply chain solutions, Hyperledger Grid allows developers to choose the best reusable components, frameworks with existing distributed ledger platform software, and business-specific applications.

Hyperledger Aries

As we discussed in Chapter 2, the *Hyperledger Aries* library is an infrastructure of interoperable tools for blockchain-rooted, peer-to-peer interactions. It includes a shared cryptographic wallet for blockchain clients, a decentralized identifier (DID) communications protocol for allowing off-ledger interactions among those clients, and key management technologies. A *shared cryptographic wallet* is a multisignature wallet that can be accessed by two or more users. Sending a transaction requires at least one "cosigner" of the wallet to be authorized by using their private keys.

Aries grew out of work on Hyperledger Indy, which is an active DLT within the Hyperledger family. Increasing demand for standalone libraries that could manage identities and boost the security of Hyperledger DLTs like Fabric and Sawtooth led to the incubation of Hyperledger Ursa and Hyperledger Aries. As covered in Chapter 2, while Ursa is focused on boosting security in the Hyperledger network, the Aries library is used in conjunction with other Hyperledger DLTs like Fabric or Sawtooth to manage their member IDs in its decentralized architecture.

Aries provides both secure secret management and hardware security functionality that utilizes the cryptographic support provided by Ursa. Aries is a blockchain interface layer (known as a *resolver*) facilitating interoperability with other identity projects and is used to create, manage, and transmit digital credentials, while Indy provides a resolver implementation.

Aries supports these features:

- A blockchain resolver interface layer for supporting multiple blockchains and creating and signing blockchain transactions
- A digital wallet for secure data store with vetted credentials
- An encrypted messaging system for off-ledger communication between clients using multiple transport protocols
- An implementation of ZKP W3C verifiable credentials using the ZKP primitives found in Ursa
- An implementation of the decentralized key management system (DKMS) specification currently being incubated in Indy
- A mechanism to build higher-level protocols and API-like use cases based on the secure messaging functionality

Figure 10-1 shows the components in the Hyperledger Aries architecture.

By providing a blockchain resolver interface layer, Aries is the agent (client) part of a decentralized identity (ledger, DIDs, verifiable credentials). In the past, the Indy SDK initiated the decentralized identity. Aries can facilitate interoperability among other DID networks, such as Ethereum, Bitcoin, Hyperledger Fabric, and Sawtooth. With a pluggable resolver interface architecture, Aries provides opportunities for the open source community to build a dynamic set of capabilities to interact with a wide variety of use cases related to blockchain-based identity. Only minimal information is needed to establish trust, including public DIDs, schemas, and credential definitions. This is handled by ZKP in the agent. Aries provides a way to communicate data over secure channels between agents.

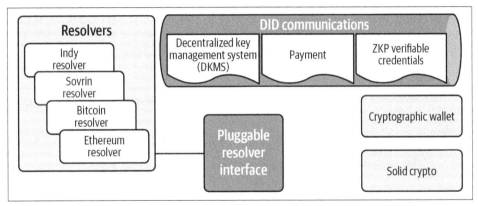

Figure 10-1. Components in the Hyperledger Aries architecture

In the current job market, an education background check is one of the critical processes used to confirm the education, training, or certification claims of candidates and identify any potential discrepancies. Aries can create, transmit, and store verifiable digital credentials (such as a college degree) to make this verification process more efficient. To demonstrate how Aries works, we will create the following two agents:

- Alice, who graduated from Faber College
- Faber College, which granted Alice's degree

Creating these agents requires two steps. First, Alice connects with the college and issues a credential about her degree. Second, Faber College will send a proof request to verify Alice's degree. To run this Aries demonstration on the local machine, we first need the following installed:

- Docker
- Docker Compose
- Git

To run this demo, we also use a *von-network* instance (a Hyperledger Indy public ledger sandbox) running in Docker locally. This instance implements an Indy ledger with four nodes.

Set Up the VON Network

Let's start by opening a bash terminal and cloning the *von-network* Git repo:

```
git clone https://github.com/bcgov/von-network
cd von-network
```

Once we clone the repo, we can start to build VON Network Docker images and start our VON Network by using the *./manage* bash script in the *von-network* folder. The script simplifies the process of building the images and brings up the network:

```
./manage build
./manage up
```

 The VON Network is a portable development-level Indy node network, which is part of the Verifiable Organizations Network (VON). The mission of VON is to build a network providing trustworthy data for organizations—locally and around the globe.

After the VON Network is up and running, you can view the node pool and ledger by visiting *http://your-machine-ip:9000* in your browser.

Run Hyperledger Aries Cloud Agent

Next, we will use Hyperledger Aries Cloud Agent Python (ACA-Py) to build and deploy two instances of the agents—one for Alice, the other for Faber College. ACA-Py is a foundation for building decentralized identity applications and services running in nonmobile environments.

Run this command to clone the ACA-Py repo and navigate to the *demo* folder:

```
git clone https://github.com/hyperledger/aries-cloudagent-python
cd aries-cloudagent-python/demo
```

Next, start the Faber agent by issuing the following command:

```
./run_demo faber
```

You should see agent terminals for Faber show their public DIDs, the schema and credential definition, and QR invitation code details.

Open another terminal window and navigate to the *demo* folder. Then issue the following command:

```
cd aries-cloudagent-python/demo
./run_demo alice
```

This brings up the Alice agent. With both agents starting, Alice is waiting for an input invitation from Faber.

Copy the Faber invitation JSON data from the Faber terminal and paste it at the Alice prompt. The agents will connect and then show a menu of options.

Once the connection is built between Alice and Faber, the Alice terminal will display a response with invitation key and DID information, as shown here:

```
Invitation response:
  {
    "their_label": "Faber.Agent",
    "invitation_key": "BLpHqGjjqPJ9NXz9wni8FVmcF74ue3LsXJBeyKV6ubTX",
    "request_id": "9b289bdb-7bd5-4804-baf1-794e66a70d60",
    "initiator": "external",
    "created_at": "2020-09-01 17:31:22.905350Z",
    "accept": "auto",
    "my_did": "MytrhNXxvaK3f5NX5ztFim",
    "updated_at": "2020-09-01 17:31:22.920279Z",
    "routing_state": "none",
    "invitation_mode": "once",
    "connection_id": "b4bddaea-f158-4910-825f-32acd0fc1ed0",
    "state": "request"
  }

Alice     | Connected
Connect duration: 0.21s
```

For Faber, we now have five options:

```
Faber | Connected
    (1) Issue Credential
    (2) Send Proof Request
    (3) Send Message
    (T) Toggle tracing on credential/proof exchange
    (X) Exit?
[1/2/3/T/X]
```

For Alice, we have three options:

```
Alice | Connected
    (1) Send Message
    (2) Input New Invitation
    (X) Exit?
```

Issue credentials

You can now test the credential exchange protocols by issuing and proving credentials from Faber. We don't need to do anything from the Alice agent. Her agent will
automatically receive credentials and respond to proof requests from the ACA-Py
demo code.

In the Faber terminal window, enter **1** to send a credential:

```
[1/2/3/T/X] 1

#13 Issue credential offer to X
Faber       | Credential: state = offer_sent, credential_exchange_id =
97a2124b-6464-4761-a7b0-
62fbc0236433
Faber       | Credential: state = request_received, credential_exchange_id =
97a2124b-6464-4761-a7b0-
```

```
62fbc0236433

#17 Issue credential to X
Faber        | Credential: state = credential_issued, credential_exchange_id =
97a2124b-6464-4761-a7b0-
62fbc0236433
Faber        | Credential: state = credential_acked, credential_exchange_id =
97a2124b-6464-4761-a7b0-
62fbc0236433
```

In the Alice terminal window, we will see this message:

```
Alice        | Credential: state = offer_received , credential_exchange_id =
e9bd52c1-364a-407d-b95b-
0e1bc1593c0a

#15 After receiving credential offer, send credential request
Alice        | Credential: state = request_sent , credential_exchange_id =
e9bd52c1-364a-407d-b95b-
0e1bc1593c0a
Alice        | Credential: state = credential_received , credential_exchange_id =
e9bd52c1-364a-407d-
b95b-0e1bc1593c0a
Alice        | Credential: state = credential_acked , credential_exchange_id =
e9bd52c1-364a-407d-b95b-
0e1bc1593c0a
Alice        | Stored credential b0030596-b025-4e95-804d-fcc6404c1788 in wallet

#18.1 Stored credential b0030596-b025-4e95-804d-fcc6404c1788 in wallet
```

After Faber issues a credential offer, Alice receives the credential. Then Alice sends
back a credential request. Faber receives Alice's message and acknowledges that Alice
has received the credential. Then Alice stores the credentials in her wallet.

Request a proof

To request a proof, enter **2** in the Faber terminal, and we will see this message:

```
[1/2/3/T/X] 2
#20 Request proof of degree from alice
Faber        | Presentation: state = request_sent , presentation_exchange_id =
6d8b4157-254f-45f2-8f52-
ca86f2ab536a
Faber        | Presentation: state = presentation_received , presenta-
tion_exchange_id = 6d8b4157-254f-
45f2-8f52-ca86f2ab536a

#27 Process the proof provided by X

#28 Check if proof is valid
Faber        | Presentation: state = verified , presentation_exchange_id =
6d8b4157-254f-45f2-8f52-
```

```
ca86f2ab536a
Faber      | Proof = true
```

The Alice terminal window will display the following message:

```
Presentation: state = request_received , presentation_exchange_id =
b6675e49-1ddd-4edf-872d-
e667fcf155f7

#24 Query for credentials in the wallet that satisfy the proof request

#25 Generate the proof

#26 Send the proof to X
Presentation: state = presentation_sent , presentation_exchange_id =
b6675e49-1ddd-4edf-872d-
e667fcf155f7
Presentation: state = presentation_acked , presentation_exchange_id =
b6675e49-1ddd-4edf-872d-
e667fcf155f7
```

We can see that after Faber sends a proof request, Alice receives a request and query for credentials in the wallet that satisfies the proof request. Then Alice generates the credential proof of degree and sends the proof back to Faber. Faber receives the proof provided by Alice and then starts to process and verify the proof.

Once the proof is verified, Faber will update and mark the proof as true to indicate it's verified. As we can see, proof is generated on Alice's side without exposing Alice's actual personal data.

Hyperledger Avalon

Blockchain is a decentralized encrypted database system. Every transaction processed by a node needs to broadcast to other nodes in the network. This behavior ensures that transactions are transparent and reflects the state of the ledger. In addition, the behavior will result in data resiliency, as many copies of this data exist across the nodes participating in the network. However, using this architecture comes at the cost of scalability with low throughput. Only a limited number of transactions in the blockchain can be processed.

The public blockchain is accessible to everyone, and every transaction can be traced back to the first genesis block. A cryptocurrency user uses their private key to access the blockchain and initiate blockchain transactions. The transaction data in blockchain is pseudo-anonymous; it is not possible to assign the data to a person without connecting to additional personal information (e.g., a digital identity). In certain applications (global trading, for example), keeping some sensitive company data confidential and logic encrypted is required, to prevent it from becoming vulnerable to corruption, stolen by competitors, or explored by outside entities frontrunning the competition.

The *Hyperledger Avalon* project was created to address scalability and privacy challenges. Through trusted off-chain computing, Avalon is used to maintain resiliency and integrity guarantees as much as possible while accomplishing additional scalability and privacy.

The core strategy to accomplishing scalability and ensuring that computation is done correctly and secretly is a trusted compute service that provides a trusted execution environment, zero-knowledge proof, and multiparty computation.

Trusted Execution Environment

Applications running in a *trusted execution environment* (*TEE*) can ensure strong data confidentiality. The Hyperledger Avalon TEE uses Intel's Software Guard Extensions (SGX). This extension to the x86 architecture has a set of security-related instruction codes to run applications in a completely isolated, secure manner. It is built into some modern Intel central processing units (CPUs). In SGX, user-level code will allocate private regions of memory, called *enclaves*. The application process is running at higher privilege levels, not only isolated from other applications on the same system, but also from the operating system and possible hypervisor. System administrators can't tamper with the application after it is started.

SGX data confidentiality brings significant benefits to the enterprise blockchain workloads and enhances a trustworthy link between off-chain and on-chain execution. SGX can handle accessing off-chain transaction resources and compute confidential data, trusted tokens, attested oracles, and more.

Zero-Knowledge Proofs

Zero-knowledge proofs (*ZKPs*) are mathematical methods that allow data to be verified without sharing or revealing that data. In a transaction using ZKPs, the basic roles are the prover and verifier. The *prover* needs to prove something based on a small piece of unlinkable information to the verifier, without telling the verifier anything else about that information. The verifier must verify that the prover is telling the truth.

A true ZKPs needs to prove three criteria:

Completeness
The statement from the prover is true and should eventually convince the honest verifier.

Soundness
If the statement is false, it cannot convince the verifier that the prover's statement is true.

Zero-knowledge
> If the statement is true, only the statement being proven is revealed.

A simple example that presents the fundamental ideas of ZKPs is *Where's Waldo*.[1] It has cryptography's favorite fictional characters, Alice and Bob. The objective of the *Where's Waldo* book series is to comb through the crowds of people to find Waldo.

Assume that Bob is the prover, and Alice is the verifier. Bob claims he has an algorithm that can find Waldo easily, but he wants to be paid to use his algorithm. Alice wants to buy it, but she wants to be sure that Bob is not lying and wants him to prove himself. As with many transactions, Alice and Bob don't fully trust each other.

Now, Bob needs proof his algorithm works. He points out the location of Waldo on the page. To make sure Bob's algorithm fully works, Alice selects other pages that also have Waldo. As Bob has the algorithm, he will always be able to find Waldo on the page that Alice gives to him. The more times Bob repeats this exercise, the more probable it is that Bob has an effective, fast algorithm.

In this example, the solutions fulfill the three properties of ZKP systems: completeness, soundness, and zero-knowledge:

Completeness
> As long as Bob is able to consistently find Waldo by using his algorithm, Bob's proof systems convince Alice that he can find Waldo.

Soundness
> Alice provides a random page of the scene to let Bob prove his algorithm, Bob's proof systems are truthful and do not let him cheat.

Zero-knowledge
> Bob proves to Alice that he has found Waldo without revealing his algorithm.

Multiparty Computation

Multiparty computation (*MPC*) is a cryptographic protocol that allows independent parties to jointly compute a shared result without revealing an individual party's data. Let's take a look at an average salary example to understand how MPC works.

Suppose Alice's salary is $50K and Bob's salary is $80K. Alice splits her salary into two randomly generated pieces: $20K and $30K, for example. Alice keeps $20K as a secret piece to herself and sends $30K to Bob. Similarly, Bob splits his salary into two randomly generated pieces: $10K and $70K. Bob keeps $70K as a secret piece to himself and sends $10K to Alice. Now Alice and Bob hold a set of values, as listed in Table 10-1.

---

1 *Where's Wally*, if you're reading this outside of North America.

Table 10-1. Divided salaries of Alice and Bob

	Alice	Bob
Total: $50K	$20K	$30K
Total: $80K	$10K	$70K

Alice and Bob know nothing about each other's salaries. They have no useful information from the other party's secret piece.

However, Alice and Bob can locally sum up their values. This will provide valuable information, as shown in Table 10-2. Then, the recombined sum divided by the number of participants yields an average salary of $65K.

Table 10-2. Combined salaries of Alice and Bob

	Alice	Bob
Total: $130K	$30K	$100K

Since MPC is complex, not many real-world projects use this technology. One well-known example is using the Sharemind MPC platform to perform research based on two private, secret, shared governmental databases; one 2015 project studied the correlation between working while attending college and failing to graduate on time.

Hyperledger Avalon Architecture

In Avalon, trusted workers (e.g., TEE, MPC, and ZKP workers) are hosted by a trusted compute service (TCS). Workers are set up by the TCS. The workers can create attestation verification that is signed by TEE SGX as attestation information. The attestation information can be published in the worker directory on the blockchain. In a TEE SGX worker case, worker attestation information is generated as an asymmetric signing/verification key pair. A requester can find the worker in the worker directory from the DLT and verifies and stores its attestation info.

A requester app or smart contract submits a work order request. The TCS receives and maintains a work order queue. By checking available workers, the TCS schedules the work orders for execution. During the work order execution stage, the trusted workers execute these work orders and record the work order response on the blockchain.

Figure 10-2 shows the Hyperledger Avalon high-level architecture.

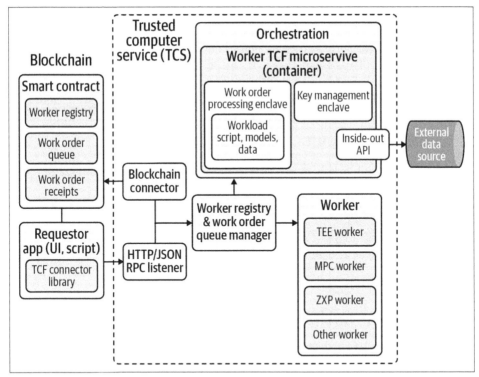

Figure 10-2. Hyperledger Avalon high-level architecture

The requestor can connect to TCS via two models: the proxy model and direct model. In the *proxy model*, a blockchain connector is used to connect requests from a smart contract (Ethereum) or chaincode (Fabric) running on the DLT. In this model, the blockchain is acting as a proxy. The *direct model* provides a JSON RPC API for passing requests submitted by requesters via a frontend UI or command-line tools.

In the middle tier, the work order queue manager will handle work order requests, delegate execution of the work orders to execution adaptors, and maintain work order queue size. The worker registry stores the list's trusted compute workers.

Between frontend and middleware components is the KV Storage Manager, a thin wrapper implemented on top of the Lightning Memory-Mapped Database (LMDB) that maintains the worker directory and work order queue.

In the worker TCF microservice component, the trusted worker executes application-specific workloads. Workloads can be either static, precompiled scripts, or scripts that are provided at runtime (e.g., Solidity or Python). Workload script logic is typically application related.

Hyperledger Besu

Hyperledger Besu, formerly known as *Pantheon*, is an open source Ethereum client designed to connect large enterprises with the public Ethereum blockchain. It is written in Java. Besu can be run on the Ethereum public network, private networks, and test networks such as Ropsten (proof-of-work testnet), Kovan (proof-of-authority testnet), Gorli (proof-of-authority testnet), and Rinkeby (proof-of-authority testnet).

As a basic Ethereum client, it has the following features:

- Connects to the blockchain network to synchronize blockchain transaction data or emit events to the network
- Processes transactions through smart contracts in an EVM environment
- Provides data storage for networks (blocks)
- Publishes a client API interface for developers to interact with the blockchain network

Hyperledger Besu Architecture

Figure 10-3 shows the high-level Hyperledger Besu architecture, which consists of three key layers.

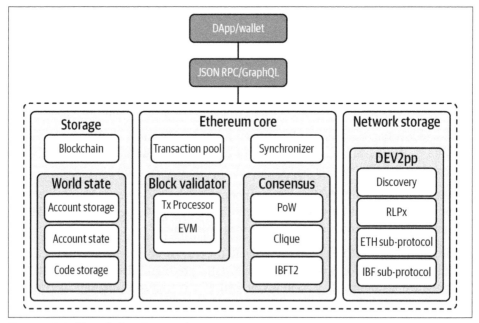

Figure 10-3. Hyperledger Besu architecture

Ethereum storage layer

The Ethereum Virtual Machine (EVM) is a powerful, Turing-complete virtual machine embedded within each full Ethereum node. Smart contracts will compile and deploy to EVM bytecode. EVM is responsible for executing contract bytecode within an Ethereum blockchain.

Besu implements proof-of-work (PoW) and proof-of-authority (PoA) consensus mechanisms via Ethash, Clique, and IBFT 2.0. As explained in Chapter 1, PoW is a consensus algorithm that relies on energy by solving a cryptographic puzzle. The puzzle is to find an input that produces a hash number with a certain number of leading zeros. The work of resolving the math problem is called PoW.

PoA is an algorithm that selects a limited number of trusted nodes. These nodes have proven their authority and are responsible for validating transactions, generating new blocks, and keeping the network working. Besu implements several PoA protocols, including Clique and IBFT 2.0.

Clique is a PoA blockchain consensus protocol. The blockchain runs the Clique protocol, maintaining the list of authorized signers. These approved signers validate transactions and blocks and take turns to create the next block without mining. Therefore, the transaction task is computationally light. When creating a block, a miner collects and executes transactions, updates the network state with the calculated hash of the block, and signs the block using their private key. By defining a period of time to create a block, Clique can limit the number of processed transactions.

IBFT 2.0 (Istanbul BFT 2.0) is a PoA Byzantine-fault-tolerant (BFT) blockchain consensus protocol. Transactions and blocks in the network are validated by authorized accounts, known as *validators*. Validators collect, validate, and execute transactions and create the next block. Existing validators can propose and vote to add or remove validators and maintain a dynamic validator set. The consensus can ensure immediate finality. As the name suggests, IBFT 2.0 builds upon the IBFT blockchain consensus protocol with improved safety and liveness. In the IBFT 2.0 blockchain, all valid blocks are directly added in the main chain, and there are no forks.

Storage layer

Besu uses a RocksDB database to store data locally. This data is divided into two parts:

Blockchain
    Blockchain data is composed of block headers and block bodies. Each block header contains sets of block metadata (the hash of the previous block, a timestamp, nonce, etc.) that is used to cryptographically verify blockchain state. Block bodies contain the list of ordered transactions included in each block.

World state

The world state is a database that holds the current value of the attributes of a business object that have been added, modified, or deleted by the set of validated and committed transactions in the blockchain. Every block header references a world state via a `stateRoot` hash. The world state is a mapping between addresses and account states. As a global state, it is constantly updated by transaction executions.

Network storage layer

Besu implements point-to-point (P2P) networking with Ethereum's DEVp2p network protocols for interclient communication and an additional subprotocol for IBFT 2.0. In the DEVp2p network, after the peer node's secure TCP connection is established, DEVp2p negotiates an application session between two connected peers. Each node will send another peer a greeting message with its own node ID, DEVp2p version, client name, and other node-related metadata. Then the nodes start transmitting application data packets over DEVp2p. DEVp2p nodes will periodically ping connected clients to ensure that their connected peers are still active. If a corresponding DEVp2p message is not received by a client within the maximum allowed idle time, the node connection will be closed.

Besu provides powerful user-facing APIs through mainnet Ethereum, and EEA JSON-RPC APIs over HTTP and WebSocket protocols, as well as a GraphQL API.

Besu's monitoring allows you to identify node and network issues. You can configure metrics and logging. Node performance is monitored by using the Prometheus Visual tool or the `debug_metrics` JSON-RPC API method. Network performance is monitored with Alethio tools such as Block Explorer and EthStats Network Monitor. You can also collect Besu log files to enable issue diagnosis.

Besu uses a private transaction manager, Orion, to implement privacy. Private transactions that were signed with the node private key are sent or received from the Besu node to the associated Orion node. Besu and Orion nodes both have public/private key pairs identifying them. Other parties cannot access the transaction content, sending party, or list of participating parties.

By enabling node permissioning and account permissioning, a permissioned network allows only specific nodes and accounts to access the network. Node permissioning is used to control connections between individual nodes. Account permissioning can limit which accounts a node can allow to perform the transactions, deny broken smart contracts, suspend accounts, and enforce onboarding or identity requirements.

Set Up Hyperledger Besu

To demonstrate how Hyperledger Besu works, we will run a private network example. It uses the Hyperledger Besu Docker image to run a private network of Besu nodes. To run this example, you must have the following installed:

- Docker
- Docker Compose
- Git
- cURL
- Node.js (version 10+)
- npm
- MetaMask

If you haven't installed Docker and Docker Compose yet, you can find the installation guide at the Docker official website. The Node.js site will give you instructions to install Node.js and npm.

MetaMask, an Ethereum wallet, is a Google Chrome browser plug-in. It can connect a blockchain network from Ethereum-based DApps. Users can invoke smart contracts to transfer coins, play games, and more. You can find the installation guide at the MetaMask site (*https://metamask.io*).

To start, we'll open a bash terminal and clone the *besu-sample-network* Git repo, and then navigate to the *besu-sample-networks* directory:

```
git clone https://github.com/ConsenSys/quorum-dev-quickstart
cd besu-sample-networks
```

Next, start the Besu sample network by running this command:

```
./run.sh
```

The script builds the images and creates a local private Besu network using Docker. The default consensus mechanism is Ethash; you can select other consensus mechanism by using -c <ibft2|clique|ethash> on your private network.

When the network starts, you should see a list of the running services in the terminal:

```
ubuntu@ip-172-31-72-58:~/besu-sample-networks$ sudo ./run.sh
*********************************
Sample Network for Besu at latest
*********************************
Start network
------------------
Starting network...
minernode uses an image, skipping
….
```

```
**********************************
Sample Network for Besu at latest
**********************************
List endpoints and services
--------------------------------
          Name                        Command
State                                 Ports
----------------------------------------------------------------------------
----------------------------------------------------------------------------
----
besu-sample-networks_bootnode_1    /opt/besu/bootnode_start.s ...   Up
(health: starting)   0.0.0.0:30303->30303/tcp, 0.0.0.0:30303->30303/udp, 8545/
tcp, 8546/tcp,

            8547/tcp
besu-sample-networks_explorer_1    /docker-entrypoint.sh ngin ...
Up                   0.0.0.0:25000->80/tcp
besu-sample-networks_grafana_1     /run.sh
Up                   0.0.0.0:3000->3000/tcp
besu-sample-networks_minernode_1   /opt/besu/node_start.sh -- ...   Up
(health: starting)   30303/tcp, 8545/tcp, 8546/tcp, 8547/tcp
besu-sample-networks_node_1        /opt/besu/node_start.sh -- ...   Up
(health: starting)   30303/tcp, 8545/tcp, 8546/tcp, 8547/tcp
besu-sample-networks_prometheus_1  /bin/prometheus --config.f ...
Up                   0.0.0.0:9090->9090/tcp
besu-sample-networks_rpcnode_1     /opt/besu/node_start.sh -- ...   Up
(health: starting)   30303/tcp, 0.0.0.0:8545->8545/tcp, 8546/tcp, 8547/tcp
```

You'll also see a list of the endpoints:

```
****************************************************************
JSON-RPC HTTP service endpoint      : http://localhost:8545
JSON-RPC WebSocket service endpoint : ws://localhost:8546
GraphQL HTTP service endpoint       : http://localhost:8547
Web block explorer address          : http://localhost:25000/
Prometheus address                  : http://localhost:9090/graph
Grafana address            : http://localhost:3000/d/XE4V0WGZz/besu-
overview?orgId=1&refresh=10s&from=now-30m&to=now&var-system=All
****************************************************************
```

JSON-RPC HTTP service endpoint

A JSON-RPC HTTP service endpoint is a lightweight remote procedure call (RPC) protocol that provides access to the Besu node service from a DApp client or cryptocurrency wallets such as MetaMask. You can run RPC requests on rpcnode by using a cURL command or other HTTP tools (for example, Postman).

Here is the command to submit a request to get the most recently mined block number. You will need to replace *<http-rpc-endpoint>* from *http://localhost:8545* with your machine IP address if you run from an external command-line terminal:

```
~/besu-sample-networks$ curl -X POST --data
'{"jsonrpc":"2.0","method":"net_peerCount","params":[],"id":1}' http://
3.237.17.164:8545
```

The response shows the most recently mined block:

```
{
  "jsonrpc" : "2.0",
  "id" : 1,
  "result" : "0x3"
}
```

JSON-RPC WebSocket

A JSON-RPC WebSocket service endpoint provides a web socket endpoint for a DApp client connected to the node service.

GraphQL HTTP service endpoint

GraphQL, a query language for the HTTP API, supports a runtime for executing queries with the existing data. It is in contrast to REST APIs that expose a suite of URLs, and each of these URLs exposes a single resource. You can connect the HTTP GraphQL node service from your DApp.

GraphQL is both a query language for your API and a server-side runtime for executing queries by using a type system you define for your data.

Web block explorer address

The web block explorer address is an online block explorer that displays the contents of individual blockchain transactions, blocks, the transaction histories, and balances of addresses.

You can access the explorer by entering the web block explorer address in the browser (Figure 10-4). It will display a summary of the private network.

Figure 10-4. Web block explorer address

In this example, the explorer indicates three peers: the one regular node, the mining node, and the bootnode. Click the block number (#1131) to display the block details (Figure 10-5).

Figure 10-5. Web block explorer block details

Prometheus address

Prometheus provides monitoring and alerting services for Besu node metrics. The data stored in Prometheus can be used in Grafana to visualize the collected data. The link for the Prometheus address can access the Prometheus dashboard.

Grafana address

The Grafana dashboard provides a visualization and analytics tool to monitor the Besu network connection, sync state, and block import rate along with CPU and memory usage statistics. The required data in Grafana comes from the Prometheus data store, which is exported directly from Besu.

With the Besu example network set up, we will now run a smart contract and DApp in the Besu test network. In this DApp example, we will use MetaMask to send transactions.

Set up MetaMask and account

Use the following steps to set up MetaMask:

1. Sign in to MetaMask.
2. In the MetaMask network list, select Custom RPC. Enter the JSON-RPC HTTP service endpoint: *http://your-machine-ip:8545*.
3. Save and return to the MetaMask main screen. MetaMask is now connected to the private network RPC node.
4. Create an account or use one of the following accounts provided by Besu for testing purposes. You can import an account into MetaMask using a private key:

```
Account 1 (Miner Coinbase Account)
Address: 0xfe3b557e8fb62b89f4916b721be55ceb828dbd73
Private key :
0x8f2a55949038a9610f50fb23b5883af3b4ecb3c3bb792cbcefbd1542c692be63
Initial balance : 0xad78ebc5ac6200000 (200000000000000000000 in decimal)
Account 2
Address: 0x627306090abaB3A6e1400e9345bC60c78a8BEf57
Private key :
0xc87509a1c067bbde78beb793e6fa76530b6382a4c0241e5e4a9ec0a0f44dc0d3
Initial balance : 0x90000000000000000000000
(2785365088392105618523029504 in decimal)
Account 3
Address: 0xf17f52151EbEF6C7334FAD080c5704D77216b732
Private key :
0xae6ae8e5ccbfb04590405997ee2d52d2b330726137b875053c36d94e974d162f
Initial balance : 0x90000000000000000000000
(2785365088392105618523029504 in decimal)
```

Figure 10-6 shows the screen in MetaMask where you import a private key.

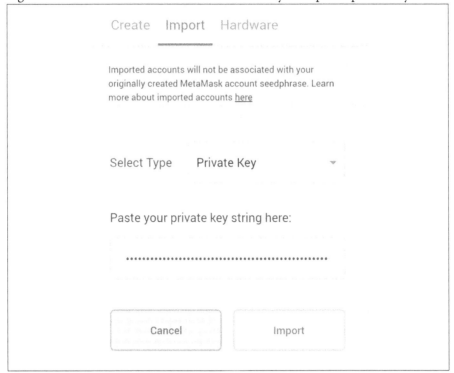

Figure 10-6. Importing a private key in MetaMask

MetaMask is a browser extension cryptocurrency wallet for accessing Ethereum blockchain. You can visit *metamask.io* to get more info.

Smart Contract and DApp in Hyperledger Besu Private Network

We will run the PetShop tutorial on the Truffle website in the Hyperledger Besu private network we just set up. PetShop is an adoption tracking system for a pet shop. Users can adopt a pet by sending ether tokens in the network.

The DApp requires you to install Truffle. For this setup, we use Truffle v5.0.15. Truffle is an end-to-end Ethereum DApp development tool that provides a development environment for writing, compiling, testing, and deploying smart contracts and DApps.

Open the command line and run the following:

```
npm install -g truffle
```

The PetShop source code for the smart contract and DApp are in the *pet-shop* folder:

```
~/besu-sample-networks/pet-shop$ ls
Dockerfile      box-img-sm.png  contracts  node_modules       package.json
test
box-img-lg.png  bs-config.json  migrations  package-lock.json  src
truffle-config.js
```

Run *./run-dapp.sh* in the *besu-sample-networks* directory to start the PetShop DApp:

```
~/besu-sample-networks$ sudo ./run-dapp.sh
```

The *run-dapp.sh* script runs npm install under the *pet-shop* folder, then uses the Truffle command to compile, migrate, and test the smart contract in sampleNetwork Wallet. If successful, it builds a container for the PetShop DApp and deploys it in *besu-sample-network*. The DApp container binds port 3001 on the system.

Once the DApp is up, you can open the browser by entering *http://your-machine-ip: 3001*, which should have PetShop running. If you click the Adopt button to adopt a pet, a MetaMask window should pop up and ask to confirm or reject the current adoption transaction (Figure 10-7).

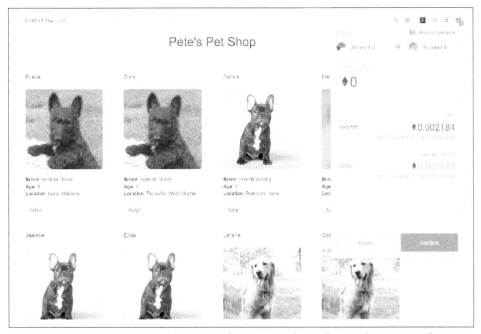

Figure 10-7. In this pet store DApp, note the MetaMask window in the upper right

After confirming the transaction, the status of the adopted pet will show Success. The MetaMask UI will keep a record of the confirmed transaction (Figure 10-8).

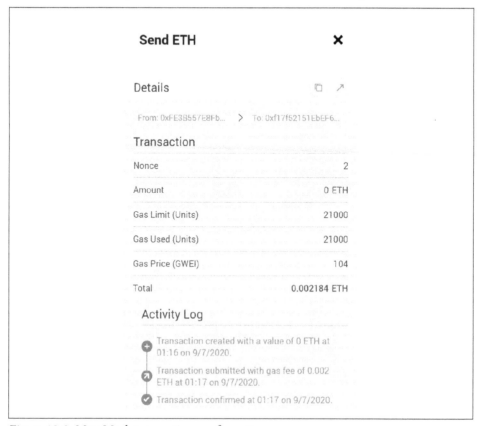

Figure 10-8. MetaMask transaction confirmation

We can also search the same transaction from the Block Explorer UI by entering the transaction hash to see the transaction detail (Figure 10-9).

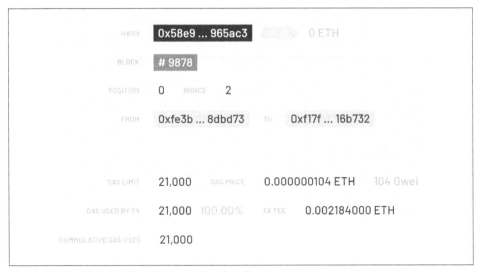

Figure 10-9. Block Explorer transaction detail

When all is completed, you can stop the private network and remove the containers:

```
~/besu-sample-networks$ sudo ./remove.sh
```

The command will shut down the private network and delete all containers and images created from running the sample network.

Hyperledger Grid

Since the blockchain is a transparent, immutable, and secure decentralized system, it enables participants to record every transaction within a supply chain; the ledger data is shared among all actors. Traditional supply chain industries using blockchain technology could improve the following areas:

- Tracking the assets from production to delivery, or through use by the end user in the entire chain
- Verifying and authenticating physical assets in the chain
- Ensuring that ledger data is immutable and shared among supply chain participants
- Providing better auditability

However, developing blockchains for supply chain applications is not an easy task, especially when building everything from scratch. The use case can contain a vast amount of information on everything from a product order, to delivery, to the number of parts contained within one item. A small bug could cause the entire supply chain application to be corrupted and worthless. Developing a full production-ready blockchain application is also time-consuming. The Hyperledger ecosystem doesn't have many reusable libraries, frameworks, domain models, or standard components that enable quickly creating supply chain solutions. This is what the *Hyperledger Grid* project is trying to solve.

Grid is a platform for building supply chain solutions that allows developers to choose the best reusable components, frameworks with existing distributed ledger platform software, and business-specific applications. Figure 10-10 shows the Hyperledger Grid platform stack.

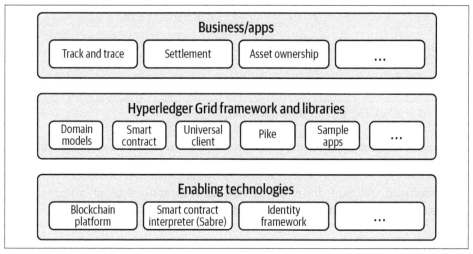

Figure 10-10. Hyperledger Grid platform stack

Grid's key components are domain models, a smart contract, a universal client, Pike, and sample apps.

Domain Models

Grid uses existing open standards such as GS1, Open Data Initiative, and Blockchain in Transit Alliance (BiTA) to implement domain-specific data models. GS1 provides a global standard business language to identify, capture, and share supply chain data—ensuring that key information about products, locations, assets, and more is accessible, accurate, and easy to understand. The best known of these standards is the barcode.

Smart Contracts

The smart contract builds business logic based on industry best practices, including product catalogs, product transformation, and batch behavior. It executes various business transactions in a decentralized way in the blockchain. The smart contracts are handled by the Sawtooth Sabre smart contract interpreter, which implements on-chain smart contracts in a WebAssembly virtual machine.

WebAssembly is an open standard inside the W3C WebAssembly Community Group. It defines a fast, efficient, and portable WebAssembly binary-code format for executable programs. The corresponding low-level textual assembly language is readable and debuggable. WebAssembly is designed to be secure, and its code is run in a safe, sandboxed execution environment. By taking advantage of common hardware capabilities, it provides interfaces for nicely facilitating interactions with other web technologies and maintains backward compatibility.

All Sawtooth Sabre objects are serialized using Protocol Buffers before being stored in state. These objects include namespace registries, contract registries, and contracts.

Pike

Pike is a smart contract that is designed to track agents and the organization's identity permissions in the supply chain. The Pike agent is a cryptographic public key, which contains role information representing an organization's relationships. These roles can be used to determine user access permission with a platform.

An agent has five attributes:

`public_key`
   An agent's unique cryptographic public key

`org_id`
   The agent's organization identifier

`active`
   The activity flag to indicate whether the agent is currently active at the organization

`roles`
   A list of roles the agent has with the organization

`metadata`
   A set of key-value data describing organization-specific information about the agent

Here is an example of a Pike agent:

```
message Agent {
    string org_id = 1;
    string public_key = 2;
    bool active = 3;
    repeated string roles = 4;
    repeated KeyValueEntry metadata = 5;
}

message KeyValueEntry {
    string key = 1;
    string value = 2;
}
```

PikePayload as a Pike transaction contains two parts: enumeration of action and transaction actions. The following Protocol Buffers code shows how to define Pike Payload:

```
message PikePayload {
    enum Action {
        ACTION_UNSET = 0;

        CREATE_AGENT = 1;
        UPDATE_AGENT = 2;

        CREATE_ORGANIZATION = 4;
        UPDATE_ORGANIZATION = 5;
    }

    Action action = 1;

    CreateAgentAction create_agent = 2;
    UpdateAgentAction update_agent = 3;

    CreateOrganizationAction create_org = 4;
    UpdateOrganizationAction update_org = 5;
}
```

SDK

Currently, Pike uses the Rust SDK to develop smart contracts. This SDK has three modules: permission, protocol, and protos. In the previous section, PikePayload is a protos module.

Sample Apps

Grid provides sample apps that can help demonstrate how to combine Grid components to build a supply chain application. The Grid Track and Trace example is the first showcase. This smart contract allows users to track goods, including a history of ownership and custodianship, as well as histories for a variety of properties such as temperature and location through a supply chain.

Summary

This chapter covered four members of the Hyperledger family: Hyperledger Aries, Hyperledger Avalon, Hyperledger Besu, and Hyperledger Grid. Specifically, we discussed how Aries works: it provides a blockchain interface layer, facilitates interoperability with other identity projects, and is used to create, manage, and transmit digital credentials. As a trusted compute framework, Avalon addresses blockchain scalability and privacy challenges through trusted off-chain processing. By exploring Besu modular architecture, you learned how this open source Ethereum client brings public blockchain to the enterprise. As a platform for building supply chain solutions, Grid allows developers to choose the best reusable components, frameworks with existing distributed ledger platform software, and business-specific applications.

Concluding Remarks

Throughout the course of this text, you have learned about all the aspects and facets to consider for developing and deploying an enterprise blockchain application using Hyperledger Fabric. We hope that we have educated you not only on all of the facets and features of Fabric application development, but also on the importance of looking at your blockchain ecosystem in a much broader sense, including things such as intra-industry consortiums, data governance, and change management.

You should walk away from this book feeling that you know how to build a private enterprise blockchain system using Hyperledger Fabric and that you know how to put together various components of Fabric to create and maintain a robust, secure, and scalable blockchain application. Because of a lack of space, some topics have been left out for you to explore on your own. Specifically, here are areas that merit further consideration:

- Using design patterns for integrating Fabric into current or legacy systems
- Considering post-production factors such as reliability, availability, and serviceability
- Implementing continuous integration and continuous delivery and DevOps best practices to achieve agility in the Fabric network
- Taking microservices and event-driven architectures into consideration while designing your enterprise Fabric architecture
- Best practices for achieving resilience and fault tolerance in a Fabric network
- Best practices for securing Fabric smart contracts and networks

Next Steps

You probably have lots of questions. That's good. Gather those questions and send them to us (via *email* or the contact form on our website (*https://www.coding-bootcamps.com*)). But in general we recommend that you don't stop here. Try to find practical problems and create and launch their solutions with Hyperledger Fabric.

Beyond practical experience, we recommend you keep reading. As always, check out the Hyperledger website (*https://www.hyperledger.org*) to follow the latest developments and see the latest projects built with Fabric, as well as to get the latest updates on Fabric versions and patches. Likewise, Fabric Wiki (*https://wiki.hyperledger.org*) pages provide developers with great hands-on resources for expanding their knowledge and expertise on all Hyperledger DLTs, tools, and libraries.

To help cement everything you have learned, you need to use it. Experience is one way we have already mentioned, but mentorship, teaching, and general presenting is another great way to learn. If you have to explain something to someone else, especially when the format is formal, like a presentation, it forces you to consolidate your ideas and commit your models and generalizations to memory. Don't fall into the trap of thinking that you are not experienced enough to talk about it. You are; you are an expert in the experiences you have had. It is very likely that you can apply, explain, or teach some of your experiences with Hyperledger Fabric in a way that nobody else could. Give it a go!

Now It's Your Turn

With that, we will hand it over to you.

As you know, you can find more resources on the accompanying website (*https://www.myhsts.org*). But we also want to hear from you. We want to hear about the projects you are working on, your challenges, your tips and tricks, and your ideas for the future of Hyperledger Fabric. We especially want to talk to you if you are thinking about applying Fabric in industry or you are struggling with a problem. We can make your life easier with solutions, tips, and assessments to reduce effort, reduce risks, and improve performance. From designing a basic proof of concept to deploying a large-scale consortium solution, we are available to help. So feel free to reach us through our website (*https://www.hashflow.us*).

Good luck!

Further Reading

- Hyperledger DLTs
  - *Hyperledger Cookbook* by Brian Wu, Chuanfeng Zhang, and Andrew Zhang (Packt Publishing)
  - *Blockchain with Hyperledger Fabric*, Second Edition, by Nitin Gaur et al. (Packt Publishing)
- Ethereum and Solidity
  - *Learn Ethereum* by Brian Wu, Zhihong Zou, and Dongying Song (Packt Publishing)

Index

O

About the Authors

Matt Zand is a serial entrepreneur and the founder of four tech startups: DC Web Makers, Coding Bootcamps, HashFlow, and High School Technology Services. He has written more than one hundred technical articles and tutorials on blockchain development for the Hyperledger, Ethereum, and Corda R3 platforms. At HashFlow, he leads a team of blockchain experts for consulting and deploying enterprise decentralized applications. As a chief architect, he has designed and developed blockchain courses and training programs for Coding Bootcamps. He has a master's degree in business management from the University of Maryland. Prior to blockchain development and consulting, he worked as a senior web and mobile app developer and consultant, investor, and business advisor for a few startup companies.

Xun (Brian) Wun is an advisor at HashFlow. He is a prolific writer on the subject of blockchain. As one of the prominent voices in the blockchain community, he has written eight books on blockchain covering popular blockchain technologies like Hyperledger and Ethereum from beginner to advanced levels. He has 20 years of extensive hands-on experience with blockchain-based enterprise application design and development, big data, cloud computing, UI, and system infrastructure solutions. He has also successfully repurposed and integrated blockchain-based applications into gaming and supply chains as well as asset device management industries. In addition to his strong background in the blockchain space, he has served as the tech lead for multiple key technology initiatives at leading financial institutions including J.P. Morgan, Citigroup, and Bank of America.

Mark Anthony Morris is an autodidact with 30 years experience. One of Mark's early startups won the FDIC RTC $50M contract for document imaging and workflow automation. Mark designed and led development of a healthcare application that was nominated by the state of Texas for best government to business application architecture and design in the States CIO Awards competition—it manages 5,700 long-term care facilities. Mark was an independent "hired gun" for IBM, Sun Microsystems, Big 6, Fortune 500, and federal and state government clients for over 20 years. He is an expert in blockchain, AI, AR, IIoT, ecommerce, security, systems integration, microservices, cryptocurrency, enterprise software systems engineering, re-engineering to cloud (Azure and AWS), internet and intranet SOA technology, and federated partner integration and single-sign-on. Mark is a world thought leader and true visionary. A sample of Mark's past clients includes LCRA, Epicor, IBM, Sun Microsystems, American Achievement Corp, InterContinental Hotels Group, Gap Inc., Sprint, FDIC, Texas Department of Human Services, Blue Cross Blue Shield Assoc., CSX Intermodal, American Airlines, Federated Systems Group, Cap Gemini Inc., EDS Federal, Comcast, Zions National Bank, Depository Trust & Clearing Corp., Federal Reserve Information Technology, and Transarc (IBM).

Colophon

The animal on the cover of *Hands-On Smart Contract Development with Hyperledger Fabric V2* is a long-tailed trogon. Often referred to as the most beautiful bird in all of North America, they are commonly found in the mountain canyon habitats of Southeastern Arizona.

Trogons are members of the *Trogonidae* family, with 40 different species of the bird distributed throughout the tropic and neo-tropic regions of the world. The species found in the canyons of Arizona are the elegant trogon and the eared trogon, with the latter being far more rare with long periods of years between verified sightings.

These colorful birds have short necks, rounded bodies, and long tails. They resemble each other in form and size across different species. The only way to tell them apart is the rich variety of their bright, iridescent plumage. Trogons are unique for their heterodactylous toes: the third and fourth digits point forward, while the first and second digits point back; and like owls, they also turn their heads 180 degrees.

In Arizona, the long-tailed elegant trogons mainly live in riverside upland oak and sycamore canyons. They eat mostly insects, which they catch by watching, completely motionless, from a perch and then erupting into fluttering flight. They sit very upright on perches, with their long square-tipped tails pointing straight down. Identifying a long-tailed trogon isn't too hard; along with their brightly colored bodies, they also make a hoarse, repetitive croaking sound that sometimes resembles the barking of a small dog.

The word "trogon" comes from the Greek word for "nibbling" and refers to the bird's habit of gnawing holes into tree trunks in order to create their nests. These fascinating birds are territorial and monogamous. They are increasingly sought after by birdwatching enthusiasts for their beauty and unique nature. Trogons are considered relatively common, with their current conservation status being of "least concern." However, they are especially sensitive to habitat destruction and have experienced some population decline over the years. Many of the animals on O'Reilly covers are endangered; all of them are important to the world.

The cover illustration is by Karen Montgomery, based on a black and white engraving from *Elements of Ornithology*. The cover fonts are Gilroy Semibold and Guardian Sans. The text font is Adobe Minion Pro; the heading font is Adobe Myriad Condensed; and the code font is Dalton Maag's Ubuntu Mono.

O'REILLY®

There's much more where this came from.

Experience books, videos, live online training courses, and more from O'Reilly and our 200+ partners—all in one place.

Learn more at oreilly.com/online-learning

Ingram Content Group UK Ltd.
Milton Keynes UK
UKHW031817260423
420834UK00008B/411